MINORITIES, MIGRANTS, AND CRIME

*Diversity and Similarity
Across Europe and
the United States*

Ineke Haen Marshall

editor

SAGE Publications
International Educational and Professional Publisher
Thousand Oaks   London   New Delhi

MINORITIES, MIGRANTS, AND CRIME

For information:

 SAGE Publications, Inc.
2455 Teller Road
Thousand Oaks, California 91320
E-mail: order@sagepub.com

SAGE Publications Ltd.
6 Bonhill Street
London EC2A 4PU
United Kingdom

SAGE Publications India Pvt. Ltd.
M-32 Market
Greater Kailash I
New Delhi 110 048 India

Printed in the United States of America

Library of Congress Cataloging-in-Publication Data

Main entry under title:

Minorities, migrants, and crime : diversity and similarity across Europe
  and the United States / editor, Ineke Haen Marshall.
      p. cm.
    Includes bibliographical references (p.) and index. ISBN 0-7619-0334-8
(cloth : acid-free paper).—ISBN 0-7619-0335-6   (pbk. : acid-free paper)
    1. Discrimination in criminal justice administration.   2. Minorities.
3. Race relations.   4. Ethnic relations.   I. Haen Marshall, I. (Ineke)
HV7419.M56   1997
364.1′08—dc21   97-4758

97 98 99 00 01 02 03 10 9 8 7 6 5 4 3 2 1

Acquiring Editor:	C. Terry Hendrix
Editorial Assistant:	Dale Mary Grenfell
Production Editor:	Michele Lingre
Production Assistant:	Karen Wiley
Typesetter/Designer:	Marion Warren
Cover Designer:	Candice Harman
Print Buyer:	Anna Chin

CONTENTS

INTRODUCTION

Ineke Haen Marshall

This book is the product of the enthusiastic collaboration of several authors living and working in the United States, Britain, Sweden, Germany, Italy, France, Belgium, the Netherlands, and Spain.[1] The objective of this book is to give some sort of general "inventory" of what is known about ethnic and racial minorities, noncitizens, foreigners, immigrants, and crime—including law enforcement priorities; punishment philosophy and practices; media coverage; and political, scholarly, and public discourse on these issues—in these European countries, as well as in the United States.

Does it make sense to bring the experiences of this wide variety of nations together? In spite of a growing sense of "we-ness" among European nations, national boundaries continue to reflect sharp differences in language, culture, history, and politics. Political, cultural, and legal variations between these European countries make most claims to comparability and generalizations about Europe open to challenge. Enter the United States into the picture, and the situation gets even more complicated. Internationally, the United States is a nation both envied and despised, admired and ridiculed.

The United States is one of the world's superpowers: It has a leading economic, political, and, to the dismay of many, cultural role in the world.[2] The "land of the great, home of the free" also has one of the highest murder rates in the industrialized world, has more inmates in prison than almost any other Western society, still executes several offenders each year, and is at a loss regarding what to do about the large numbers of babies born to teenage girls, or how to resolve the structural unemployment problems of the decaying inner cities. It struggles with outbursts of racial violence; its citizens are increasingly polarized: the "haves" who hide themselves in distant well-kept suburbs, and the "have nots" living on the streets, or in poor housing in rural areas or inner cities. There is no doubt: The contrasts in the United States are much more extreme than those found in most Western European countries. In many ways, the cultural gap that separates the United States and Europe is more formidable than the mere 6,000 miles or so of Atlantic Ocean between the two continents (see, for example, Kroes, 1992).

How then do we make the connection between American experiences and Europe? A different, but related question is, How do we link race, ethnicity, migration, and citizenship issues? I will elaborate on this in the last chapter of the book, but for now let us pretend for a minute that it is possible to forget all we know about history; pretend that we descend from the planet Mars—our assignment being to provide an overview of the diverse social groupings living in Europe and the United States. The astute Martian observer will note that some social groups have very little power to influence social, political, or economic events; members of these relatively powerless groups often are visibly different from the rest of society; they are stereotyped, and frequently discriminated against by the rest of society. The Martian observes such groups all over the world, including in the Netherlands, Germany, France, Belgium, and the United States. But the creature from outerspace is puzzled: Sometimes, concepts such as ethnicity or race are used when earthlings talk about these groups—whereas other times, it is citizenship, nationality, immigration status. Could it be that these terms are secret earthly codewords for something else? It does not take long before the visitor figures out that the key to it all really is quite straightforward; all these groups seem to have two things in common: (a) a marginal social position in society (in terms of employment, education, housing, political influence), and (b) a distinct ethnic-cultural position, characterized by prejudice and stereotyping, self-identification, and shared customs (cf. Penninx, 1994). "Minority" status is the thread that unites migrants, foreigners, indigenous ethnic minorities, and nonnative resident ethnic groups; it is the minority concept that reveals international parallels and similarities, sometimes over-shadowing important national differences and local specificities; it is the minority perspective that builds a bridge between the United States and Europe.[3]

Why do we start these chapters with this cultural outlier, this "exceptional" case of the United States? The reason is simple: The United States' very complex immigrant heritage, together with its long and checkered race relations history, makes this society a uniquely valuable source of insight and experience with regard to the volatile mixture of race, ethnicity, nationality, and immigrant status. If we want to accomplish cross-fertilization of the different approaches to minority research and theory, whether it takes place under the conceptual umbrella of race studies, ethnicity studies, or immigration studies, we must be open to the possibility of shared experiences and commonalities between recent developments in Europe and the United States. Some have vehemently rejected such efforts as artificial, misguided, and useless. These arguments, however reasonable they might have appeared years ago, are less and less convincing in the 1990s. We know so much more now than we did even 10 years ago. We know more about migrants and ethnic minorities, more about the push and pull factors of migration, more about criminality—in both Europe and the United States. We know more about the socio-political-economic dynamics of world change. There is no doubt that scholars on both continents have come a long way since the early beginnings of research and theory on migration, race, ethnicity and crime (Bonger, 1943; Ferracuti, 1968; Sellin, 1938). Not only has our knowledge grown tremendously, there also have been substantial changes in (type and motivation of) migrants, host countries, as well as in global context (cf. Schmid, 1996; Sun & Reed, 1995) over the last decade—changes that are shared by many of the European countries. Changes that make the leap across the Atlantic Ocean less formidable than ever before.

NOTES

1. The author of the chapter on France lives in the United States.

2. For an excellent example of the cultural impact of the United States on the rest of the world, see Ritzer, 1993.

3. Not all foreigner or migrant criminality should be analyzed from a minority view (see Albrecht, Chapter 4, this volume). Some recent developments are better captured by a migration perspective or a political approach.

REFERENCES

Bonger, W. A. (1943). *Race and crime.* New York: Columbia University Press.

Ferracuti, F. (1968). European migration and crime. In M. E. Wolfgang (Ed.), *Crime and culture. Essays in honor of Thorsten Sellin* (pp. 189-219). New York: John Wiley.

Kroes, R. (1992). *De leegte van Amerika. Een massacultuur in de wereld* [The emptiness of America. A mass culture in the world]. Amsterdam: Prometheus.

Penninx, R. (1994). *Raster en Mozaiek.* Amsterdam: Universiteit van Amsterdam, Instituut voor Migratie-en Ethnische Studies (IMES).

Ritzer, G. (1993). *The McDonaldization of society.* Newbury Park, CA: Pine Forge.

Schmid, A. (Ed.). (1996). *Migration and crime.* Milan, Italy: International Scientific and Professional Advisory Council of the United Nations Crime Prevention and Criminal Justice Program (ISPAC).

Sellin, T. (1938). *Culture conflict and crime.* New York: Social Science Research Council.

Sun, H. -E., & Reed, J. (1995). Migration and crime in Europe. *Social Pathology, 1*(3), 228-252.

ACKNOWLEDGMENTS

This book is the product of the collaboration of a large number of individuals. I owe a debt of gratitude to each of them. First and foremost, I want to express my appreciation to the contributing authors: Marian FitzGerald, Hanns von Hofer, Jerzy Sarnecki, Henrik Tham, Hans-Joerg Albrecht, Uberto Gatti, Daniela Malfatti, Alfredo Verde, Patrick Hebberecht, Willem de Haan, Pamela Irving Jackson, Rosemary Barberet, and Elisa García-España. Without them, this book could not have happened. I thank them for their enthusiasm, for their patience with my questions, for keeping within the deadlines, for writing original and outstanding chapters. Because the individual chapters were not allowed to exceed a particular number of pages, I had to eliminate substantial parts of some of the original manuscripts. I thank the authors for their gracious acceptance of my editorial decisions, even in those cases where my editorial knife sliced away more deeply or differently than preferred.

There are many other individuals to whom I owe thanks. I appreciate the reviews of the manuscript by Carl Pope (the University of Wisconsin) and Kimberly Kempf-Leonard (University of Missouri-St. Louis), also those by Richard Bennett (American University) and Frank Bovenkerk (University of Utrecht, The Netherlands). I had a great experience working with Sage Publications and its editors, Terry Hendrix and Dale Grenfell; Michele Lingre was laudable as a production editor; Monika Treadway was outstanding as a copy editor. When this book was still in its embryonic stage, the University Committee on Research of the University of Nebraska at Omaha provided me with a Summer Fellowship to do the background research. The Department of Criminal Justice of the University of Nebraska at Omaha has provided me with clerical assistance; I am particularly grateful to Angela Patton for her generous and patient word processing support. Last but not least, I am especially indebted to my husband and colleague Chris Marshall (University of Nebraska at Omaha). His encouragement and unwavering support, his competent and even-tempered assistance with frustrating computer problems, logistic crises, and miscellaneous other obstacles, have made a tremendous difference.

It is with mixed feelings that I see this book go to press. Judging by the attention of the mass media and politicians in both Europe and the United States, the minority/crime issue will not go away quietly. Discussions on minorities, migrants, and crime provide a most sensitive, potentially explosive mixture. I dread that publications such as this book will contribute to the reification of concepts such as "race," "ethnicity," "nationality," or "crime" as inherently meaningful categories. This is not the intention of this book. To the contrary. I can only hope that this book will help illustrate the socially constructed nature of race, ethnicity, and crime, thereby leading to the indisputable conclusion that ultimately, the minority/migrant/crime "problem" is of our own making.

1

MINORITIES, CRIME, AND CRIMINAL JUSTICE IN THE UNITED STATES

Ineke Haen Marshall

The purpose of this chapter is to provide an overview of minorities, crime, and criminal justice in the United States. This is not a simple assignment. The sheer volume of work by American scholars on the topics of race, ethnicity, and crime, as well as on the interrelationships among these concepts, is mind-boggling; to capture the essence of this body of work in one brief summarization is difficult. To complicate matters further, the fabric of modern American society is woven of an extremely complex patchwork of minority groups—based on race, ethnicity, national origin, citizenship, or all of these. Some "minorities" have been part of American society for a long time, others are foreign-born, recent legal immigrants, or undocumented aliens; some come from Europe, others from Asia, South America, or Africa; they are political refugees, migrant workers, members of international organized crime groups, or highly educated professionals. Some are white, others are people of color. In the United States, the measuring rod for normal behavior and appearance continues to be the "Americanized" white (Northern and Western) European; this reduces, by definition, all other ethnic, national, and racial groups to minorities. I organize my discussion around (a) studies in which the primary focus is on "race" or "ethnicity," and (b) analyses with primary emphasis on citizenship or immigrant status ("foreigners").

CRIME AND THE ENEMY WITHIN: BLACKS, HISPANICS, ASIAN AMERICANS, NATIVE AMERICANS

The racial and ethnic classifications employed by government agencies are not neutral statistical devices; to the contrary, they determine the types of comparisons that can be made; they reinforce racial, ethnic, and national distinctions; they shape people's self-identification. The impact of these classification schemes on research and policy in the areas of race/ethnicity is most convincingly illustrated by the manner in which the American government statistically cuts its population into four grossly oversimplified "racial" groups: American Indians/Native Americans, African Americans/blacks, Asian Americans, and Caucasians/whites. Each of these four racial categories consists of a large number of subgroups with often widely divergent national, ethnic, or racial characteristics.

In addition to "race,"[1] the U.S. Bureau of the Census uses "ethnic" background (defined as Spanish-speaking or not): About 9% of the population in 1990 was classified as Hispanic; the remaining 91% as non-Hispanic. Someone classified as Hispanic, incidentally, may be either white, black, Asian, or Native American.

Figure 1.1 presents the racial/ethnic composition of the approximately 250 million people living in the United States in 1990. This scheme fails to capture essential distinctions and commonalities among and between minority groups; the researcher who has to rely on formal statistics (i.e., police, court, prison data) has no choice but to work within the limits imposed by these artificial distinctions between population groups. The bulk of American research on minorities, then, makes rather crude black/white comparisons, with only occasional Asian American, Native American, or Hispanic/non-Hispanic contrasts. Driven by this classification, most reviews of the field (e.g., Flowers, 1988; Mann, 1993) classify research and theory into these four "minority" groups (blacks, Hispanics, Asian Americans, Native Americans).

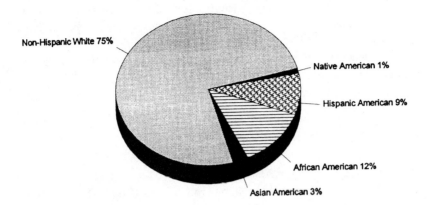

Figure 1.1. U.S. Population in 1990
SOURCE: Adapted from Parillo, 1996, p. 78; U.S. Bureau of the Census, 1992.

AFRICAN AMERICANS

White perceptions of blacks have always included an assumption of criminality (Myers, 1995, p. 146). In American society, public concern with crime (and fear of personal victimization) continues to be primarily focused on blacks—an overly broad category that includes Americans born of long-ago African ancestry, recent African immigrants (Ethiopians, Nigerians, Ghanians), and those who are from a Carribean background (Haitians, Jamaicans; Parrillo, 1996, p. 127). African Americans are America's largest minority group; they continue to lag seriously behind white Americans in education, income, quality of housing, life expectancy and health, and political power (Hacker, 1992; Parrillo, 1996). Not only the public and politicians have long equated "crime" with "black crime": American scholars, too, have a lengthy history of discussions about the crime rates of blacks versus whites (see Hawkins, 1995a; Tonry, 1995).

Research and writing on the involvement of blacks with the criminal justice system have exploded over the last 20 years, reflecting the impact of urban race riots, the continuing evidence of racial disproportionality in rates of crimes and punishment (Hawkins, 1995a, p. 28; see, also, LaFree & Russell, 1993), the practical concerns about the costs of prison construction, the growing intolerance of unequal justice, and last but not least, the rapidly growing supply of academic researchers who have made crime their business. Research funding is more generous, publication outlets more ample, and the obstacles to access to information less formidable when studying America's blacks (or Hispanics or Native Americans) than when investigating the deviance of powerful corporations, government agencies, or politicians.

Official Statistics on Black Crime

"On an average day in America, 1 out of 3 African American men aged 20 to 29 was either in prison or jail, on probation or parole" (the Sentencing Project as cited in Donziger, 1996, p. 105); 5 years ago, "only" 1 in 4 black males was under criminal justice supervision. This statement underscores the urgency of the problem of race and justice in America. The United States is "on the verge of a social catastrophe because of the sheer number of African Americans behind bars—numbers that continue to rise with breathtaking speed and frightening implications" (Donziger, 1996, p. 99). The United States, a country that already has a high incarceration rate relative to other industrialized nations, locks up African American men at a rate six time that of white men (1,860 vs. 289 per 100,000; Table 2.1 in Tonry, 1995, p. 62). More than a half million blacks were incarcerated in U.S. prisons and jails in 1990; blacks make up nearly 50% of those in prison on an average day (Tonry, 1995, p. 49). Historically, African Americans have always been overrepresented in jails and prisons, but the differences have widened tremendously over the last decades. Donziger (1996, p. 103) explains that in 1930, 75% of all prison admissions were white and 22% were African American, but that ratio roughly reversed in 1992—29% of prison admissions were white, while 51% were African American and 20% were Hispanic.

In every stage of the criminal justice system from arrest through incarceration, blacks are present in numbers greatly out of proportion to their presence in the population. In 1994, for example (see Table 1.1), blacks made up about 12% of the U.S. population but 44.7% of those arrested for violent index crime (murder, forcible rape, robbery, and aggravated assault).[2]

More than one half of the arrests for homicide (56.4%) and robbery (60.8%) in 1994 involved a black suspect; about one third of the arrests for index property crimes (burglary, larceny-theft, car theft, and arson) was cleared by the arrest of an African American. The 1994 data (not presented in Table 1.1) show a somewhat lower degree of overrepresentation of blacks for vandalism, sex offenses (other than rape and prostitution), driving under

TABLE 1.1 Total Arrests, Distribution by Race, United States, 1994

	Total Arrests					Percentage Distribution[a]				
Offense Charged	Total	White	Black	American Indian or Alaskan Native	Asian or Pacific Islander	Total	White	Black	American Indian or Alaskan Native	Asian or Pacific Islander
Murder/nonnegligent manslaughter	18,475	7,705	10,420	126	224	100.0	41.7	56.4	0.7	1.2
Forcible rape	29,759	16,683	12,419	327	330	100.0	56.1	41.7	1.1	1.1
Robbery	146,793	55,055	89,232	737	1,769	100.0	37.5	60.8	0.5	1.2
Aggravated assault	449,179	264,466	176,062	4,063	4,588	100.0	58.9	39.2	0.9	1.0
Burglary	319,466	215,363	97,867	2,844	3,392	100.0	67.4	30.6	0.9	1.1
Larceny-theft	1,235,016	796,212	407,231	12,803	18,770	100.0	64.5	33.0	1.0	1.5
Motor vehicle theft	166,119	95,216	66,544	1,562	2,797	100.0	57.3	40.1	0.9	1.7
Arson	16,727	12,555	3,853	168	151	100.0	75.1	23.0	1.0	0.9
Violent crime[b]	644,206	343,909	288,133	5,253	6,911	100.0	53.4	44.7	0.8	1.1
Property crime[c]	1,737,328	1,119,346	575,495	17,377	25,110	100.0	64.4	33.1	1.0	1.4
Crime Index total[d]	2,381,534	1,463,255	863,628	22,630	32,021	100.0	61.4	36.3	1.0	1.3
Total	11,846,833	7,894,414	3,705,713	126,503	120,203	100.0	66.6	31.3	1.1	1.0

SOURCE: Uniform Crime Reports, 1994.
NOTES: a. Because of rounding, the percentages may not add to total.
b. Violent crimes are offenses of murder, forcible rape, robbery, and aggravated assault.
c. Property crimes are offenses of burglary, larceny-theft, motor vehicle theft, and arson.
d. Includes arson.

the influence, liquor law violations, drunkenness, curfew and loitering law violations, and runaways: Approximately one of every five arrests for these offenses involved a black suspect. For all 29 offense types included in the Uniform Crime Reports data (see Table 1.1), 31.3% of the arrests nationwide were cleared by the arrest of an African American.

Aggregate national data such as those presented in Table 1.1 only provide a very crude index of the involvement of blacks in the criminal justice system. There are major geographic variations; there is a greater overrepresentation in cities (in 1994, 48.5% of arrests for violent index crimes in cities was African American) than in suburban areas (32%), or in rural counties (24.5%). Over half of the African American population lives in the big cities of the North and the Midwest.

Impact of the "War on Drugs"

In spite of public beliefs to the contrary, rising violent crime rates among blacks are not responsible for the alarming growth in the locking up of America's blacks (Chambliss, 1995); the proportion of African American arrests for violent crime has not changed significantly for 20 years (Mauer, 1995; Tonry, 1995, 1996). Today, young blacks (under 18) are twice as likely as young whites to be arrested for one of the index crimes—this risk is about five times higher for a black adult (18 or older) than for a white adult. This was true in 1979, and it still holds true today.

Drug law enforcement (the "war on drugs") is primarily responsible for the increase in incarceration of African Americans (and Hispanics). The drug-related arrest rates for blacks have increased much faster than those for whites (see Tonry, 1996, Fig. 6, p. 51) Of current prison admissions for drug offenses, 90% are African American or Hispanic. Since 1980, non-white drug arrest rates have increased steadily and then skyrocketed—so that by 1988 they were five times higher than white rates (Tonry, 1996, p. 49).

Are blacks that much more involved in drug use and dealing than whites, then? Although African Americans are estimated to constitute about 13% of drug users,[3] they make up 35% of arrests for drug possession, 55% of convictions, and 74% of prison sentences for drug possession (Mauer, 1995). There is a growing consensus among American scholars that the skyrocketing of drug-related arrests of African Americans is a result of the oversurveillance of the inner-city black area in the name of the war on drugs (Mauer, 1995; Tonry, 1995, 1996).[4]

Self-Report and
Victimization Surveys

When self-report studies of offending (mostly among youth) were first done some 40 years ago, black/white differences in self-reported offending were found to virtually disappear, or to diminish greatly (compared to arrest statistics)—a finding that supported the discrimination thesis. This is no longer the case. Most researchers now believe that differences between race and crime estimates from the FBI's Uniform Crime Reports and from self-report surveys exist largely because self-reports overemphasize less serious forms of crime and juvenile delinquency (Elliott & Ageton as cited in LaFree & Russell, 1993, p. 278). Black/white differences in offender reports are trivial for nonserious offenses (such as drunkenness, truancy, drug violations), but race differences are "unmistakable" (Harris & Meidlinger, 1995, p. 125) for the more serious forms of delinquency.

Confidence in the validity of Uniform Crime Report (UCR) arrest data regarding race has also grown because of the results of the National Criminal Victimization Survey (NCVS). For instance, comparisons of crime rates by race for the UCR and NCVS show "remarkable correspondence" (LaFree & Russell, 1993, p. 278) between the percentage of robbery offenders identified as black by victims and the percentage of blacks among UCR arrests for robbery; a similar finding was made with regard to burglary. NCVS data also suggest that racial differences in victim reporting to the police are minor, thus eliminating another potential source of racial bias in police statistics.

The NCVS shows that African Americans report a higher level of personal victimization than whites. In 1993, the violent crime annual victimization rate for persons aged 12 or older was 66.1 per 1,000 blacks and 49.7 per 1,000 whites. Blacks experienced higher annual victimization rates than whites for rape (2.7 vs. 2.3), robbery (12.7 vs. 5.1), and aggravated assault (18.7 vs. 11.3), but there were virtually no differences from whites in simple assault (32.1 vs. 31; Bureau of Justice Statistics [BJS], 1994a, p. 232, Table 3.5).

Crimes against black Americans cause greater injury than similar crimes committed against persons from other races; they are also more likely to involve guns (Bureau of Justice Statistics, BJS, 1994b). In large cities, blacks have higher annual robbery and household burglary rates than whites, regardless of the age or family income of the victim or the household head.

Violence, Guns, Drugs, and
Gangs in America's Ghettos

It is true that, compared to some 100, 50, or even 20 years ago, black Americans have made considerable progress on their long voyage to economic, educational, and political equality with their white counterparts. But, blacks in the United States continue to experience a much lower quality of life (measured in terms of income, jobs, education, health, housing, personal safety) than white Americans (Hacker, 1992). As a matter of fact, the National Minority Advisory Council on Criminal Justice (as cited in Young & Sulton, 1994, p. 4) concludes that the relative involvement of African Americans in crime is not disproportionate at all, considering their ranking on the "misery index."

The last decades have witnessed the increasing polarization of America's black population: a growing, well-to-do, black middle class, separated from an expanding number of poor "underclass" blacks whose homes tend to be clustered in slum neighborhoods of the larger American cities. Of course, there are also white poor Americans: 16% of white children in 1990 lived below the poverty line, compared with about 45% of black youngsters (Hacker, 1992, p. 99). Most of America's white poor, however, live in rural areas or in the suburbs; there are few white ghettos. Urban black families are more visibly segregated: 70% of these households are concentrated in what commonly are referred to as ghettos. It is in America's slum areas that crime (violent crime in particular) has grown to be a tremendous problem. How do these recent disturbing developments in the American crime story fit with the picture painted by national crime statistics?

At first glance, the most recent developments in the crime statistics for the nation as a whole are encouraging. Victimization data show a pattern of overall decline in victimization of the population since 1975. For instance, the NCVS violent crime rate in 1992 was lower than in the early 1980s. Police data show that the violent crime rate in 1994 (716 per 100,000) was 2% below the 1990 rate (732); the property crime rate for 1994 (4,658) was 8% lower than the 1990 rate (5,088). This reflects a reversal of the trend during the 1980s of increasing violent (and stable property) crimes for the "average" American (BJS, 1994a). That is the good news.

The bad news is that these global crime statistics paint an oversimplified picture of reality. The average American is merely a statistical construct; developments in crime (measured both by police statistics and victim surveys) are not the same for the young and the old, for blacks and whites, for males and females, for city dwellers or rural folks. Victimization among whites is decreasing, but among certain segments of the black population, crime (violent crime in particular) is now touching more, rather than fewer, lives.

Violence, especially homicide, has historically affected the African American population disproportionally. Today, the odds of being a homicide victim are about seven times higher for blacks than for whites. In the United States, nonwhites have always been more likely to be murdered than whites; however, with the exploding drug-trafficking business in the mid-1980s, gun-related lethal violence has started to grow disproportionately among the very young: A "dramatic change in violent crime committed by young people" (Blumstein, 1995, p. 3) has taken place, particularly among black inner-city youth. The 1992 UCR data show that black males aged 12 to 24 represented 17.2% of single-victim homicides (they make up 1.3% of the population); this translates to a homicide rate of 114.9 per 100,000 black males in this age range (BJS, 1994b)—more than 11 times higher than the U.S. average rate.

NCVS data on assault, rape, and robbery parallel the trends seen in recent homicide statistics. Between 1973 and 1992, the rate of violent victimizations of young black males increased about 25% (BJS, 1994b). The average rate of handgun victimizations per 1,000 black males aged 16 to 19 was 39.7 from 1987 through 1992—four times the rate for white males. Persons under age 21 committed two thirds of the victimizations of black males between 12 and 21.

Heart-wrenching journalistic and biographical accounts of life in the ghetto (e.g., Kotlowitz, 1991) echo the bleak picture painted by cold police statistics, emergency room information, and survey data. There is, then, no doubt that violent crime (in particular, gun-related violence) has made life in some areas in large cities increasingly unsafe: "The combination of inner-city economic dislocation, the allure of the drug trade, and the ready availability of guns have taken a great toll on many communities" (Mauer, 1995). Indeed, much of the violence is associated with the sale of drugs (crack, cocaine, heroin; Sanders, 1994; see also, Block & Block, 1993; Schatzberg & Kelly, 1996).

Intraracial Nature of Black Crime

One of the few undisputed facts about street crime is that crime is intraracial; black offenders tend to choose black victims, and whites victimize whites. Both NCVS data and studies based on police statistics confirm this. In 1994, about 40% of murders (involving a single victim and a single offender) involved a white offender and a white victim; 46% a black offender and a black victim (Federal Bureau of Investigation, 1996, p. 17, Table 2.8). Among the victims of rape, robbery, and assault aged 12 to 24, 82% of the victimizations of black males (and 71% of the victimizations of white males) involved an offender or offenders of the same race (BJS, 1994b). And, contrary to political rhetoric and public opinion, victim reports consistently show that the bulk of all street crime—assault, rape, theft, burglary—with the exception of robbery (the majority of the victims of black robbers are white), is committed by whites against whites.

Antiblack Hate Crimes: On the Rise?

Besides the crime of robbery, there is another very important exception to the intraracial character of America's street crime: These are the so-called hate crimes, motivated by racism and xenophobia, which are most commonly committed by whites against blacks or other minorities. Not only have black Americans a disproportionate burden of "common" victimization, many believe that crimes motivated by racial hate may be on the rise (Garofalo, 1991, p. 164).[5]

Antiblack Bias in the Criminal Justice System

The blatantly racist treatment of blacks, considered normal a century or even 30 years ago, is today much more likely to be indirect, and therefore more difficult to prove (see Zatz, 1987). Partly because of legislative pressures, partly because of more general social changes, the most egregious racial inequalities in the criminal justice system have been reduced or eliminated. This has led a few researchers (e.g., Wilbanks, 1987) to conclude that the problem of racial discrimination by police and other criminal justice agencies is exaggerated and as good as gone. There are, however, only very few scholars who make the unqualified claim that there is no racism in the system. How could one expect a completely bias-free criminal justice system in a society that remains racist?

Antiblack racism in the criminal justice system continues to exist in particular structural contexts (e.g., Chiricos & Crawford, 1995), but in general, with the exception of drug law enforcement, the influence of the offender's race on official decisions concerning individuals is considered to be "slight" (Tonry, 1995, p. 50). Some scholars and policy analysts take exception to the dominant view and argue that institutional racism remains a reality in the American criminal justice system (Mann, 1993, 1995). Donziger (1996), for example, argues that there are "so many more African Americans than whites in our prisons that the difference cannot be explained by higher crime among African Americans, racial discrimination is also at work and it penalizes African Americans at almost every juncture in the criminal justice system" (p. 99).

Thus, research no longer supports the allegation of pervasive and systematic discriminatory treatment based on race. But there remain some troubling and well-documented pockets of racial discrimination in the American system of justice (discussed in next sections). Whenever a study finds evidence of differential treatment based on race, this is typically to the disadvantage of blacks, very seldom to the disadvantage of whites. There is also not much evidence for leniency toward blacks (Kleck as cited in Chiricos & Crawford, 1995, p. 300).

The analysis of "empirical race bias" (cf. Harris & Meidlinger, 1995) is limited to decision-making points in the criminal justice system. Racial bias, however, enters discussions on "race and crime" much earlier: By analyzing police statistics and victimization studies most researchers limit themselves to street crime, a focus that will exaggerate the involvement of blacks in criminality. High-profit, low-risk crime remains the privilege of the well-to-do middle class (primarily whites). This "a priori race bias" (Harris & Meidlinger, 1995) also is seen in legislative decisions, law enforcement priorities, and media coverage of "criminality." If the scholarly and popular focus were on white-collar crime, for instance, the *under*representation of blacks as offenders would be one of the most striking observations.

Black Experience With the Police

The much-publicized Rodney King incident, in which Los Angeles law enforcement officers brutally beat a fleeing black suspect, exemplifies the tense relationship that continues to exist between police and blacks in the United States. Police use of excessive force, including deadly force, against racial minorities has become the cause célèbre of the 1990s. The federal government has initiated a nationwide data collection effort in police abuse cases; research funds have been made available, and there is a growing interest in the improvement of the handling of citizen complaints (Walker & Wright, 1995). Early studies concluded that police officers were more likely to shoot and use excessive force when dealing with blacks; more recent research indicates that the racial disparity in people shot and killed by police has declined (Walker, Spohn, & DeLone, 1996, pp. 93-95).

"Many minority communities in America feel both overpoliced and underprotected" (Donziger, 1996, p. 160). Black Americans, more so than white Americans, feel verbally and physically harassed by the police; police protection in black neighborhoods is viewed as worse than in white neighborhoods. Response to 911 calls in black neighborhoods is often slow. Violence associated with gangs and the drug trade make assignment to the impoverished black inner-city neighborhoods one of the least desirable job assignments for police officers, thus placing the youngest and least experienced officers in charge of the most violent precincts. Police gang and drug sweeps in predominantly black housing projects (e.g., Operation Clean Sweep in Chicago) often involve blatant disregard for the residents' rights and dignity.

Several cities now are using "community policing models" to improve police relations with minority communities. Yet black citizens who encounter police (be it as a victim or a suspect) continue to have a lesser chance of receiving civil and fair treatment than whites. A recent report by the Criminal Justice Institute at Harvard Law School (reported in Donziger, 1996, p. 169) based on hearings in six cities on the issue of police brutality against minorities, found that for minorities any encounter with police "carries the risk of abuse, mistreatment, or even death."

Death Penalty

Capital punishment is now used with growing frequency in the United States. Since the Supreme Court reinstated the death penalty in 1976, 24 states have executed 257 prisoners. More than one third (100) of the executions took place in 3 years (1992, 1993, and 1994). Between 1977 and 1994, 98 black non-Hispanic men were executed (compared to 139 white non-Hispanic men). Currently 1,197 black persons are under sentence of death (compared to 1,645 whites; BJS, 1995c). Death penalty research has consistently and thoroughly documented that this ultimate punishment is definitely not color blind (Baldus, Pulaski, & Woodworth, 1983). To the contrary—a rather uniform pattern of discrimination based on race of the victim has been found; offenders killing whites are more likely to be given the death penalty than those killing blacks (Gross as cited in Smith, 1995). One interpretation of this finding is that the death penalty system is more lenient toward black murderers, because the large majority kill black victims. More convincing is the counterargument that the lives of black victims simply have less value in the criminal justice system than do those of whites.

Blacks as Workers in the Criminal Justice System

In the United States, efforts by the police, courts, and corrections to recruit more racial minorities have taken place for several reasons: It is required by law, it is believed to reduce racism, and it is believed to improve the relationship between the criminal justice system and racial minorities. Federal affirmative action programs have helped to increase the presence of racial minorities in the criminal justice system (Hacker, 1992). Most large U.S. cities now have a sizable proportion of black officers (in 1992, Washington, D.C., had a 67.8% black police force; Detroit, 53.3%; Atlanta, 54.6%); and, in most of the 50 largest cities in the United States between 1983 and 1992, the situation improved (Walker & Turner as cited in BJS, 1995c, p. 49, Table 1.36). Yet, only a handful of these cities (e.g., Los Angeles and Washington, D.C.) have a representation of black officers equal to their proportion in the general population. Several large cities have a black mayor or a black police chief.

Similar trends, albeit less pronounced, are seen in other branches of the criminal justice system. The United States now has more black prosecutors, judges, and correctional officers then ever before in history; however, they are still seriously underrepresented. In 1992, 20% of all correctional personnel were black (and 5% Hispanic; Walker et al., 1996, p. 211). Using the proportion of arrestees for index crimes (one third), or the proportion of blacks in the prison population (almost 50%), even these considerable gains are not satisfactory. As history has shown, U.S. prisons (Attica!) are hotbeds of racial tension, occasionally exploding in violent rioting. Often, urban black offenders are incarcerated in prisons away from the city, in a rural setting, guarded by working-class whites. Unfortunately, the recent increase in minority correctional personnel may come to an abrupt halt with the dismantling of federal affirmative action programs and the backlash of the "white angry male" against preferential hiring and promotion practices. The increasingly tough stance on prisons (i.e., federal funds for inmate education have been eliminated, together with exercise equipment and other "frills") will only escalate the smoldering racial unrest in U.S. prisons.

HISPANICS

U.S. census forms include one question about race and another question about ethnicity (Hispanic or not; Hispanics may be of any race). The category of Hispanics (or Latino) includes a wide variety of Spanish-speaking groups: people of Mexican heritage, Puerto Ricans, Cubans, people from Central or South America; a mixture of long-term habitants of the United States and newcomers, Latino immigrants and refugees, and their descendants (Parrillo, 1996, p. 131). In 1990, about 22.4 million people (9% of the U.S. population) was Hispanic (see Figure 1.1).

Paralleling the experiences of black Americans, Hispanics as a group are relatively powerless, they have been (or are) seen as "different," often threatening, problematic, or deviant; they have been subject to discriminatory laws and regulations, prejudice, and negative stereotyping; the focus of public fear and violence; and targets of political campaigns. On average, they are less educated, more likely to be unemployed, poorer, and less healthy than the non-Hispanic population (Hacker, 1992). But there are huge differences among the different Latino groups: Some are wealthier and better educated than the rest of the United States (e.g., Cubans who came to the United States to escape from Castro in the 1960s); whereas others rank at the bottom of the scale (i.e., Puerto Ricans, Mexicans).

In a recent volume on criminal justice and Latino communities, Lopez (1995) laments the lack of research on criminal justice and the Latino community. The absence of official data (Hispanics are often categorized as white) is one explanation; another reason is the assumption that Hispanic crime is a "mirror image of that of blacks, who have been studied extensively" (Flowers, 1988, p. 96). Furthermore, criminological research has stereotyped images of Latinos: "These images have influenced the objectivity of the research" (Lopez, 1995, p. ix). Most of the research is on Mexican Americans, who are numerically the largest Hispanic group; this is also the group that has attracted most of the public fear and allegations of crime by illegals.

Official Statistics on Hispanic Crime

For a short time period (1980 to 1986), the FBI collected arrest information on Hispanics. National aggregate arrest data on Hispanics are no longer available. Prison statistics, on the other hand, do distinguish between Hispanic and non-Hispanic inmates, but there are substantial variations in classification procedures, as well as a large percentage of "unknowns" (in 1993, 14.9% were missing), which make these statistics of questionable utility. (The government counts most Hispanics with the white population.) According to the 1993 census of jails, Hispanics made up 12.8% of the nation's inmate population and 27% of the federal prisoners; Hispanic

inmates were incarcerated disproportionally for drug-related offenses. Hispanics constituted the fastest growing minority group in prison from 1980
to 1993. During that period, the proportion of inmates of Hispanic origin
increased from 7.7% to 14.3% and the rate of imprisonment for Hispanics
more than tripled, from 163 to 529 prison inmates per 100,000 Hispanic
residents (Donziger, 1996, pp. 103-104). In 1990, 10.4% of all Latino males
were either on probation, on parole, or in prison (Poupart, 1995, p. 179). In
1994, 224 Hispanics were on death row (8.4% of inmates with a known
ethnicity).

Other Data on Hispanic Crime

Victim surveys show that Hispanic households have higher victimization rates (445 per 1,000 households—for burglary, car theft, and household
larceny combined) than non-Hispanic households (313 per 1,000). Hispanics
also run a slightly higher risk of personal victimization (62.5 per 1,000
respondents aged 12 and over, compared to 53.2 per 1,000 non-Hispanics),
in particular for robbery (10.8 vs. 5.8 per 1,000 individuals; BJS, 1995b). A
large proportion of criminal victimization is intraethnic (i.e., Hispanics
victimizing other Hispanics), which is consistent with the overrepresentation
of Hispanics in arrest and incarceration statistics.

Hispanics also figure prominently in the youth gang literature (Klein,
Maxson, & Miller, 1995; Sanders, 1994); life in the urban "barrios" has
historically been associated with gangs, and since the 1980s guns, drugs, and
violence have become a more central feature of these gangs. The notions of
machismo and the subculture of violence are among the more popular
explanations of gang membership (see Erlanger, 1995 for a critical note). In
a later section, I will discuss explanations of minority crime; it is sufficient
to note now that explanations for criminal involvement of Hispanics parallel
those of other minorities (Mann, 1993, p. 101) and include the following:
oversurveillance, prejudice, and discrimination; adjustment and acculturation problems (for the new arrivals), social disorganization particularly in
the urban areas; and low economic status and poverty.

Anti-Hispanic Bias in the Criminal Justice System

Some of the Hispanic overrepresentation in police and prison cells may
reflect the impact of discriminatory treatment by the criminal justice system. Studies have documented that Chicanos (compared to Anglos) receive

harsher treatment at each stage of the criminal process in Monterey County, California (Garza, 1995); that Hispanics (compared to the general population) in Texas feel less safe, do not trust the police, and do not feel they have adequate police protection (Carter, 1995a, 1995b); that Mexican-origin defendants (and blacks) are considerably more likely to receive a severe sentence than comparable Anglo defendants (Holmes & Daudistel, 1995); that there has been a marked increase in racial violence against Latinos (Hernandez, 1995); that Hispanic criminal defendants received less favorable pretrial release outcomes, were more likely to be convicted in jury trials, and received more severe sentences than whites in Tucson, Arizona and El Paso, Texas (LaFree, 1995). Language barriers handicap many Latino criminal defendants (Lopez, 1995), contributing to misunderstandings and reinforcing prejudice among police (Mann, 1993, p. 103).

ASIAN AMERICANS

The Generic term *Asian* includes not only Japanese and Chinese and Koreans, but also Indonesians and Indians along with Burmese and Thais, Fillipinos, and Pakistanis (Hacker, 1992, p. 5)—a strange mixture of racial, national, and cultural identities that together constitute 3% of the American population. Some Asian American groups are doing extremely well, both socially and economically (e.g., the Japanese), whereas others (some Chinese, Fillipinos) barely are able to survive economically. This population group has been the subject of legal discrimination, police harassment, and hate crimes (Flowers, 1988, Hacker, 1992; Jacobs & Henry, 1996; Mann, 1993), both in the past and present.

Not a "Model Minority"

Asian Americans have a lower arrest rate (1.0%) than their presence in the population (3%; see Table 1.1)—lower than whites, blacks, and American Indians. Asian Americans also have a very low rate of incarceration; of the 7.5 million, 5,408 were incarcerated in 1993 (.57% of the total federal and state inmate population). Seventeen Asian Americans were on death row in 1994, less than their proportion in the general population. May we conclude then, that Asian Americans are a "model minority," and that the relative absence of research on Asian American criminal involvement and contacts with criminal justice agencies is therefore justified? I don't think so.

First, there exist important variations in criminality when comparisons are made among the diverse Asian groups. Japanese Americans have consistently had lower crime rates than Chinese Americans (Mann, 1993, p. 94), explained, among other things by strong family ties. But although Chinese crime rates within Chinese communities were low prior to 1965 (Chin, 1995, p. 46), crime and violence among Chinese have increased since then, partly because of the influx of young immigrants from Hong Kong who have formed youth gangs (see later section), and partly because of the "extremely high unemployment rates, depressing poverty, and disheartening living and social circumstances" of the people living in Chinatowns (Takagi & Platt as cited in Mann, 1993, p. 97).

A second reason to challenge the notion of Asian Americans as "model citizens" is the fact that arrest statistics do not fully capture the involvement of Asian groups in organized crime; both Chinese and Japanese organized criminals have been active in drug trafficking, gambling, and prostitution in the United States from the early beginnings of immigration. Also, national statistics do not reflect the fact that Asian Americans are concentrated in a few states (California, Washington, New York, Nevada). State-level statistics indeed do provide a less favorable picture than national data. To illustrate, the California Youth Authority reports that Asians and Pacific Islanders constitute 6% of incarcerated youth, but 9% of new admissions, mostly immigrants from Southeast Asia, China, and the Phillipines (Donziger, 1996, p. 104).

NATIVE AMERICANS

This is the smallest "racial" group identified by the U.S. census data; according to the 1990 census, there are about 1,800,000 Native Americans—American Indians, Eskimos, and Aleuts—.7% of the U.S. population. The identification of who is and who is not Indian is a serious problem in studying this minority. Indians tend to be a loose residue of tribes, rather than a racial entity (Hacker, 1992, p. 5). Another factor that makes research difficult is the problem of multiple jurisdictions: Tribal members are subject to the tribe, the state, and the federal government jurisdiction, depending on the type of crime, whether it happened on or off the reservation, and whether Indians or non-Indians were involved (Zatz, Chiago Lugan, & Snyder-Joy, 1991,

p. 101). American Indians have the lowest life expectancy, as well as very high rates of illiteracy, unemployment, infant mortality, suicide, and alcoholism.

Crime, Criminal Justice, and American Indians

The most current profile of crime, delinquency, arrest, prosecution, and incarceration among Native Americans "paints an extremely grim picture" (Armstrong, Guilfoyle, & Melton, 1996, p. 81). Guilfoyle (as cited in Armstrong et al., 1996, p. 81) states that adult Indians have the highest rate of arrest, conviction, incarceration, and recidivism among all racial and ethnic groups. Table 1.1 shows that American Indians account for 1.1% of the total arrests. These aggregate official police statistics tell only a small part of the story. The arrest figures for homicide (.7%), in particular, are grossly misleading because they do not include crimes committed on reservations, where about half of the Indian population lives. The homicide rate for American Indians is much higher on-reservation than off-reservation. For instance, Bachman (as cited in Snyder-Joy, 1995, p. 318) reports that the national homicide rate for American Indians is 9.6 per 100,000 population, but the rate may be over 100 per 100,000 population in some reservation counties. Homicide accounts for 3.2% of all Native American deaths in comparison to 1.1 % of the larger American population (Armstrong et al., 1996, p. 81).[6] Alcohol use plays a large role. This is seen in the overrepresentation of Native Americans in the arrest statistics related to drunkenness, liquor law violations, driving under the influence, and disorderly conduct. Arrest data show that Native American youth were more likely to be arrested for status offenses and nonserious crimes (in particular drug and alcohol offenses, and less likely for serious offenses) than their white or black counterparts (Armstrong et al., 1996, p. 80). American Indian youths in the past have had little involvement with street gangs, but recently, as reported by the Associated Press (cited in Nielsen & Silverman, 1996), Indian youth gangs have emerged, resulting in the development of tribal gang intervention units.

American Indians are overrepresented in federal prisons (in 1994, they made up 1.5% of the 1994 federal prison population; BJS, 1995c); this may be explained by the fact that there is federal jurisdiction over particular offenses committed by Indians. About 6 of every 10 juveniles in federal custody are Native American (Donziger, 1996, p. 104). In 21 states, the Indian inmates make up 1% or more of the state prison population

(Grobsmith, 1996, p. 226). States with a heavy concentration of American Indians have an overrepresentation in their state prisons; for example, in South Dakota, Indians constitute 7% of the state population, but represent about 26% of the prison inmates; in Montana, 18.3% of the inmates are American Indian (three times the state proportion); and in North Dakota, 22.2% (more than five times the state proportion; Grobsmith, 1996, p. 225). In 1994, 23 American Indians were on death row (.8% of the total).

Discrimination and oversurveillance in Indian communities may explain the higher arrest rates (Mann, 1993, p. 98), as well as the higher incarceration rates of American Indians. Few studies have examined the involvement of American Indians in the criminal justice system (Snyder-Joy, 1995, pp. 316-317; Zatz et al., 1991, pp. 100-101). Native Americans are more likely to receive a prison sentence than non-Indians; they serve a longer portion of their sentence before parole release (Snyder-Joy, 1995, p. 317). Some studies, however, have found that American Indians in some cases receive more lenient treatment than non-Indians (Bachman, Alvarez, & Perkins, 1996, p. 199). Theories of criminality among American Indians make use of the concepts of social disorganization, culture conflict, and economic deprivation (Mann, 1993).

CRIME AND THE THREAT FROM WITHOUT: RECENT IMMIGRANTS AND CRIMINAL ALIENS

America is a nation of immigrants; it is thus only natural that the crime of foreign-born and recent immigrants has always been an issue, although at times overshadowed by interest in crime by blacks (Hawkins, 1995a).[7] In the past few years, there has been a renewed interest in the link between immigrants and criminality; concepts such as "country of origin," "nationality," and "citizenship" are making a comeback in American scholarly and public debate. It is not difficult to see why that is happening.

The nature of criminality in the 1990s has changed; ordinary street crime no longer ranks as the primary crime problem. Characterized by keywords such as *globalization* and *internationalization,* official attention is now drawn to "transnational crime, drug traffickers, terrorism, traffic in weapons of mass destruction, money laundering, and other forms of corruption" (Winer, 1996, p. 9). A senior government official states that "international organized crime groups represent a major threat to U.S. national security interests and to the democratic world order" (Clarke, 1996, p. 5). Highly publicized violent terrorist acts committed by foreigners on U.S. territory, or against U.S. citizens or property (i.e., the World Trade Center bombing, the Lockerbee airplane bombing) shape the public image of "the foreigner" as dangerous. With the spotlight on the international character of crime comes a renewed interest in the foreigner as criminal.

As Table 1.2 shows, the bulk of noncitizens legally admitted to the United States are nonimmigrants: The number of refugees and asylees (126,000 in 1994) has grown since 1988 (87,000). Most noncitizens entering the United States are legal aliens; however, substantial numbers of illegal aliens are removed by the Immigration and Naturalization Service (INS; more than 1 million annually; BJS, 1996, p. 3). The exact number of illegal aliens is not known, but the INS estimates their number to be between 3 and 4 million (BJS, 1996, p. 3), increasing by approximately 299,000 per year. The vast majority of illegal immigrants apprehended are Mexican nationals intercepted at the border (BJS, 1996, p. 3).

Some foreign born obtain citizenship quickly, although others choose to remain permanently a legal alien resident, thus inconveniently muddling the analytical waters for social scientists relying on official government statistics. About 7.9% (20 million) of the nation's population was foreign born in 1990, the highest proportion in the past four decades. The number of foreign-born persons entering the United States has increased steadily since the early 1960s, from 1.5 million in 1960-1964, to a peak of 5.6 million in 1985-1990. One third of the foreign-born population lives in California.

The sheer magnitude of these figures makes current interest in immigrants' and foreigners' crime certainly understandable. I focus on the three, sometimes overlapping, issues related to crime, citizenship, nationality, and immigrant status around which current public, political, and scholarly interest revolves: (a) the growing numbers of foreigners in U.S. prisons, (b) aliens and ethnic organized crime, and (c) aliens and ethnic gangs.

Foreigners in the
Criminal Justice System

During the 1980 "freedom Flotilla," Castro sent a large number of Cuban immigrants to America's shores, some of whom had a criminal record or history of mental illness. In November 1987, these "Mariel" Cuban prisoners took over two federal detention centers, resulting in extensive media coverage (Clark, 1991, p. 113). This incident fueled the popular fear that large numbers of (mostly illegal) immigrants are driving up the crime rate in the United States. The belief that immigrants are responsible for many social

TABLE 1.2 Number of Noncitizens Admitted to the United States, 1984 to 1994 (in 1,000s)

Type of Entry	1984	1986	1988	1990	1992[a]	1994
Immigrants	**544**	**602**	**643**	**1,536**	**974**	**804**
Refugees	80	62	87	116	127	126
Refugees[b]	68	58	80	110	123	114
Asylees[c]	12	4	7	6	4	12
Non-immigrants	**9,293**	**10,471**	**14,592**	**17,574**	**20,911**	**22,118**
Tourists	6,595	7,342	10,821	13,418	16,441	17,154
Business	1,623	1,938	2,376	2,661	2,788	3,164
Other	1,075	1,191	1,395	1,495	1,682	1,800
Total	**9,917**	**11,135**	**15,322**	**19,226**	**22,012**	**23,048**

SOURCE: Bureau of Justice Statistics, 1996.
NOTE: a. The number of nonimmigrants admitted during 1991 to 1993 reflects the revised number published by the Immigration and Naturalization Service (INS) in the 1994 *Statistical Yearbook*.
b. The number of refugees represents the number admitted.
c. The number of asylees reported represents the number of individuals granted asylum by the INS district directors and asylum officers.

ills, including poverty, alcoholism, and crime, has been deeply ingrained in U.S. popular thinking virtually since its colonial beginnings (Bailey, 1991; Parrillo, 1996; Purcell, 1995; Steinberg, 1989). The alleged link between immigration and crime has been studied extensively in the United States, particularly in the first half of this century (see Hawkins, 1993, 1994; Sellin, 1938).

Today's popular belief that criminality by migrants and aliens is becoming a more serious problem appears to be supported by both court and prison data. For example, the number of noncitizens who were prosecuted in U.S. district courts from 1984 to 1994 increased an average of 10% annually, from 3,462 to 10,352 (BJS, 1996, p. 5; compared to an 2% annual increase in overall federal caseload). The growth in the number of noncitizens prosecuted between 1986 and 1989 was generally attributable to an increase in the number of noncitizens charged with drug and immigration offenses (BJS, 1996, pp. 5-6). Drug and immigration offenses account for the majority of the offenses for which noncitizens are prosecuted in federal court (BJS, 1996, Table 5); in 1994, these two offenses accounted for over 78% of the prosecutions of noncitizens in federal court (up from 69% in 1984). Although in 1984, 35% of noncitizens prosecuted in federal court were charged with a drug offense, by 1994, the proportion charged with a drug offense had increased to 45% (BJS, 1996, p. 1).

In 1994, two thirds of those convicted of an immigration offense were convicted of illegally entering the United States of reentry after deportation, 18.7% were convicted of alien smuggling, and 12.4% of trafficking in fraudulent entry documents (BJS, 1996, p. 7, Table 7). Only 1.4% of the noncitizens in federal courts were prosecuted for a violent offense, compared with 8.5% of citizens (13.3% for property offenses, and 6.8% for public order offenses other than immigration). It is important to note that 55% of the noncitizens prosecuted in U.S. district courts were legal aliens (BJS, 1996, p. 3). Nearly one half (48.6%) of all noncitizens convicted were from Mexico, 14.6% from South America, 14.2% from the Carribean Islands— conspicuously absent (but consistent with the composition of current immigrants) are Western European offenders (BJS, 1996, p. 3, Table 2).

Of noncitizens convicted of a federal offense in 1994, 88% received a prison sentence. Comparable to trends in prosecution, the number of noncitizens serving a sentence of imprisonment in a federal prison between 1984 and 1994 increased on average 15% annually—from 4,088 to 18,929; the overall federal prison population increased on average 10% annually—from 31,105 to 87,437 (BJS, 1996, p. 1). For example, in 1992, more than 20% of federal inmates were non-U.S. citizens, from over 120 countries (Tanton & Lutton, 1993, p. 217). Table 1.3 presents data on the number of noncitizens serving a prison sentence in federal prison, 1984 through 1994.

According to the most recent figures, about 75% of noncitizens incarcerated were convicted of a drug offense, 13% were convicted of an immigration offense, and less than 2% were convicted of a violent offense (BJS, 1996, p. 9). After completion of their sentence, those citizens identified as "criminal aliens" are deported. Noncitizens received prison sentences with an average of 50.1 months (69.9 months for drug offenses).

Foreigners (noncitizens) are becoming increasingly visible in the American criminal justice system. For many of these noncitizens, the only illegal act is their failure to possess a legal residence permit; they are law-abiding people who have come to the United States in search of a better life. Some of them may drift into an illegal way of life when the "American Dream" turns out to be an illusion (see next two sections). For yet another category of (legal and illegal) aliens, however, criminal motives are the sole reason for crossing U.S. borders. It is this latter group that exemplifies a qualitatively new type of "foreigner" crime (i.e., terrorism, drug trafficking, trafficking in humans, and in human organs)—illegal behavior not captured by traditional theories on "crime by immigrants" (first, second, or third generation) developed some half century ago (e.g., Sellin, 1938).

TABLE 1.3 Noncitizens Serving a Sentence of Imprisonment in a United States Federal Prison, 1984 to 1994

Most Serious Offense of Conviction	1984	1989	1994
Violent offenses	290	313	343
Property offenses	228	509	658
Fraudulent	144	376	522
Other	84	133	136
Drug offenses	2,270	7,647	14,226
Public-order offenses	1,251	2,125	3,614
Regulatory	69	96	95
Other	1,182	2,029	3,519
Immigration	872	1,542	2,478
Total[a]	4,088	10,658	18,929

SOURCE: Bureau of Justice Statistics, 1996.
NOTE: Data represent the federal prison population on December 31.
a. Includes cases for which the offense category could not be determined.

Aliens and Ethnic Organized Crime

Scholarly and public interest in differences among white ethnic groups started to wane some 50 years ago, with one important exception: White ethnic groups remained persistently tied to organized crime (Hawkins, 1994). Migrants have always played an important role in organized crime in the United States. Woodiwiss (as cited in Bailey, 1991, p. 12) describes the "nativist xenophobia" in the years after World War II, the fear of "alien conspiracies" by Sicilians and Italians, the belief that something called the Mafia was responsible for U.S. organized crime problem. Indeed, organized crime has long been thought of as an underworld enterprise composed almost exclusively of traditional white ethnic (immigrant) groups such as Italians, Irish, and Jews. Organized crime has provided a "vehicle for upward mobility for lower-income ethnic minorities in their odyssey toward the fulfillment of the American Dream" (O'Kane, 1992, p. 139).

Recent evidence suggests that new ethnic groups, no longer only white ethnics, have been "waiting their turn" on the ethnic queue: Blacks (American and Carribean), Hispanics (Cuban, Mexican, Puerto Rican, Colombian, Venezuelan), and Asians (Chinese, Japanese, Vietnamese, Filipino, and Korean), Soviet Jews, Nigerians, Ghanians (O'Kane, 1992, p. 89). Many of the ethnic criminal organizations exist in their native countries and simply expand into the United States. Some of these groups consist primarily or solely of U.S. born, others are mostly made up of foreigners or recent immigrants. "The ethnic membership of the migrants makes the formation of gangs of the same origin easier because the language can be a natural barrier against intrusive investigations by the police" (Schmid & Savona, 1996, p. 21). Furthermore, "The bonds resulting from a common place of origin and its cultural and social rituals and values are exploited by organized crime to reproduce the same structures of hierarchy, complicity, conspiracy of silence and the same cohesion to which migrants where used to, and in some cases wanted to escape from, in their country of origin" (Schmid & Savona, 1996, p. 21).

More and more, the U.S. organized crime picture reflects global political changes and population movements. For instance, since the collapse of the Soviet Union, police departments throughout the United States have come in contact with Russian organized emigre crime networks (Finckenauer, Waring, & Barthe, 1996). Furthermore, the Asian-based organized criminal influence in the United States is rapidly becoming a very visible problem, particularly in cities such as Los Angeles and New York. The increasing number of Chinese immigrating to the United States has affected the stability of the Chinese communities (Chin, 1995, p. 46); unable to absorb the large influx of immigrants, Chinese gangs have developed in San Francisco, Los Angeles, Boston, Vancouver, and New York City. Chinese gangs' involvement in heroin trafficking, money laundering, high-tech thievery, and other racketeering activities have led to the prediction that "Chinese criminal organizations will emerge as the number one organized crime problem in the 1990s" (Chin, 1995, p. 46). Most gang members are young immigrants; few are U.S. born. Asian gangs include not only Chinese "organized criminal groups involved in street crime" (Operation Safe Streets Gang Detail [OSS], 1995, p. 14) such as the Wah Ching gang, comprised of Cantonese Chinese with youthful, illegal immigrants as members (p. 43), but also Viet-Chings (Vietnamese of Chinese ethnicity), Koreans, and Filipinos. Organized Chinese criminal groups are increasingly involved in the smuggling of illegal immigrants. As many as 600,000 undocumented Chinese immigrants have been smuggled into the United States in recent years by ethnic Chinese syndicates charging $25,000 to $35,000 a person. An FBI review in 1995 found Chinese criminal enterprises active in 24 of the nation's 94 federal districts; in a 1992 review, they were reported active in 15 districts ("Ethnic Chinese," 1996).

There appears to be a serious escalation of Japan-based Yakuza activity in the United States: Yakuza members are thought to be involved with factions of La Cosa Nostra on the east coast (OSS, 1995, p. 44). Reuter (1996) suggests that the Italian Mafia is no longer a serious threat to the United States; instead, new ethnic gangs mostly from East Asia, have "become wealthy through their control of large-scale illicit drug distribution systems" (p. 33).

Although the obvious problems involved in studying these highly secretive, often very violent profit-oriented criminal enterprises are formidable, scholarly research in this area has started to develop at a fast-growing rate.[8] The most recent evidence based on participant observation, police intelligence, and government investigations suggests that O'Kane's (1992, p. 234) prediction ("ethnic organized crime among current minority newcomers is flourishing and ever expanding, with no end in sight") may be right on target.

Aliens and Ethnic Gangs

Historically, American scholarly debate kept the domain of "organized crime" distinct and separate from that of "gangs." This separation begins to blur more and more, now that more youth gangs are getting involved in organized criminal activity, and criminal syndicates operate more frequently through youth gangs.

Decades ago, discussion of youth gangs involved white youth organized along ethnic lines (Irish, Polish, Italian). Interest in these white ethnic youth gangs diminished (with the exception the present interest in supremacist groups such as Skinheads), to be replaced by preoccupation with "home-grown" (primarily) black gangs (Bloods and Crips) a decade or so ago. The extreme violence associated with these street gangs (and their conflicts with some long-established Hispanic gangs)[9] received national attention in the 1980s, and the (youth) gang phenomenon acquired a clear racial (black and Latino) connotation.

With the influx of new immigrants, new gangs have emerged, and the youth gang picture is no longer dominated by these "domestic" urban (black and Hispanic) gangs. Today, the U.S. urban landscape provides an increasingly complex amalgamation of gangs: For instance, in Chicago, there are black and Hispanic gangs, but also Chinese, Cambodian, Vietnamese, Filipino, and Greek; in Los Angeles, Pacific Islander gangs (Samoan, Tongan, Guamanian, and Hawaiian) have emerged (OSS, 1995, p. 44), as well as

Filipino, Salvadoran, Mexican, Korean, and Vietnamese. More often than not, these gangs are involved in a variety of crimes.

THEORETICAL EXPLANATIONS

Because race, ethnicity, and immigrant status are central concepts in U.S. social science, most, if not all, mainstream criminological theories have been applied at one time or another to accommodate the apparent racial and ethnic differences in arrest and punishment experiences (see Flowers, 1988; Harris & Meidlinger, 1995; Hawkins, 1993, 1994, 1995a, 1995b; Joseph, 1995; LaFree & Russell, 1993; Mann, 1993).

Sociobiological Theories

Among the oldest, most persistent, and most popular crime theories are the genetic, biological, and biosociological perspectives. These perspectives attribute personality traits associated with criminal offending to innate genetic, biochemical, and neurological characteristics of offenders (Regulus, 1995, p. 46). In the oldest theories, blacks were viewed as biologically inferior and inherently criminal. (White ethnic groups, in particular recent immigrants, in the past have also been depicted as biologically inferior.) Presently, such claims are seldom explicitly stated, but some still maintain, by inference, that racial (and ethnic) differences in offending have sources in the biological constitutions of these groups (see Wilson & Herrnstein, 1985).

These theories find little support among most of today's U.S. criminologists, because of conceptual and theoretical problems, lack of sound empirical research, and questionable policy implications (Regulus, 1995). For instance, Wilson and Herrnstein's (1985) claim that the higher incidence of crime among blacks may be evidence of biologically inherited propensities, has been denounced as "thoroughly racist" (Fraser, 1995; Joseph, 1995, p. 61)—and rightly so. Still, as long as biologically based theories continue to be included in discussions about the causes of crime among ethnic and racial minorities, such explanations of the race/crime link cannot be summarily dismissed as irrelevant. References to biologically based theories are frequently critical (e.g., Harris & Meidlinger, 1995; Joseph, 1995), but their presence in contemporary discourse about race and crime continue to provide legitimacy to the ill-conceived attempts to link the socially constructed concept of race—a concept that long has been discarded by physical anthropologists as unscientific (Wheeler, 1995)—to the culture-bound concept of criminality.

Sociological Theories

Hawkins (1993) uses the distinction between "economic deprivation/inequality" theories and "cultural variance" theories to group the different (sociological) theoretical approaches to race, ethnicity, and crime. Economic deprivation/inequality theories attribute higher rates of crime for certain ethnic/racial groups to their marginal socioeconomic status and their social and political subordination. Within this approach, ethnicity and race are treated as "proxies or near proxies for social class status" (Hawkins, 1993, p. 93; see, also, Myers & Simms, 1988). Structural factors including the family structure, ghetto environment, overcrowding, social isolation, and social disorganization contribute to feelings of powerlessness, despair, social alienation, and crime (Joseph, 1995, p. 65). Groups of (primarily) blacks and Hispanics, who suffer joblessness, economic deprivation, and poverty and who are seen as economic failures for generations, are said to belong to an "underclass" (Lewis as cited in Joseph, 1995, pp. 65-66; Wilson, 1987). Underlying themes of many of the economic deprivation/inequality theories include persistent racism and historical experience, which have taught blacks to be violent (e.g., Silberman, 1978). The historical past and structural factors of poverty, inadequate education, disorganized and deprived environments, unemployment, and other social ills interact to lessen the degree of social integration of minorities in society (Joseph, 1995, p. 68). Parallel reasoning (minus the historical past) applies to crime by immigrants (see, also, Sun & Reed, 1995).

The cultural-variance perspective, on the other hand, emphasizes the etiological importance of cultural differences in explaining crime rates across ethnic and racial groups; culture, rather than poverty, constitutes the primary cause of racial/ethnic group differences in the rate of crime (Hawkins, 1994, p. 102; see, also, Curtis, 1975; Erlanger, 1995; Wolfgang & Ferracuti, 1967). Sellin's (1938) notion of "culture conflict" as an explanation of crime by immigrants fits in this tradition.

In the last 30 years, one of the major tenets of criminology has been that "the most important task of criminology is not to study etiology, but rather to study the creation and application of law" (LaFree & Russell, 1993). In the context of the race/ethnicity/crime debate, it boils down to the hypothesis that the overrepresentation of minorities in crime statistics simply reflects discrimination by lawmakers and by the criminal justice system. The discrimination interpretation is the theoretical outgrowth of the labeling and conflict (Chambliss & Seidman, 1982) perspective. This body of research has evolved from rather simplistic tests of the main conflict hypothesis (i.e., minorities will be treated more severely than majority members by criminal justice officials), to much more sophisticated conceptual formulations. A good example is the "power-threat hypothesis," which suggests that as minority group membership grows, majority members will intensify their efforts to maintain dominance (Brown & Warner, 1995; Jackson, 1995; see, also, Chamblis, 1995).

A "Minority Perspective"

Several African American social scientists have begun to challenge the domination of U.S. criminology by Anglo Americans (Mann, 1993, 1995). Some include the colonial model (Fanon as cited in Joseph, 1995, p. 63) in the black view: African Americans have suffered greater social, political, and economic oppression than their white counterparts; blacks are subjected people, totally dependent on whites for their existence, excluded from decision-making processes, resulting in alienation and crime (Joseph, 1995; Tatum, 1994). Whether there is a distinct theoretical paradigm that can be classified as the "African American perspective" is subject to debate (Young & Sulton, 1994).

Toward a Political Economy of Criminality

In the last few years, major transformations have taken place in the U.S. experience with crime, race, and ethnicity as a consequence of both domestic developments and international forces. How have U.S. criminologists responded to the newest challenges?

There are those who remain primarily interested in the etiology of criminal involvement by racial/ethnic minorities. The last few years, there has been a renewed interest in individualistic biological and psychological approaches (Gottfredson & Hirschi, 1990; Wilson & Herrnstein, 1985), reverting back to theories with more manageable policy implications than those of structural (sociological) theories. Others remain involved in the further expansion of social-psychological theories, exploring whether the same variables that may be used to explain the behavior of whites may also be used to explain the behavior of minorities, sometimes adding structural and cultural variables to the conceptual mix (Bernard, 1990). Much outstanding work continues in the tradition of (cultural variance, economic deprivation/inequality, or both) sociological theories.

There is no doubt, however, that the recent developments in "domestic" minority crime, crime by (legal and undocumented) immigrants, and transnational crime require a greater investment of criminologists in the study of the nature and extent of newly emerging forms of crime, such as transnational drug-production and distribution systems, international terrorism and sabotage, transnational organized crime, nuclear material trafficking, electronic international fraud, and trafficking in people. Crime theories need to incorporate the influence of global developments on the nature and distribution of crime in the United States, including its inner cities (see Chapter 10, this volume).

FUTURE DEVELOPMENTS

By the middle of the next century, according to U.S. census projections, the U.S. population will almost be evenly divided between non-Hispanic white and minorities. (By 2010, Hispanics will be the largest minority group in the U.S., outnumbering blacks; the Asian group is also expected to grow at a very fast rate.) The white (northern and western) European will no longer be the measuring rod of "appropriate" behavior, and no longer in control of political, economic, and social life in the United States. Power balances will change, with a corresponding shift in the types of people most involved in criminality, and differences in what kind of activities will be criminalized.

Meanwhile, there is a strong backlash against immigration and immigrants. The year 1996 was a bad year for immigrants in the United States. A bill severely limiting the rights of undocumented and legal noncitizens has been signed into law by the president. Budget allocations for agencies dealing with detecting undocumented aliens and patrolling the borders have been expanded. Children of undocumented immigrants no longer have the right to receive public education (including school lunches). Welfare guarantees have been severely undercut by recent federal law, with potentially disastrous effects on the quality of life of some recent immigrants. The new federal welfare bill also will have a disproportionate effect on the economic and physical well-being of many blacks, Hispanics, Native Americans, and some Asian groups. In the short run, then, the prospects seem pretty grim. The (mostly minority) underclass segregated in inner-city ghettos will balloon, the size of the homeless population will grow, guns and drugs will continue to be more effective means of communication than kind and civil language. The penal climate will harden even more. Political rhetoric will become more extreme and divisive. Fear of crime will continue to curtail the daily routines of many U.S. citizens. Private security business will continue to boom; the flight to the suburbs will persist. But the pendulum is bound to swing back, be it for ideological, humane, or pragmatic reasons. There are only so many prison cells, so many executions, so many beggars, so many locks on doors that a nation like the United States is willing to tolerate. (If nothing else, it keeps the tourists away!) There will be a point where inclusion rather than exclusion will be seen as the key to preserving the American Dream. Once that happens, ordinary "garden-variety" (violent and property) street crime will not disappear, but the further escalation of violence may be prevented.[10]

The handwriting is on the wall; a distinct qualitative shift in the nature of criminality is taking place. The internationalization and globalization of criminality implies that U.S. citizens can no longer simply deal with their fears by moving, buying a gun, or installing sophisticated security equipment in their homes. Keeping the borders sealed will not work. Stiffening prison sentences will not work. An effective crime policy must address the political-economic bases of criminality, not only within, but also outside U.S. national borders. It is very simple, really: The economic deprivation/ inequality theory applies not only to the United States, but to all members of the global village.

NOTES

1. "Race" is placed between quotation marks to signify the socially constructed nature of this concept. In the remainder of the chapter, these quotation marks have been omitted.

2. This disproportionality becomes even more marked when one considers that the majority of arrests for serious crime involves males, and that black males make up only about 6% of the general population.

3. These estimates are based on national drug use surveys; they probably underestimate the extent of serious drug abuse among marginal populations. Recent trends indicate a decline in casual use, a growing abstinence among middle-class users, and the spread of addiction among the poor and unemployed, pointing to the increasing importance of race and class in shaping patterns of drug abuse (Schatzberg & Kelley, 1996, p. 165)

4. Also, federal sentencing guidelines require much more severe penalties for crack than for powder cocaine. Crack is most typically used by African Americans, whereas powder cocaine is more commonly used among whites.

5. But for a convincing counterargument, see Jacobs and Henry's (1996) strong challenge of the "uncritical acceptance of a hate crime epidemic" (p. 391).

6. See Silverman (1996) for a challenge of the high level of overrepresentation across most offense categories of Indian crime.

7. Hawkins must be credited with reintroducing the concept of ethnicity in the study of minorities and crime (Hawkins, 1993, 1994, 1995a, 1995b).

8. See, for example, publications in two recent professional journals, *Trends in Organized Crime* and *Transnational Organized Crime*.

9. In Los Angeles, the "gang capital of the world," almost 600 gang-related killings took place in 1989; the L.A. gang population was estimated around 100,000 in 1989.

10. Declining rates of lethal violence during the past few years suggest that there may be a time lag between official and public response to crime and the seriousness of the crime problem.

REFERENCES

Armstrong, T. L., Guilfoyle, M. H., & Melton, A. P. (1996). Native American delinquency: An overview of prevalence, causes, and correlates. In M. O. Nielsen & R. A. Silverman (Eds.), *Native Americans, crime, and justice* (pp. 75-88). Boulder, CO: Westview.

Bachman, R., Alvarez, A., & Perkins, C. (1996). Discriminatory imposition of the law: Does it affect sentencing outcomes for American Indians? In M. O. Nielsen & R. A. Silverman (Eds.), *Native Americans, crime, and justice* (pp. 197-208). Boulder, CO: Westview.

Bailey, F. Y. (1991). Law, justice, and "Americans": A historical overview. In M. J. Lynch & E. Britt Paterson (Eds.), *Race and criminal justice* (pp. 10-21). Albany, NY: Harrow and Heston.

Baldus, D. C., Pulaski, C., & Woodworth, C. (1983). Comparative review of death sentences: An empirical study of the Georgia experience. *Journal of Criminal Law and Criminology, 74,* 661-753.

Bernard, T. (1990). Angry aggression among the "truly disadvantaged." *Criminology, 28,* 73-96.

Block, C., & Block, R. (1993). *Street gang crime in Chicago* (National Institute of Justice: Research in brief. Office of Justice Programs, U.S. Department of Justice). Washington, DC: Government Printing Office

Blumstein, A. (1995, August). Juvenile homicides. *National Institute of Justice Journal, 229,* 2-9.

Brown, M. C., & Warner, B. D. (1995). The political threat of immigrant groups and police aggressiveness in 1900. In D. F. Hawkins (Ed.), *Ethnicity, race, and crime: Perspectives across time and place* (pp. 82-98). Albany: State University of New York Press.

Bureau of Justice Statistics. (1994a). *Highlights from 20 years of surveying crime victims.* Washington, DC: Government Printing Office.

Bureau of Justice Statistics. (1994b). *Young black male victims.* Washington, DC: Department of Justice.

Bureau of Justice Statistics. (1995a). *Capital punishment, 1994.* Washington, DC: Department of Justice.

Bureau of Justice Statistics. (1995b). *Criminal victimization in the United States, 1993.* Washington, DC: Government Printing Office.

Bureau of Justice Statistics. (1995c). *Sourcebook of criminal justice statistics, 1994.* Washington, DC: Government Printing Office.

Bureau of Justice Statistics. (1996). *Noncitizens in the federal criminal justice system, 1984-1994.* Washington, DC: Department of Justice.

Carter, D. L. (1995a). Hispanic interaction with the criminal justice system in Texas: Experiences, attitudes, and perceptions. In A. S. Lopez (Ed.), *Latinos in the United States. Volume 3. Criminal justice and Latino communities* (pp. 57-72). New York: Garland.

Carter, D. L. (1995b). Hispanic perception of police performance: An empirical assessment. In A. S. Lopez. (Ed.), *Latinos in the United States. Volume 3. Criminal justice and Latino communities* (pp. 73-86). New York: Garland.

Chambliss, W. J. (1995). Crime control and ethnic minorities: Legitimizing racial oppression by creating moral panics. In D. F. Hawkins (Ed.), *Ethnicity, race, and crime. Perspectives across time and place* (pp. 235-258). Albany: State University of New York Press.

Chambliss, W. J., & Seidman, R. (1982). *Law, order, and power* (2nd ed.). Reading, MA: Addison-Wesley.

Chin, K. (1995). Chinese gangs and extortion. In M. W. Klein, C. L. Maxson, & J. Miller (Eds.), *The modern gang reader* (pp. 46-52). Los Angeles: Roxbury.

Chiricos, T. G, & Crawford, C. (1995). Race and imprisonment: A contextual assessment of the evidence. In D. F. Hawkins (Ed.), *Ethnicity, race, and crime: Perspectives across time and place* (pp. 281-309). Albany: State University of New York Press.

Clark, D. D. (1991). Ethnic bias in a correctional setting: The Mariel Cubans. In M. J. Lynch & E. Britt Paterson (Eds.), *Race and criminal justice* (pp. 113-125). Albany, NY: Harrow and Heston.

Clarke, R. (1996). Interview with R. Clarke, Special Assistant to the President. *Trends in Organized Crime, 1*(3), 5.

Curtis, L. A. (1975). *Violence, race, and culture.* Lexington, MA: Lexington Books.

Donziger, S. R. (Ed.). (1996). *The real war on crime: The report of the National Criminal Justice Commission.* New York: HarperCollins.

Erlanger, H. S. (1995). Estrangement, machismo, and gang violence. In A. S. Lopez (Ed.), *Latinos in the United States. Volume 3. Criminal justice and Latino communities* (pp. 207-220). New York: Garland.

Ethnic Chinese now no. 1 in crime, say U.S. experts. (1996, October 14). *Omaha World Herald,* p. 2.

Federal Bureau of Investigation. (1996). *Crime in the United States 1995.* Washington, DC: Government Printing Office.

Finckenauer, J. O., Waring, E. J., & Barthe, E. (1996). Law enforcement perceptions of Soviet emigre crime networks in the United States. *Trends in Organized Crime, 1*(3), 37-40.

Flowers, R. B. (1988). *Minorities and criminality.* New York: Praeger.

Fraser, S. (1995). *The bell curve wars: Race, intelligence, and the future of America.* New York: Basic Books.

Garofalo, J. (1991). Racially motivated crimes in New York City. In M. J. Lynch & E. Britt Paterson (Eds.), *Race and criminal justice* (pp. 161-173). Albany, NY: Harrow and Heston.

Garza, H. (1995). Administration of justice: Chicanos in Monterey County. In A. S. Lopez (Ed.), *Latinos in the United States. Volume 3. Criminal justice and Latino communities* (pp. 47-56). New York: Garland.

Gottfredson, M. R., & Hirschi, T. (1990). *A general theory of crime.* Stanford, CA: Stanford University Press.

Grobsmith, E. (1996). American Indians in prison. In M. O. Nielsen & R. A. Silverman (Eds.), *Native Americans, crime, and justice* (pp. 224-227). Boulder, CO: Westview.

Hacker, A. (1992). *Two nations: Black and white, separate, hostile, unequal.* New York: Ballantine.

Harris, A. R., & Meidlinger, L. R. (1995). Criminal behavior: Race and class. In J. F. Sheley (Ed.), *Criminology* (2nd ed., pp. 115-144). Belmont, CA: Wadsworth.

Hawkins, D. F. (1993). Crime and ethnicity. In B. Forst (Ed.), *The socioeconomics of crime and justice* (pp. 89-120). Armonk, NY: M. E. Sharpe.

Hawkins, D. F. (1994). Ethnicity: The forgotten dimension of American social control. In G. S. Bridges & M. A. Myers (Eds.), *Inequality, crime, and social control* (pp. 99-116). Boulder, CO: Westview.

Hawkins, D. F. (1995a). Ethnicity, race, and crime: A review of selected studies. In D. F. Hawkins (Ed.), *Ethnicity, race, and crime: Perspectives across time and place* (pp. 11-45). Albany: State University of New York Press.

Hawkins, D. F. (Ed.). (1995b). *Ethnicity, race, and crime: Perspectives across time and place.* Albany: State University of New York Press.

Hernandez, T. K. (1995). Bias crimes: Unconscious racism in the prosecution of "racially motivated violence." In A. S. Lopez (Ed.), *Latinos in the United States. Volume 3. Criminal justice and Latino communities* (pp. 139-158). New York: Garland.

Holmes, M. D., & Daudistel, H. C. (1995). Ethnicity and justice in the Southwest: The sentencing of Anglo, black, and Mexican origin defendants. In A. S. Lopez (Ed.), *Latinos in the United States. Volume 3. Criminal justice and Latino communities* (pp. 125-138). New York: Garland.

Jackson, P. M. (1995). Minority group threat, crime, and the mobilization of law in France. In D. F. Hawkins (Ed.), *Ethnicity, race, and crime: Perspectives across time and place* (pp. 341-360). Albany: State University of New York Press.

Jacobs, J. B., & Henry, J. S. (1996). The social construction of a hate crime epidemic. *Journal of Criminal Jaw & Criminology, 86,* 366-391.

Joseph, J. (1995). Black youths, delinquency, and juvenile justice. Westport, CT: Praeger.

Klein, M. W., Maxson, C. L., & Miller, J. (1995). *The modern gang reader.* Los Angeles: Roxbury.

Kotlowitz, A. (1991). *There are no children here.* Garden City, NY: Doubleday.

LaFree, G. D. (1995). Official reactions to Hispanic defendants in the Southwest. In A. S. Lopez (Ed.), *Latinos in the United States. Volume 3. Criminal justice and Latino communities* (pp. 159-184). New York: Garland.

LaFree, G. & Russell, K. K. (1993). The argument for studying race and crime. *Journal of Criminal Justice Education, 4*(2), 273-289.

Lopez, A. S. (Ed.). (1995). *Latinos in the United States. Volume 3. Criminal justice and Latino communities.* New York: Garland.

Mann, C. R. (1993). *Unequal justice: A question of color.* Bloomington: Indiana University Press.

Mann, C. R. (1995). The contribution of institutionalized racism to minority crime. In D. F. Hawkins (Ed.), *Ethnicity, race, and crime: Perspectives across time and place* (pp. 259-280). Albany: State University of New York Press.

Mauer, M. (1995, October 16). Disparate justice imperils a community. *Legal Times,* p. 1.

Myers, M. A. (1995). The new South's "new" black criminal: Rape and punishment in Georgia, 1870-1940. In D. F. Hawkins (Ed.), *Ethnicity, race, and crime. Perspectives across time and place* (pp. 145-168). Albany: State University of New York Press.

Myers, S. L., & Simms, M. C. (Eds.). (1988). *The economics of race and crime.* New Brunswick, NJ: Transaction Books.

Nielsen, M. O., & R. A. Silverman (Eds.). (1996). *Native Americans, crime, and justice.* Boulder, CO: Westview.

O'Kane, J. M. (1992). *The crooked ladder: Gangsters, ethnicity, and the American dream.* New Brunswick, NJ: Transaction Books.

Operation Safe Streets. (1995). Street gang detail. L.A. style: A street gang manual of the Los Angeles County Sheriff's Department. In M. W. Klein, C. L. Maxson, & J. Miller (Eds.), *The modern gang reader* (pp. 34-45). Los Angeles: Roxbury.

Parrillo, V. (1996). *Diversity in America.* Thousand Oaks, CA: Pine Forge.

Poupart, L. M. (1995). Juvenile justice processing of American Indian youth: Disparity in one rural county. In K. L. Leonard, C. E. Feyerherm, & W. H. Feyerherm (Eds.), *Minorities in juvenile justice* (pp. 179-200). Thousand Oaks, CA: Sage.

Purcell, L. E. (1995). *Immigration.* Phoenix, AZ: Oryx.

Regulus, T. A. (1995). Race, class, and sociobiological perspectives on crime. In D. F. Hawkins (Ed.), *Ethnicity, race, and crime: Perspectives across time and place* (pp. 46-65). Albany: State University of New York Press.

Reuter, T. (1996). The decline of the American Mafia. *Trends in Organized Crime, 1*(3), 27-34.

Sanders, W. B. (1994). *Gangbangs and drive-bys: Grounded culture and juvenile gang violence.* Hawthorne, NY: Aldine de Gruyter.

Schatzberg, R., & Kelly, R. J. (1996). *African American organized crime.* New York: Garland.

Schmid, A. P., & Savona, E. U. (1996). Migration and crime: A framework for discussion. In A. P. Schmid (Ed.), *Migration and crime* (pp. 5-42). Milan, Italy: International Scientific and Professional Advisory Council of the United Nations Crime Prevention and Criminal Justice Program [ISPAC].

Sellin, T. (1938). *Culture conflict and crime.* New York: Social Science Research Council.

Silberman, C. E. (1978). *Criminal violence, criminal justice.* New York: Random House.

Silverman, R. A. (1996). Patterns of Native American crime. In M. O. Nielsen & R. A. Silverman (Eds.), *Native Americans, crime, and justice* (pp. 58-74). Boulder, CO: Westview.

Smith, M. D. (1995). The death penalty in America. In J. F. Sheley (Ed.), *Criminology* (2nd ed., pp. 557-572). Belmont, CA: Wadsworth.

Snyder-Joy, Z. (1995). Self-determination and American Indian justice: Tribal versus federal jurisdiction on Indian lands. In D. F. Hawkins (Ed.), *Ethnicity, race, and crime. Perspectives across time and place* (pp. 310-322). Albany: State University of New York Press.

Steinberg, S. (1989). *The ethnic myth: Race, ethnicity, and class in America.* Boston: Beacon.

Sun, H.-E., & Reed, J. (1995). Migration and crime in Europe. *Social Pathology, 1*(3), 228-252.

Tanton, J., & Lutton, W. (1993). Immigration and criminality in the U.S.A. *Journal of Social, Political, and Economic Studies, 18*(2), 217-234.

Tatum, B. (1994). The colonial model as a theoretical explanation of crime and delinquency. In A. T. Sulton (Ed.), *African American perspectives on crime causation, criminal justice administration, and crime prevention* (pp. 33-52). Newton, MA: Butterworth-Heinemann.

Tonry, M. (1995). *Malign neglect: Race, crime, and punishment in America.* New York: Oxford University Press.

Tonry, M. (1996). The effects of American drug policy on black Americans, 1980-1996. *European Journal on Criminal Policy and Research, 4*(2), 36-62.

U.S. Bureau of the Census. (1992). *Current population reports* (Series P25-1092). Washington, DC: Government Printing Office.

Walker, S., Spohn C., & DeLone, M. (1996). *The color of justice: Race, ethnicity, and crime in America.* Belmont, CA: Wadsworth.

Walker, S., & Wright, B. (1995). *Citizen review of the police, 1994: A national survey.* Washington, DC: Police Executive Research Forum.

Wheeler, D. L. (1995, February 17). A growing number of scientists reject the concept of race. *Chronicle of Higher Education, 17,* A8, A9, A15.

Wilbanks, W. (1987). *The myth of a racist criminal justice system.* Monterey, CA: Brooks/Cole.

Wilson, J. Q., & Herrnstein, R. (1985). *Crime and human nature.* New York: Simon & Schuster.

Wilson, W. J. (1987). *The truly disadvantaged.* Chicago: University of Chicago Press.

Winer, J. (1996). Interview with J. Winer, Deputy Assistant Secretary of State. *Trends in Organized Crime, 1*(3), 9.

Wolfgang, M. E., & Ferracuti, F. (1967). *The subculture of violence: Toward an integrated theory in criminology.* Beverly Hills, CA: Sage.

Young, V., & Sulton, A. T. (1994). Excluded: The current status of African American scholars in the field of criminology and criminal justice. In A. T. Sulton (Ed.), *African American perspectives on crime causation, criminal justice administration, and crime prevention* (pp. 1-17). Newton, MA: Butterworth-Heinemann.

Zatz, M. S. (1987). The changing forms of racial/ethnic biases in sentencing. *Journal of Research in Crime and Delinquency, 24,* 69-92.

Zatz, M. S., Chiago Lugan, C., & Snyder-Joy, Z. K. (1991). American Indians and criminal justice: Some conceptual and methodological considerations. In M. J.Lynch & E. Britt Patterson (Eds.), *Race and criminal justice* (pp. 100-112). New York: Harrow and Heston.

2

MINORITIES, CRIME, AND CRIMINAL JUSTICE IN BRITAIN

Marian FitzGerald

The academic and political debate over race and crime in Britain has tended to focus on the black[1] groups as the cause of concern with regard to offending. That debate has been conducted quite separately from the more recent, less academic, and relatively politically consensual discussion about racial harassment. The main focus here has tended to be the Asian groups, and the discussion has rarely been set in the context of general victimisation. That is, both the debate on offending and that on victimisation have been conducted in highly "ethnicised" terms. Moreover, the failure of criminologists to make any connections between the two debates clashes with their increasing recognition that victims and offenders are not discrete categories. Rather, they overlap in ways that have not only conceptual implications but that raise important questions for criminal justice practitioners. By

EDITOR'S NOTE: Because of the multinational nature of this book, British spellings have been retained in this chapter. British Crown copyright 1996. Published with the permission of the Controller of Her Britannic Majesty's Stationery Office. The views expressed are those of the author and do not necessarily reflect the views or policy of the Home Office, Her Britannic Majesty's Stationery Office, or any other British Government Department.

sustaining the dichotemisation of minorities as *either* offenders *or* victims, criminologists have effectively consigned them to a one-dimensional ethnic niche outside mainstream developments in criminological thinking and have blocked the light that the evidence on victimisation could throw on the highly charged debate on ethnic minority offending.

This chapter affords an opportunity to refocus the discussion of ethnicity and offending in Britain by referring also to the evidence on ethnicity and victimisation. It is presented in three parts. The first is background, including some history. The second divides into two and concerns the available evidence on ethnic minorities as suspects and offenders, followed by data on ethnic minorities as victims of crime including questions of what in Britain is often (though not uncontroversially) termed "racial harassment." The final section draws out some of the patterns that emerge from the juxtaposition of these two sets of evidence and the implications for our understanding of ethnicity and offending.

BACKGROUND

Most of the minority groups with whom the British research has been concerned have their origins in the postwar immigration of visible minorities from countries of the former British Empire, in particular the "Asian" groups from the Indian subcontinent and the "black" groups from the West Indies. Most primary migration took place in the 1950s, 1960s, and 1970s and the majority of these immigrants, once here, had the right to settle (or acquired it fairly readily) because they were British citizens, British subjects, or both.[2] Currently the largest of the groups with their origins in this migration are the Indians (some of whom had previously been settled in East Africa). The two next-largest groups have their origins in the Caribbean or Pakistan (see Table 2.1).

It is important to note, however, that the timing both of primary immigration and of immigration for family reunion took place in different stages for different groups. The result of this is, broadly speaking, that the black Caribbean group (to use the classification introduced in the 1991 national census) is the longest established ethnic minority group in Britain and is now into the third generation whereas the Bangladeshis are the most recent and still completing the phase of family formation. It also means that there is considerable variation in the proportion of each group who were actually born in the United Kingdom and in their age structures. On average, all are

TABLE 2.1 Population Composition of Great Britain by Ethnic Group

	Thousands	Percentage of Population	Percentage of All Ethnic Minorities
Black			
Caribbean	500	0.9	17
African	210	0.4	7
Other	180	0.3	6
Indian	840	1.5	28
Pakistani	480	0.9	16
Bangladeshi	160	0.3	5
Chinese	160	0.3	5
Other Asian	200	0.4	7
Other	290	0.5	10
All minority ethnic groups	3,020	5.5	100
White	51,870	94.5	

SOURCE: 1991 census.

younger than the white population, but in particular the Pakistanis and Bangladeshis along with the "Black Other" and the "Other" groups. For the first two of these groups, this is associated with migration patterns, whereas the two Other groups tend to comprise people of mixed ethnic origin, a high proportion of whom were born in Britain (see Table 2.2).

Two other points are also worth bearing in mind with regard to the demography of these groups. The first is that, as previous migrants here and elsewhere, all tended to settle mainly in urban areas; and, the broad patterns of initial settlement remain. Their distribution across those areas, however, has been uneven and it has also been uneven within the urban areas where they have settled. London has been the most important urban area for all groups (and particularly for the black groups[3]) except for the Pakistanis, less than 20% of whom are found in the capital, with slightly more in the West Midlands, and only slightly fewer in West Yorkshire.

Second, there are important socioeconomic differences among and within the minorities themselves. In terms of their economic status, the Indian population is not dissimilar to (and in some respects more privileged than) the average for whites. The black Caribbeans, however, are much more disadvantaged; and, the Pakistanis and Bangladeshis are in some respects worse off again, with high levels of unemployment among these groups compounded by low income and poor housing conditions.

In the early years, discrimination was totally unchecked by legislation (which was first introduced in 1965) and racial tensions were largely ignored

TABLE 2.2 Percentage[a] Born in the United Kingdom and Age Structure

	Ethnic Group	Aged 0-4	Aged 5-15	Born in United Kingdom
Black	Black Caribbean	7.6	14.3	53.7
	Black African	11.8	17.5	36.4
	Black Other	20.3	30.3	84.4
Asian	Indian	8.8	20.7	41.9
	Pakistani	13.1	29.5	50.5
	Bangladeshi	15.1	32.2	36.6
Other	Chinese	7.1	16.3	28.4
	Other Asian	8.0	16.4	21.9
	Other	16.4	25.3	59.8
White	White	6.4	13.0	95.8

SOURCE: 1991 census.
NOTE: a. Percentage of total in each ethnic group.

by politicians. The group from the West Indies, the earliest arrivals, were certainly harassed and that harassment led to riots in the late 1950s in both London and the provincial city of Nottingham. The same group also began, around this time, to complain of harassment by the police, and this issue was taken up by campaigning groups and in the literature by the 1960s (Hunte, 1966; Rose et al., 1969).

The police acknowledged the deterioration in their relationship with this group (Simpson, 1967; Whitaker, 1964) but rejected claims of harassment made by "West Indians" (to use the terminology of that period). They also maintained an official position at least until the mid-1970s that there was no problem of crime among ethnic minorities. Giving evidence in 1972 to a House of Commons Select Committee on Police Immigrant Relations, police forces acknowledged widespread concern about "growing tensions" but concluded "beyond doubt" that

> Coloured immigrants are no more involved in crime than others nor are they generally more concerned in violence, prostitution, and drugs. The West Indian crime rate is much the same as that of the indigenous population, the Asian crime rate is very much lower. (House of Commons Select Committee, 1972, p. 71)

But by the late 1970s, there had been a significant escalation, polarisation, and indeed politicisation of the debate around race and crime. The police had

rescinded their previous position only 4 years after they gave the evidence
cited here, when the Select Committee took evidence on the situation of "the
West Indian community" more generally. The Metropolitan Police submitted
a memorandum that concluded that although further evidence was needed on
"this sensitive and emotive subject"

> already our experience has taught us the fallibility of the assertion that
> crime rates among those of West Indian origin are no higher than those of
> the population at large. (House of Commons Select Committee, 1977,
> p. 182)

And, when they were challenged on this apparent departure from their
previous position, they submitted a further memorandum stating that "from
current statistics available, our overall experience of 1971 no longer holds
good" (House of Commons Select Committee, 1977, p. 689).

During the same time period there was the rise of the Scrap Sus campaign, which was formed and led largely by black people. The campaign
drew heavily on a report (Demuth, 1978) showing that the police (in particular in London) were using the provisions of a Vagrancy Act dating back to
1824 to arrest black people disproportionately *on suspicion* of being about
to commit an offence. There was also a sustained upsurge of interest in the
phenomenon of "mugging," which the media identified strongly with people
of West Indian origin (Hall, Critcher, Clarke, Jefferson, & Roberts, 1978).
This phase in the development of mounting antagonism between the police
and this particular section of the communities of postwar immigrant origin
culminated in a press release from the Metropolitan Police in 1982 that
selectively used police figures to reinforce the perception that black people
were disproportionately involved in street crime (Scotland Yard press release, March 10, 1982).

That press release overlapped with a new turn of events. In 1980, the
British mainland was shaken by the first major public disorder in the postwar
period, with clashes in Bristol between the police and what were by now
coming to be referred to as black youth. Similar events occurred in the
summer of 1981 and were more widespread, affecting parts of London and
Liverpool as well as other cities and large towns (Scarman, 1981). They
recurred in London and Birmingham in 1985, this time with the loss of three
lives. These events and the political debates they engendered added to
popular negative stereotypes of "the black mugger," associating people of
West Indian origin in the 1980s with social disorder generally (Solomos,
1988).

Meanwhile, the phenomenon referred to as "Paki-bashing" (racially motivated assaults on people of Asian origin) had been well known in East London, certainly throughout the 1970s and indeed earlier. Three influential publications translated the problem of racial harassment (associated primarily with Asians[4]) into a political issue in the late 1970s and early 1980s. The first, called *Blood on the Streets,* was a report on the problem in an area of East London produced by a local labour organisation (Bethnal Green & Stepney Trades Council, 1978). The second was a national survey conducted by the Joint Committee Against Racism (JCAR), which had been founded jointly by the leadership of the main political parties in the context of the vigorous antiracist movement of the mid-1970s (JCAR, 1980). The third was a Home Office study that the government initiated in direct response to the JCAR report (Home Office, 1981). Certainly the question of racial harassment became a significant policy concern of the 1980s for campaigning groups, for local government, and for central government (FitzGerald, 1996). The subject was examined by a House of Commons Select Committee in 1985 to 1986 and the government set up a Racial Attacks Group, involving all relevant government ministries and representatives of the police and other statutory agencies in 1988.

All this time, however, remarkably little attention had been given in British criminology as such, to issues of race and crime. Apart from reports by campaigning organisations and journalism, the published works that are most memorable for raising the issues were written mainly (although not exclusively) by political or social scientists and certainly there was very little empirical work of rigour. The topic was covered within the first major study of British race relations in 1969 (Rose et al., 1969). In 1978, a major sociological critique called *Policing the Crisis* (Hall et al., 1978) wove the issues on the thread of what its authors saw as a moral panic over mugging. The report by Lord Justice Scarman, which was commissioned by the Government (Scarman, 1981), seized the opportunity to put the riots of the early 1980s into the wider context of police relations with minorities and of the political and economic circumstances of black people—its status as one of the seminal works in this field confirmed by its publication as a commercial paperback. And a study undertaken around the same time, on behalf of the Metropolitan Police, produced a four-volume oeuvre in 1983 on the force's relations with the public with particular reference to ethnic minorities (Smith, 1983).

In addition, small-scale studies and surveys of varying degrees of statistical and intellectual rigour appeared in connection with questions both of the criminal involvement of ethnic minorities and of "racial" victimisation.[5]

The first major empirical breakthrough undertaken by a criminologist, however, did not occur until the early 1990s with the publication of Roger Hood's study of sentencing in the Crown Court in the West Midlands (Hood, 1992).

In view of wider political developments and debates, however, issues of race and crime were increasingly forcing themselves onto the research agenda. Yet interpreting the data posed dilemmas for liberal-minded criminologists, and it is probably no coincidence that they tended to be addressed by those with a particular policy orientation. Much, if not most, of the empirical research that was undertaken from the late 1970s in this area was undertaken by the Research and Planning Unit of the British Home Office. The Unit was responsible for the 1981 study of racial harassment referred to previously but had already, by that time, produced a report titled *Race, Crime, and Arrests* (Stevens & Willis, 1979) and another on *Ethnic Minorities, Crime, and Policing: A Survey of the Experiences of West Indians and Whites* (Tuck & Southgate, 1981).

Academic criminologists, meanwhile, inasmuch as they addressed the issue, tended to rely on secondary sources and seem to have tied themselves in quite a number of knots. Their work has been confined almost exclusively to questions of criminality; and, those who have sought to prove racial discrimination and police harassment in this area, have wrestled ineffectually with the apparently contrasting experience of the Caribbean and Asian groups. Some have risked drawing superficial and potentially dangerous "parallels" from the extensive American literature, assuming that the black groups in each country can be equated (a point taken up again in the next discussion section). Unconstrained by empirical evidence, some have generalised so sweepingly in their attempts to "explain" the apparent differences between the different ethnic groups that they have come close to stereotyping, as the following offering from the British New Left Realist school illustrates:

> The question arises of the differences between Asian and West Indian youth. As a result of discrimination, the unemployment rate for ethnic minority youth in general has risen at a much faster rate than for their white counterparts, but between youth of West Indian and Asian parentage there are two differences that have the effect of comparatively insulating the latter from the process of relative deprivation. First, by comparison with West Indian youth, Asians have a more substantive opportunity structure within their own community; this is due to the larger size of the professional and business class in the Asian community. Second, the distance between Asian culture and indigenous British culture is greater than that between the latter and West Indian culture. Assimilation to indigenous British

standards and aspirations has thus *probably* been a more rapid process for youth of West Indian parentage and hence relative deprivation is felt more acutely with the consequent fostering of a counterculture. (Cowell, Jones, & Young, 1982, p. 8, emphasis added)

Against this background, it is appropriate to turn now to examining the evidence that exists on ethnic minorities as suspects and offenders.

THE EVIDENCE

Suspects and Offenders

The most robust and longest established source of information on ethnic minorities as suspects and offenders is the prison statistics. Ethnic monitoring of the British prison population began in 1983 and since 1985 has produced data on a comparable basis over time. For nearly 10 years the figures have consistently shown overrepresentation of black people in British prisons, with a dramatic increase over that time among black women (see Table 2.3).

The prison statistics also show apparently different patterns of offending by different ethnic groups (see Table 2.4) and different sentence lengths (a point returned to later).

There are two main limitations to the prison data for purposes of establishing levels and patterns of offending among different ethnic groups:

1. They are unable to differentiate between British ethnic minorities and those normally resident abroad.
2. They also represent the end point of the criminal justice system. That is, they refer to a very small proportion of all offenders and it is, therefore, unclear to what extent they reflect the underlying reality in terms of the levels and patterns of crime that they indicate.

With regard to their inability to differentiate between British ethnic minorities and those normally resident abroad, there has been a refinement since 1992 in the system of classification used in prisons, and also in the procedures for recording. This has at least produced reasonably reliable breakdowns of British prisoners by nationality. It is important to note that residence cannot necessarily be inferred from nationality; but, it certainly

TABLE 2.3 Ethnic Composition of the Prison Population (England and
Wales), June 1985 to June 1995 (row percentages)

	White	Black	Asian	Chinese/Other/ Not Recorded
Males				
1985	83	8	2	7
1995	83	11	3	3
Females				
1985	78	12	2	8
1995	76	20	1	4

SOURCE: Home Office Prison Statistics.

provides us with a better approximation than was previously available. What
it does show is that in June 1995, black prisoners with U.K. nationality
accounted for just under 10% of the total male prison population, whereas
the total black figure is nearly 2% higher. The corresponding figures for
women, however, show a much starker contrast at 11% and 20%, respectively. The reasons for the apparent major difference in the figures for women
relate to the very high proportion of black women in prison who are foreign
nationals, mostly from African countries, and in prison for drug smuggling
(Home Office Statistical Bulletin, 1994).

The prison statistics are the only national data set capable of showing
trends over time; but, they represent the end point of the system. It is,
therefore, necessary to piece together the more disparate evidence concerning the key points in the criminal justice process before the stage of imprisonment.

At the beginning of the process we have two major unknowns. One is
that we know little or nothing about actual rates of offending by different
ethnic groups as reported by themselves to self-report surveys.[6] Also, we
know very little about whether crimes committed by different ethnic groups
are more or less likely to be reported. Few British studies have examined
whether there is a greater likelihood that crimes in which the offender is from
an ethnic minority will be reported than crimes committed by whites. There
is some evidence for this in Smith's (1983) study with further tentative
confirmation by the present author (FitzGerald & Hale, 1996) but, as yet,
nothing conclusive on this point.

There is, however, some evidence that black people are disproportionately brought into the system through proactive policing. The most robust

TABLE 2.4 Adult Sentenced Prisoners: Offence Group by Ethnic Origin and Gender, 1995 (column percentages)

	White		Black		Asian
	Males	*Females*	*Males*	*Females*	*Males*
Violence against the person	23	21	20	8	24
Rape	5	—	6	—	5
Other sexual offences	6	1	1	—	3
Burglary	17	5	10	1	6
Robbery	13	8	23	5	12
Theft/handling	10	23	5	7	6
Fraud and forgery	3	7	2	7	7
Drug offences	8	20	20	61	16
Other offences	12	10	6	7	16
N	31,555	1,111	3,975	276	1,044

SOURCE: Home Office Prison Statistics.

data come from various studies of stops by the police. In particular, Wesley Skogan's (1990) analysis of the 1988 British Crime Survey in which, taking all relevant factors into account in a sophisticated multivariate analysis, he still finds that there is disproportionate stopping of blacks by the police that is unattributable to any other obvious factor except their ethnicity. More recently, the Inspectorate of Police has since April 1993 required the police to record the ethnic origin of all persons they stop and search using their powers under the Police and Criminal Evidence Act of 1984. These data are limited because, to the present, they have not provided any breakdown within ethnic minority groups but are simply presented in terms of whites versus nonwhites.

Overall, ethnic minorities appeared to be five times as likely to be stopped as whites, with 36.0 stops per 1,000 population in the first year of recording compared with 6.8 stops for whites. There were, however, variations in the level of overrepresentation both between and within forces; and, some have made available figures broken down further within the ethnic minority category. These show a starker overrepresentation of black people, which is often masked in the aggregate data by average or lower than average rates for the Asian groups.[7] It is, however, important to remember that only a small proportion of stops actually result in arrest. Much less is known about other forms of proactive policing, although the Hood (1992) report tends to confirm previous studies (including Stevens & Willis, 1979), which suggest that black people are more likely to be brought into the system as a result of police initiatives. Hood notes that, among his sample, black defendants sentenced at the Crown Court were "disproportionately involved in the supply of drugs, usually cannabis" and reports that

> these convictions regularly arose from police activity rather than from a complaint by citizens. . . . If these offences were excluded, the proportion of black males dealt with at the West Midlands courts would have been . . . equivalent to 20% lower. (Stevens & Willis, 1979, p. 180)

Certainly evidence is mounting that fewer black people are likely to be cautioned[8] than whites rather than charged and prosecuted, while Asians (if anything) are more likely to be cautioned—although the figures for blacks appear to be largely explained by the lower likelihood that they are prepared to admit the charges brought against them (Commission for Racial Equality, 1992). In addition, black people are more likely to be charged with "indict-able-only" offences such as robbery (Walker, 1988; Walker, Jefferson, & Seneviratne, 1989), which may only be tried at Crown Court and may, for this reason, incur heavier penalties for those found guilty than offences triable in Magistrates' Courts. It is also important to remember in this regard both that the charge that is brought is subject to some discretion, especially in offences of medium seriousness, and that there are considerable variations by area in charging practices (points that will be returned to in the discussion).

Not only does a higher proportion of black offenders and defendants go to the Crown Court because this group has a higher charge rate for indictable offences, they are also more likely to be tried at Crown Court because in cases that could either be tried there or in a lower court, they are less likely than whites to be tried in (lower) Magistrates' Court (Brown & Hullin, 1992; Hood, 1992; Shallice & Gordon, 1990; Walker 1988, 1989; Walker et al., 1989). The evidence leaves it unclear, however, whether the reason for this is primarily the choice of the defendant or the choice of magistrates and, again, it is known that magistrates' patterns of committal for Crown Court trial vary considerably by area, anyway.

A further influence on different groups' trajectory through the criminal justice process is the rate at which they are remanded in custody before trial. Hood (1992) has shown that, taking everything else into account, black defendants were far more likely than whites to be remanded in this way. One of the consequences of this was that they were disproportionately brought to trial from custody and this, in turn, increased the probability that if they were found guilty they would be given a custodial sentence. Often overlooked is the fact that black people have a higher acquittal rate, in part because they tend disproportionately to plead not guilty to the charges against them, although the corollary is that, if they are found guilty, they are liable to heavier penalties (Moxon, 1988; Shallice & Gordon, 1990; Walker 1988, 1989). For this reason, it is unsurprising that black defendants who are found guilty are less likely to receive noncustodial sentences (Brown & Hullin, 1992; Home Office, 1989, 1994; Hood, 1992; Moxon, 1988; Voakes & Fowler, 1989; Walker et al., 1989); and, the prison statistics have consistently shown that both black and Asian defendants receive longer prison sentences. Home Office analyses indicate that when account is taken of age, type of offence, and court of sentence, the difference in sentence length, although it reduces, remains longer for black and Asian prisoners. Although this calculation does not take plea into account, or other important factors (in particular, seriousness within offence category, plea, and previous convictions), Hood (1992) does so and finds an unexplained excess in the proportion of adult male black offenders sentenced to prison. Once allowance is made for all relevant factors, however, the rate of imprisonment for Asians in Hood's sample was, if anything, slightly lower than for comparable whites. For both minorities, sentence lengths were significantly greater than for whites.

So the overall picture is that, for various reasons, not all of them clearly identified as yet or fully understood, black suspects and offenders seem disproportionately more likely to be brought into the criminal justice process in the first place and disproportionately less likely to be filtered out of it at each of the key stages before the end point of imprisonment. The picture for Asians is much less clear but, inasmuch as any tendency is discernible, it is in the opposite direction right up to the point of sentencing.

Ethnic Minorities as Victims of Crime and Racial Harassment

The picture we now have, certainly with regard to the black group, from the point of apprehension to the point of disposal remains patchy; but, the gaps are being filled all the time with new research and, in particular, the extension of ethnic monitoring within the criminal justice system.[9] Set against this, the evidence concerning the victimisation of ethnic minorities is much thinner.

The upsurge of concern about the problem of racial harassment in the early 1980s spawned a number of local surveys and these in turn led to various estimates of the scale of the problem. Part of the reason for the variation was that many studies used different methodologies, including different methods of sampling, but they also reflect genuine local differences. The estimates of the proportion of ethnic minorities who suffer racial harassment ranges from 5% to 50% depending on the groups covered; the area in which the survey was undertaken; and, the questions that were asked, including the timescale referred to, but in particular what types of incidents were referred to in the survey (that is, whether the survey concentrated on only the most serious offences and crimes or whether it also covered what is called low-level harassment such as racial abuse; FitzGerald & Ellis, 1992).

Once the debate reached the political agenda, there was increasing criticism of the police response to racial harassment and also controversy over the definition of racial harassment, not only among the police but other agencies and, in particular, local authorities. One result was that from the mid-1980s the police adopted the following definition of a racial incident that was to be followed by all forces in England and Wales for the purposes of recording:

1. any incident in which it appears to the reporting or investigating officer that the complaint involves an element of racial motivation; or
2. any incident that includes an allegation of racial motivation made by any person.

The figures generated by the police and the questions that they raise are returned to later; but, first it is important to note a major development in 1988, when the Home Office decided to boost the number of ethnic minority respondents to its British Crime Survey to provide large enough numbers for meaningful analysis. This was repeated again in the following British Crime Survey of 1992 and again in 1994. The British Crime Survey sample normally covers about 10,000 respondents in each sweep and asks them about their experience of selected crimes and threats during the previous year. The opportunity was taken in 1988 and in 1992 to ask ethnic minority respondents whether, if they had been a victim of crime, they thought that that crime was "racially motivated.[10]

Published reports on the British Crime Survey in 1988 and 1992 (Mayhew, Aye Maung, & Mirrlees-Black, 1993; Mayhew, Dowds, & Elliott, 1989) described the main findings about ethnic minority victimisation and perceptions of racial motivation, breaking the ethnic groups down into whites, Afro Caribbeans (i.e., black people), and Asians. Combining data from both years has produced a sample that is large enough to permit further disaggregation of the Asian group into Indians and Pakistanis. (There are within the Asian group some Bangladeshis but the numbers, in fact, are too small for analysis even once the 2 years are combined.)

As Table 2.5 shows, all ethnic minorities are significantly more likely to be victimised than whites for both household and personal offences. There are, however, some differences by offence group; and, the gap from whites is less pronounced for Indians in personal offences. Pakistanis are the most likely to be victimised in terms of both household and personal offences. Afro Caribbeans are slightly less likely than the Asian groups to suffer household crime but they are still significantly more so than whites and they are in fact the most vulnerable of all groups to burglary. Along with the Pakistanis, Afro Caribbeans also suffer very high levels of personal victimisation.

It is, however, important to note that these apparently ethnic differences are due to many factors and combinations thereof. In particular, higher ethnic minority victimisation is often accounted for by the extent to which the minorities' age profiles, socioeconomic status, and geographic distribution differ from those of whites (and from each other). That is, ethnicity as such is not always a significant factor when all else is taken into account; where it is indicated as significant, it is rarely, if ever, the most important explanation for what are apparently ethnic differences at the overall level (FitzGerald & Hale, 1996).

Ethnic minorities who had been victims of crime differed, however, in the extent to which they said they thought the incident was racially motivated. Far fewer household crimes were perceived in this way than personal crimes and in both categories of crime, Afro Caribbean respondents were slightly less likely to perceive racial motivation than Indians, whereas Pakistanis were the most likely of all to do so.

In fact, 23% of Afro Caribbean victims of personal crime, 28% of Indian victims of personal crime, and 47% of Pakistani victims of personal crime definitely thought that the incidents involved had been racially motivated (and these figures would have been much higher if noncontact thefts had been excluded). But it must be remembered that only a small minority of all respondents of any ethnic group had been victims of crime at all and that personal crime is very much rarer than household crime.

Thus, only a small proportion of ethnic minorities overall thought that they had been victims of racially motivated crime in the previous year. If we

TABLE 2.5 Differential Ethnic Risk of Victimization (percentage victimized once or more; 1988 and 1992 British Crime Statistics combined)

	White	Afro Caribbean	Asian	Indian	Pakistani
Household vandalism	4.3	3.5	6.2**	5.6*	7.1**
Burglary					
Attempts	5.8	11.1**	7.8**	8.1**	7.5
No loss	3.1	5.4**	3.6	3.5	4.2
With loss	3.0	6.7**	4.6**	5.2**	3.9
Vehicle crime (owners)					
Vandalism	9.1	10.0	11.5**	10.4	15.3**
All thefts	19.12	7.3**	21.0	20.8	22.6
Bicycle thefts (owners)	5.0	9.1**	4.7	3.5	7.8
Other household theft	6.8	5.7	5.8	5.7	6.7
All household offences	30.8	34.8**	36.2**	35.9**	39.5**
Assault	3.3	5.9**	4.0	3.3	5.1
Threats	2.5	3.3**	4.5**	3.7	6.2**
Robbery/theft from person	1.2	3.2**	3.0**	2.9**	2.1
Other personal theft	3.9	4.5	3.1	3.0	3.5
All personal offences	9.6	13.8**	13.0**	11.8*	14.7**
Unweighted N	19,294	1,776	1,976	1,236	596

NOTE: * Significant at the 10% level; ** significant at the 5% level.

restrict the estimate to those respondents who, in the previous year, had been victims of crimes that they definitely thought were racially motivated, 4% of all Afro Caribbeans, 5% of all Indians, and just under 8% of all Pakistanis had been victims of racially motivated crime.

Yet, the percentage of ethnic minority victims who thought crimes had been racially motivated considerably exceeds the extent to which ethnicity as such can be shown statistically to be associated with crime in a model that takes all relevant factors into account. This is not to say that the perception of racial motivation by victims is mistaken. Rather, it is both valid and preferable to treat racial motivation as a seriously aggravating factor in crimes, which statistically speaking, might have happened anyway.

Using the British Crime Statistics (BCS) data, other authors have estimated that 130,000 racial incidents take place in the United Kingdom each year (Aye Maung & Mirrlees-Black, 1993). This estimate has been taken from the number of incidents reported to the BCS in 1992, which were definitely believed by the victims to have been racially motivated. The number was then grossed up to the population at large using the 1991 census. Using the same method, they went on to estimate the number of such incidents that would have been reported by victims to the police. This came out as 50,000. Yet, police forces nationally in England and Wales recorded just under 8,000 racial incidents in the same year despite (a) the fact the police definition is not restricted to the limited categories of crime picked up by the BCS and (b) the fact that the BCS only asked Afro Caribbean and Asian respondents whether the crimes were racially motivated, whereas the police are supposed to record all incidents reported to them irrespective of the ethnic origin of the victim.

Yet a further major disparity arises between the BCS and the police data. Between 1988 and 1992 the BCS shows the following:

1. A slight rise in the levels of victimisation—but this is comparable for all groups; that is, the likelihood of victimisation for ethnic minorities did not increase relative to whites over this period.
2. There is a commensurate rise in the number of incidents believed to be racially motivated; that is, because ethnic minorities such as whites experienced more crime over this period they also experienced more racially motivated incidents, but the proportion of crimes against them that were attributable to racism was no higher.

In short, the BCS gives no evidence of an escalation in the problem between 1988 and 1992.

By contrast, the police figures for the same period show a dramatic rise from 4,383 to 7,734—an increase of 77%, with the figures doubling over the 4 years in forces outside London.

This is not only improbable (given the evidence of the BCS), it becomes even more so when one looks at the rise in individual forces. In Sussex, for example, the numbers went from 14 in 1988 to 214 in 1992 and in Nottinghamshire from 4 to 264—increases of 1,300% and 6,500%, respectively. It seems likely that most of the increase in racial incidents as shown by the police data is due to (a) increased reporting, but above all, (b) increased conscientiousness on the part of the police in recording what is reported to them. It is important to note that the police clearly still have a long way to go. That is, improvements in police recording are still required and may suggest a further massive "rise"[11] without in any way reflecting the underlying reality.

DISCUSSION

The literature and statistical data in the United Kingdom on minorities and crime go back further than in many other European countries, but they are still patchy and unreliable. Moreover, analysis to date of what does exist has often been deficient in three respects. It has treated offending data in isolation from data on victimisation. It has taken ethnic differences at face value—risking reification and ignoring important commonalities among different ethnic groups. And it has taken insufficient account of the limitations of official statistics. Not only do these give only part of the overall picture, but the official statistics are often unreliable and, as the disparity between the BCS and the police figures on racial incidents has demonstrated, where race or ethnicity are involved, they may be highly volatile.

The starting point for discussion, therefore, is that the data we have to work from may give a distorted picture of the underlying reality. That is not to say that ethnic statistics are not needed. Once the data stabilise, they will be important indicators of trends for that minority of cases that get into the criminal justice system at all. They will also act as a barometer for how the system actually handles them. It is important to stress, however, that considerable caution is needed in conducting any debate about ethnic involvement in offending on the basis of official statistics alone.

Subject to that health warning, the discussion looks in turn at the three lines of "explanation" that have tended to be advanced with regard to apparent black overinvolvement in offending (relative to whites), by contrast with the Asians. Some commentators have leaned heavily toward one or the other of these explanations; the political debate (in which the media have a privileged role) has tended to be especially polarised. Others, however, have rehearsed all three explanations without definitively opting for any, but have left open the possibility of some combination, and even interaction, of all three (Jefferson, 1988; Reiner, 1989). The explanations are as follows:

Socioeconomic factors
Discrimination by the criminal justice system

Ethnic-specific differences (including differences in rates and patterns of offending, which cannot be explained by socioeconomic factors alone)

Taking proper account of socioeconomic factors calls into question the simplistic assumption that the disproportionate victimisation of ethnic minorities is driven by racial hostility on the part of the majority. Rather, the evidence given here suggests that the age profile, the socioeconomic position, and the geographical distribution of the minorities have far more influence on the extent to which they are victims of crime than does ethnicity per se. This is not to say that ethnicity is irrelevant. We have evidence both of its independent influence on victimisation and of its interactive relationship with socioeconomic factors. Moreover, if ethnicity is not the main cause of their excess victimisation, the collective experience of excess victimisation may be ethnic in its effect (FitzGerald & Hale, 1996). Ethnicity, however, is not the place to start.

By the same token, if ethnicity is not the place to start in understanding differences in rates of victimisation, nor is it the place to start in interpreting apparently different patterns of offending. By contrast with the victimisation data, however, socioeconomic information has rarely been available on offenders of known ethnic origins[12] so, although socioeconomic factors tend generally to be highly correlated with offending, there has been almost no way of taking them into account in interpreting apparent ethnic differences. It is, therefore, illuminating, but hardly surprising, that analysis of the National Prison Survey of 1992 shows that the socioeconomic profile of black and white prisoners is far more similar than the profile of these groups in the population at large (FitzGerald & Marshall, 1996).

Some inferences can be drawn, however, about the likely involvement of different groups in offending from their demographic and socioeconomic profiles in the population at large. They do not provide answers to all the outstanding questions about ethnicity and offending, but they do raise some new questions. In particular, they cast doubt on the convention of treating Asians as a meaningful group in this contex, for the Asians are very diverse. The group is dominated numerically by the Indians, whose socioeconomic profile is similar to that of whites and, in some respects, better. Yet it contains two groups that are still more disadvantaged in socioeconomic terms than the black Caribbeans. The effects of this diversity are already apparent in some of our victimisation data; one particular factor that is worth highlighting in the context of offending is the question of age structure. In part for reasons that go back to the timing of the main phases of immigration, there are important differences in the average ages of the minorities (see

Table 2.2). The Pakistanis and Bangladeshis are much younger than the black groups and larger numbers than previously are just about now hitting their late teens, which is the peak period for offending. In 1991, 19% of whites were aged 0 to 15 years, compared with 22% of black Caribbeans, and 29% of Indians. The figures for Pakistanis and Bangladeshis were 43% and 47%, respectively.

It seems possible, therefore, that, if only because of socioeconomic and demographic factors, we are facing an upsurge in criminal involvement among these groups; but, it will continue to be masked as long as it is subsumed within an omnibus Asian category. We still lack systematic empirical evidence on this point, but local feedback from the police and other agencies has increasingly been supporting this view and it was dramatically illustrated by events in Bradford in June 1995. An apparently minor incident involving the police and young people in a neighbourhood where the Asian population is predominantly of Pakistani origin triggered a long weekend of disturbances involving the deployment of hundreds of police and damage to property estimated to have cost over 1 million pounds sterling. Parallels have been drawn with the disturbances of the 1980s where the young people involved were primarily black.

Socioeconomic factors may explain a large amount of the apparent ethnic differences in both levels and patterns of offending. But they are unlikely to explain them away completely and the next step must be a move to examining the role of discrimination. This will require going beyond crude notions of direct discrimination (i.e., illegitimate action stemming from conscious racial animus). The court-focused studies that are able to control for socioeconomic factors (Hood, 1992; Walker, 1988; Walker et al., 1989) tend to find that most of any remaining ethnic differences can be explained in terms of apparently race-neutral legal factors such as charge, plea, prior remand in custody, and court of trial. Yet my earlier work for the Royal Commission on Criminal Justice (FitzGerald, 1993) shows how many of these apparently neutral factors are themselves variously open to discretion and influenced by socioeconomic considerations that may disproportionately adversely affect outcomes for minority suspects.

The scope for discretion includes many key decision-making points in the criminal justice process in Britain. Examples include the following: whether to charge a suspect or simply caution them; whether to bring a charge of actual bodily harm or common assault; whether to impose a custodial or a noncustodial sentence. Many of these decisions have a knock-on effect to the next stage of the process (for example, in terms of the court of trial and the penalty available to sentencers). Some rest completely on individual decisions, but some (such as whether certain offences should be cautioned or prosecuted) may reflect differences in practice by area. There is less scope for discretion at the least and at the most serious ends of the scale; there can be considerable variation in processing the large volume of offences that are of medium seriousness.

The most obvious example of the influence of socioeconomic factors is the effect of employment status. Unemployed suspects may be less likely to be fined (because they do not have the wherewithal to pay the fine) and more likely to be remanded in custody before trial, both of which increase the likelihood of their receiving a custodial sentence if they are found guilty. Black people in general are more likely to be unemployed than whites; this was true also of the suspects in Hood's (1992) sample who de facto went into the process at a disadvantage.

More research attention needs to turn to these factors, which may indirectly penalise the outcomes for some groups relative to others, rather than continuing to expend most of our intellectual effort trying to unearth "the will o' the wisp of 'pure' discrimination" (Reiner, 1993). This is not to say that direct discrimination does not occur or that it is not an appropriate area for research; it is important to counter the argument that there is no discrimination in the system because of the apparently different treatment of Black Caribbeans and the Asian group. The claim of no discrimination was recently expressed thus:

> The theory that Afro Caribbeans but not South Asians are singled out for discriminatory treatment by crime victims and the police does not fit with the wider picture of racial discrimination and disadvantage in Britain. (Smith, 1995)

This argument is contestable on three grounds. One is that different stereotypes are held for different groups. The contention of this chapter is that there has up to now been a stereotype of the black criminal and the Asian victim—even though (as the evidence here has shown) black people, like Asians, are disproportionately more likely than whites also to be victims of crime. If such assumptions, however unconsciously, influenced the legitimate use of discretion in decisions made by criminal justice practitioners, one would expect to find black suspects and offenders benefiting from such discretion to a lesser extent than whites, and Asians benefiting slightly more. This is consistent with the overall picture that emerged from the evidence of offending summarised previously.

The second objection is that, as has already been emphasised, the Asian group is not a meaningful category: The experiences of Indians, Pakistanis, and Bangladeshis are likely to be very different. But the third objection is that, echoing the black groups 30 to 40 years ago, these groups themselves (in particular the Pakistanis and Bangladeshis) have begun to allege police discrimination, and not only in response to them as victims.[13]

In looking for direct discrimination, however, it is important to abandon the idea that it is endemic at each point in the system.[14] Rather, the issue is to identify (a) the minority of incidents in which it occurs, (b) the minority of individuals involved, and (c) the circumstances that have allowed them to exercise their prejudices in this way.

Finally, we turn to the third of our explanations for ethnic differences in levels and patterns of offending. Once the influence of socioeconomic factors has been explored with rigour and the possibility of discrimination has been examined in all its dimensions, the thorny question will remain of whether there are, in fact, real ethnic differences in levels and patterns of offending. This is clearly a sensitive area; yet it would appear that neither socioeconomic factors nor discrimination, whether direct or indirect, provides obvious explanations for all of the differences in the evidence summarised previously. There are still unanswered questions, of which the two best examples include the following:

> Why are there such striking differences in the offence patterns of different groups?
> Why do the black Caribbean groups disproportionately plead not guilty and elect to be tried at the Crown Court?

Attempts to link ethnicity per se with offending have usually been ideologically driven, labeling certain groups as inherently more "criminal" than others. This has made it difficult seriously to explore any ethnic dimension to observably different patterns; those who have tried may have lent themselves to this labeling. These problems have arisen for two related reasons:

> A failure to consider ethnicity in the context of the effects of socioeconomic factors and the possibility of discrimination (whether by effectively ignoring the other two explanations or by giving ethnicity primacy over them);
> The use of a reified notion of ethnicity, which allows qualities such as criminality to be treated as the property of particular groups.

Ethnicity, however, is not some essential "given." It is one aspect of identity, which has more or less salience for individuals in different situations (Yinger, 1986). It is constantly modified through contact with new influences and is moulded by external factors such that it must be considered inextricably linked with them rather than treated separately. This understanding fits our evidence that ethnicity per se rarely explains patterns of victimisation, but that its relationship to victimisation is twofold. It is indirectly associated with victimisation because of the socioeconomic and demographic factors that are directly correlated and that disproportionately characterise certain minorities. It is directly associated with victimisation in interactions with these factors. Extending this understanding to questions of offending may safeguard against the potential pathologizing inherent in some of the literature (see, for example, Smith, 1987, pp. 8-71). But fully to illuminate the complex interactions between ethnicity and both socioeconomic factors and the experience of discrimination requires the addition of a time dimension, for we are looking at a dynamic process of interactions that goes back nearly 50 years for the black group. This suggests that where ethnic differences remain that are not explicable immediately in terms of socioeconomic factors or discrimination, they should be understood in the light of the following interrelated factors:

> The adaptation of different groups to their economic circumstances, and the social and political environment that determines the forms this adaptation may take;
> The different minority groups' experiences of the criminal justice agencies, and the mutual perceptions and interpretations each party brings to these;
> The collective experience and perception sedentarised as folk memory—not simply among the minorities but among other key actors, including the statutory agencies and the majority population;
> Intergenerational differences, and the economic and political developments of the formative years of each generation.

In sum, further serious academic attention needs to be given to each of the three explanations for the overall picture of criminal involvement by different groups. In Britain, it could usefully start with the socioeconomic explanation and model the likely representation of particular groups in official criminal justice statistics using population data, which are now well established. It also needs to look in more sophisticated ways at the question of discrimination, exploiting fully the potential of the ethnic data that the police are beginning to generate and using qualitative methods to explore the patterns they reveal. It needs to examine the role of ethnicity (as defined previously), not separately from the other two explanations but in the context of and in interaction with them. Specifically, it will need to look not just at the effects of ethnic differences in lifestyle but, more important, at the implications of

> ethnic differences in opportunity structures;
> ethnic differences in the experience of the criminal justice system;

ethnic differences in the ways groups have adapted, and continue to adapt, to these differences in opportunity structures and differences in the experience of the criminal justice system.

These differences have not received serious attention in the British literature; and, although some American studies offer inspiration and possible methodologies (see, for example, Sullivan, 1989) it would be ill advised to read across uncritically from their results, because the groups in question in the two countries are very different in terms of their ethnic range, size, histories, and interrelationships—as are the political, social, and criminal justice contexts within which patterns of crime have developed.

No doubt there will be parallels both with the United States and with other countries; but, there will also be very important local specificities. As in many fields, international comparisons are often most illuminating for what is revealed by differences and the reasons for these rather than from similarities that are often only skin deep (and that not infrequently stretch the imagination). Above all, any international parallels will need to be sought in the social, political, and organisational processes at work rather than in inferences about the inherent characteristics of individual ethnic groups.

NOTES

1. In British terminology, *black* refers mainly to people of Caribbean or African ethnic origin and to people of these origins who also have a white parent. The Asian group mainly comprises people with origins in the Indian subcontinent (that is, India, Pakistan, and Bangladesh). These categories were established by the 1991 census and their usage should be apparent from the census data included in this chapter. Where other sources use a different form of classification, this has been retained. Broadly speaking, the use of *Asian* is consistent in all sources and Afro Caribbean equates to black, although most people described by it are of Caribbean origin.

2. Initially, both groups (as defined by the 1948 British Nationality Act) had free right of entry to the United Kingdom, but this was progressively eroded by immigration legislation from 1962, culminating in the current Nationality Act of 1981.

3. According to the 1991 census, nearly 60% of Black Caribbeans and nearly 80% of Black Africans live in London.

4. It is worth noting, en passant, that the debate about West Indians had by now lost sight of them completely as victims of crime even though figures continued to be published that demonstrated their higher rate of victimisation (Home Office, 1989).

5. For an overview of the work on criminal involvement, see FitzGerald, 1993; for racially motivated victimisation, see FitzGerald and Ellis, 1989.

6. One recent study, however, suggests comparable rates for black and white youths with lower figures for Asians (Bowling, Graham, & Ross, 1994).

7. This, of course, also suggests that part of the variation between areas may be explained by differences in their ethnic makeup. The situation may also become clearer in the future because forces have been required beginning April 1996 to collect the figures broken down into: White, Black, Asian, and Other.

8. A caution is a formal warning issued to the offender by the police as an alternative to prosecuting the case through the courts.

9. The extension of ethnic monitoring by the police to arrests and cautions beginning April 1996 will, within the foreseeable future, provide a basis for routine monitoring of decisions by the Crown Prosecution Service and the courts.

10. In 1994 this was asked of all victims, regardless of ethnicity. The BCS core sample size was 14,500 in 1994.

11. For the year 1995, the figures peaked at just under 12,000.

12. It should be noted that the main British cohort studies of delinquency have not held (or used) ethnic data on their subjects and that, in any case, numbers would probably have been too small for robust analyses.

13. Television and radio interviews after the events in Bradford in the summer of 1995, for example, produced views of the police not dissimilar from those expressed by youths of Caribbean origin after the riots of the early 1980s.

14. This is not to ignore the fact (see FitzGerald, 1993) that the cumulative effects of discrimination at each stage may indeed be significant.

REFERENCES

Aye Maung, N., & Mirrlees-Black, C. (1994). *Racially motivated crime: A British Crime Survey analysis* (Home Office Research and Planning Unit Paper 82).

Bethnal Green and Stepney Trades Council. (1978). *Blood on the streets.*

Bowling, B., Graham, J., & Ross, R. (1994). *Self-reported offending among young people in England and Wales.* In J. Junger-Tas, G. Terlouw, & M. Klein (Eds.), *Delinquent behavior among young people in the western world. First results of the International Self-Report Delinquency Study* (pp. 156-185). Amsterdam: Kugler.

Brown, I., & Hullin, R. (1992). A study of sentencing in the Leeds Magistrates Courts. The treatment of ethnic minority and white offenders. *British Journal of Criminology, 32,* 41-53.

Commission for Racial Equality. (1992). *Juvenile cautioning—Ethnic monitoring in practice.* London: Author.

Demuth, C. (1978). "Sus" a report on the Vagrancy Act 1824. Runnymede Trust.

FitzGerald, M. (1993). *Ethnic minorities and the criminal justice system* (Research Study No. 20, Royal Commission on Criminal Justice). London: Her Majesty's Stationery Office.

FitzGerald, M. (1996). Racial harassment: Issues of measurement and comparison. In Z. Layton-Henry & C. Wilpert (Eds.), *Challenging racism and discrimination in Britain and Germany.* Frances Pinter.

FitzGerald, M., & Ellis, T. (1992). Racial harassment: The evidence. In C. Kemp (Ed.), *Current issues in criminological research, 2.* Bristol and Bath Centre for Criminal Justice.

FitzGerald, M., & Hale, C. (1996). *Ethnic minorities: Victimisation and racial harassment* (Home Office Research Study No. 154). London: Her Majesty's Stationery Office.

FitzGerald, M., & Marshall, P. (1996). Ethnic minorities in British prisons. In R. Matthews & P. Francis (Eds.), *Prisons 2000.* London: Sage.

Hall, S., Critcher, C., Clarke, J., Jefferson, T., & Roberts, B. (1978). *Policing the crisis*. New York: Macmillan.

Home Office. (1981). *Racial attacks: Report of a Home Office study*. London: Government Statistical Service.

Home Office. (1989). *The ethnic group of those proceeded against or sentenced by the courts in the Metropolitan Police District in 1984 and 1985*. London: Government Statistical Service.

Home Office. (1994). *Probation statistics England and Wales 1993*. London: Government Statistical Service.

Home Office Prison Statistics England and Wales (Annual). London: Her Majesty's Stationery Office.

Home Office Statistical Bulletin 5/89. *Crime statistics for the metropolitan police district by ethnic group, 1987: Victims, suspects, and those arrested*.

Home Office Statistical Bulletin 21/94. *The ethnic origins of prisoners: Ethnic composition of prison populations 1985 to 1993; study of population on 30 June 1990 and persons received in 1990*.

Hood, R. (1992). *Race and sentencing*. Oxford, UK: Oxford University Press.

House of Commons Select Committee on Race Relations and Immigration. (1972). *Police/immigrant relations*. London: Her Majesty's Stationery Office.

House of Commons Select Committee on Race Relations and Immigration. (1977). *The West Indian community*. London: Her Majesty's Stationery Office.

Hunte, J. A. (1966). *Nigger-hunting in England?* West Indian Standing Conference.

Jefferson, T. (1988). Race, crime, and policing. *International Journal of the Sociology of Law, 16*, 521-539.

Joint Committee Against Racism—JCAR. (1981). *Racial violence in Britain*. Author.

Mayhew, P., Aye Maung, N., & Mirrlees-Black, C. (1993). *The 1992 British Crime Survey* (Home Office Research Study No. 132). London: Her Majesty's Stationery Office.

Mayhew, P., Dowds, L., & Elliott, D. (1989). *The 1988 British Crime Survey* (Home Office Research Study No. 111). London: Her Majesty's Stationery Office.

Moxon, D. (1988). *Sentencing practice in the Crown Court* (Home Office Research Study No. 103). London: Her Majesty's Stationery Office.

Reiner, R. (1989). Race and criminal justice. *New Community, 16*(1), 5-21.

Reiner, R. (1993). Race, crime, and justice: Models of interpretation. In L. Gelsthorpe (Ed.), *Minority ethnic groups in the criminal justice system*. Cambridge, UK: Cambridge University Press.

Rose, E. J. B., and Associates. (1969). *Colour and citizenship*. Oxford, UK: Oxford University Press, Institute of Race Relations.

Scarman, ?. (1981). *The Brixton disorders: Report on an inquiry by the Rt. Hon. Lord Scarman OBE*. London: Her Majesty's Stationery Office.

Shallice, A., & Gordon, P. (1990). *Black people, white justice? Race and the criminal justice system*. Runnymede Trust.

Simpson, J. (1967, August 12). *Man to man* [Editorial]. *The Job*.

Skogan, W. (1990). *The police and public in England and Wales: A British Crime Survey Report* (Home Office Research Study No. 117). London: Her Majesty's Stationery Office.

Smith, D. (1983). *Police and people in London*. London: Policy Studies Institute.

Smith D. (1987). Policing and urban unrest. In J. Benyon & J. Solomos (Eds.), *The roots of urban unrest*. Oxford, UK: Oxford University Press.

Smith, D. (1995). Youth crime and conduct disorders. In M. Rutter & D. Smith (Eds.), *Psychosocial disorders in young people: Time trends and their causes*. New York: John Wiley.

Solomos, J. (1988). *Black youth, racism, and the state*. Cambridge, UK: Cambridge University Press.

Stevens, P., & Willis, C. (1979). *Race, crime, and arrests* (Home Office Research Study No. 58). London: Her Majesty's Stationery Office.

Sullivan, M. (1989). *"Getting paid": Youth, crime, and work in the inner city.* Ithaca, NY: Cornell University Press.

Tuck, M., & Southgate, P. (1981). *Ethnic minorities, crime, and policing: A survey of the experiences of West Indians and whites* (Home Office Research Study No. 70). London: Her Majesty's Stationery Office.

Voakes, R., & Fowler, Q. (1989). *Sentencing, race, and social enquiry reports.* West Yorkshire, UK: West Yorkshire Probation Service.

Walker, M. (1988). The court disposal of young males by race in London in 1983. *British Journal of Criminology, 28,* 441-460.

Walker, M. (1989). The court disposal and remands of white, Afro Caribbean, and Asian men, London 1983. *British Journal of Criminology, 29,* 353-367.

Walker M., Jefferson, T., & Seneviratne, M. (1989, July). *Race and criminal justice in a provincial city.* Paper presented at the British Criminology Conference, Bristol.

Whitaker, B. (1964). *The police.* New York: Penguin.

Yinger, M. (1986). Intersecting strands in the theorisation of race and ethnic relations. In J. Rex & D. Mason (Eds.), *Theories of race and ethnic relations.* Cambridge, UK: Cambridge University Press.

3

MINORITIES, CRIME, AND CRIMINAL JUSTICE IN SWEDEN

Hanns von Hofer
Jerzy Sarnecki
Henrik Tham

SWEDEN—THE WELFARE STATE

With the death of King Charles the XII in 1718 during the war between Sweden and Denmark/Norway, Sweden withdrew from the international scene as a great power. With the loss of Finland to Russia in 1809, Sweden's territory was further reduced, to its present borders with an almost entirely Swedish-speaking population. The addition of Norway 5 years later was temporary, and in 1905 the two countries split peacefully. The territorial losses, although mourned at the time, were a prerequisite for a remarkably long period of peace. Sweden has not participated in any war since 1814, including the two world wars. This has been a contributing factor to the development in Sweden of what has until recently been regarded as the welfare state par excellence.

The road to the welfare state, however, was a long one. During the 19th century, Sweden was one of the poorest countries in Europe. By the outbreak of World War I, more than one million people had emigrated to find their livelihood elsewhere, primarily in the United States. After World War II, however, prosperity spread rapidly. Contributing factors included the natural resources of forests and iron ore, industry that was still intact after the war, and a well-functioning labor market.

Because prewar prosperity was slow to develop in Sweden, so was democracy. A predominantly rural country with few towns of substantial size, Sweden did not develop a strong tradition of liberalism in the late 19th century. Political opposition, necessary for the development of democracy, emerged largely within the nonconformist churches, the temperance movement, and the labor movement. The political wing of the labor movement, the Social Democratic Party, eventually grew into one of the most powerful in Europe. The Social Democrats have governed since the 1930s, with the exception of the periods 1976 to 1982 and 1991 to 1994 when the center-right blocs were elected into office.

The Swedish model of the welfare state has been based on two cornerstones: an active labor market policy and a universal social security system, each dependent on the other. The social insurance system has been characterized by a virtual universal coverage of the population and high levels of compensation. By the 1980s, this policy had resulted in uniquely low income differentials as well as high coverage and compensation levels for old age pensions, sickness and parental allowances, access to day care facilities, and benefits for single mothers (Erikson & Fritzell, 1988; Fritzell, 1991; Kangas, 1991; Palme, 1990; Wennemo, 1994). Another result, however, of the Swedish model is that those who remain outside the labor market, such as immigrants and school dropouts who are unemployed, receive relatively low levels of compensation (Marklund & Svallfors, 1987).

The social insurance system is based on work incentives. The proportion of women in the labor force is nearly as large as that of men, which means that a high percentage of women with preschool children are employed, many part-time. A prerequisite for this high level of labor market participation has been the public day care system. As many as 70% of Swedish children are enrolled in this system from about age one.

For this system to work, it is important that as many individuals as possible are gainfully employed. It is the role of the proactive labor market policy to ensure this. When during the 1980s, unemployment figures for the European Union rose to between 6% and 10%, Swedish figures remained at 2% to 3% (Organization for Economic Cooperation and Development, 1994). When unemployment rates rise, the Swedish system becomes very expensive. This has been the case during the 1990s as the jobless rate has risen to 8%—and much higher among immigrants and young people.

There are other demographic and social characteristics relevant for the development of crime as well. The country is on the whole scarcely populated. Only one third of the population live in towns with more than 50,000 inhabitants, and only the greater Stockholm metropolitan area surpasses one million in population. The birthrate in Sweden has been higher than in most West European countries. Divorce is common and increasing but so is remarriage. Cohabitation without formal marriage is also fairly common. Compared to North America and several European countries, Swedish cities are less segregated. Housing is generally of a high standard and slum areas are virtually nonexistent. Some areas dominated by public rental housing, however, experience clearly above average rates of vandalism, substance abuse, and social assistance recipients. Furthermore, trends toward increased segregation are also discernible (Wikström, 1994, p. 31).

Like many other sectors of Swedish life, the criminal justice system has been affected by the welfare state ideology. Punishment philosophies of social defense and treatment have played central roles. The Swedish prison system has also gained a reputation as a relatively open system with liberal policies for visitors and furloughs, seen as important steps for preparing prisoners for their ultimate release. The guiding criterion for determining sanctions—that of rehabilitating the offender—was, however, replaced in 1989 by "just deserts" (i.e., the choice of a criminal sanction should be based on the gravity of the offense). Prison regimes have also become stricter in recent years, motivated in large part by the presence of narcotics. These shifts in the criminal justice system can be seen as reflecting some of the many criticisms aimed at the welfare state, which have been voiced in the Swedish political debate since the 1980s.

Crime and Criminal Justice

Reported crime has risen sharply since World War II. The data on convictions in Figure 3.1 also show such an upswing. Among persons convicted for nontrivial offenses today, women constitute approximately 10%, a proportion that has increased somewhat during the postwar period. The development of crime is fairly similar to that in the other Nordic countries (Nordic Statistical Secretariat, 1991). In terms of lethal violence, Sweden is about average among European countries (Statistics Sweden, 1993, p. 492). In an international victimization study, Sweden ranked high on bicycle theft, held a middle position regarding car theft, and scored low on residential burglary, robbery, and assaults (van Dijk & Mayhew, 1993).

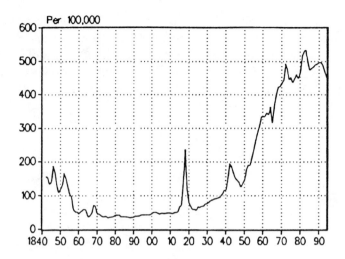

Figure 3.1. Number of Criminal Convictions per 100,000 Population (fines excluded), Sweden, 1841 to 1994

Criminal policy and public debates have partly followed the development of "real" crime (as reflected in police statistics) and partly followed a course of their own. In the 1970s, economic crime became a political issue, whereas the focus in the 1980s was on violence against women, followed by crime among immigrants; the focus then shifted to youth violence in the mid-1990s. The central criminal policy issue since the late 1960s, however, has been drugs. Sweden has a relatively minor drug problem compared to many other Western countries. The Swedish drug policy has also been quite harsh. Officially, this policy has been claimed a success—a claim that is the subject of debate (Kühlhorn, Bejerot, Käll, Romelsjö, & Stenbacka, 1995; Tham, 1995a, 1995b).

Average prison sentences are short; one third of all sentences do not exceed one month, only one tenth exceed one year. Of prison capacity, 40% is found within open prisons, that is, institutions without real means for preventing escapes. In prison, single cells are the rule. Conditional release is in most cases granted after two thirds of the prison sentence has been served. Foreign citizens can be deported after the sentence (there are 500 to 600 such cases per year).

Since the 1970s, the Swedish prison population has increased by one fourth. In 1991, Sweden ranked 18th among 23 Council of Europe member-states in terms of size of the prison population (Council of Europe, 1992, p. 18). Alternatives to imprisonment are being sought. Terms of probation, community service, and civil commitment (usually in the form of a treatment program for drug addicts) can be specified. House arrest through electronic monitoring is being used. Young lawbreakers between 15 (the age of criminal responsibility) and 17 are usually not sentenced by criminal courts, but are often directed to social services (for further details, see Svensson, 1995).

ETHNIC MINORITIES, FOREIGN CITIZENS, AND IMMIGRATION

Among a population of almost 9 million, 6 million are between the ages of 15 and 69 years (Statistics Sweden, 1996, Table 35). Of these, 5.2 million are native Swedes, 0.4 million naturalized Swedes, and 0.4 million domiciled foreign citizens. The number of nondomiciled foreign citizens is not known. Furthermore, about 0.4 million Swedish and non-Swedish citizens could be labeled "second-generation immigrants," that is, those born in Sweden with at least one parent born outside Sweden.

There are two small, but officially recognized minority groups living in Sweden: the Laplanders (Sami) and the Finns who live close to the Finnish border in sparsely populated areas in the very north of Sweden. The Laplanders are an ethnic and linguistic minority who live throughout Northern Scandinavia and on the Kola Peninsula. Today, there are a total of about 60,000 Laplanders of which 17,000 live in Sweden. No criminological studies have yet been conducted dealing with these minorities (Laplanders and Finns), who are more or less integrated into the Swedish society. In the public debate, it is sometimes claimed that gypsies (Romani) living in Sweden are highly involved with crime, but no published studies on this topic exist. In Sweden, the public debate on crime and ethnicity is concentrated almost entirely on immigrants and foreign citizens.

Immigration to Sweden has a long tradition. For instance, Germans (linked with the Hansa) immigrated here as early as the 13th century. In the 16th and 17th centuries, Finns came. In the 17th century, merchants and craftsmen arrived from Holland and France as well as miners from Wallonia (Belgium). In modern Swedish history, the first immigration of any substantial size occurred toward the end of World War II, when many refugees fled from Norway, Denmark, and the Baltic countries. After the war, an organized transfer of labor power to certain Swedish industries began (labor immigration). This practice culminated in 1969 to 1970. At that time, most immigrants came from Finland and Southern European countries. During the

1970s, immigration to Sweden consisted primarily of relatives of immigrants already living in Sweden (family immigration). Since the middle of the 1980s, immigration has been dominated by refugees (refugee immigration). In all, over the past 50 years, the Swedish population has increased by 2.2 million people (from 6.6 to 8.8 million) of which fully one half is due to immigration (see Figure 3.2).

In the 1970s, about half of the arriving immigrants originated from other Nordic countries, primarily Finland. Thereafter, the composition of the immigrant population changed; after 1985, the majority of immigrants have originated from non-European countries, especially from the Middle East. In the early 1990s, about 60,000 refugees from former Yugoslavia were granted asylum in Sweden. Still, Finns continue to constitute the largest group of immigrants living in Sweden, followed by Norwegians, ex-Yugoslavians, and Iranians (Statistics Sweden, 1996, Table 61). It should be noted, that in comparison with many other Western nations, the non-white immigrant population is very small in Sweden.

The extent and composition of immigration is determined by geographical, economic, political, and other factors in both the countries of origin and in Sweden. Such factors include differences in population growth and standard of living, revolutions and counterrevolutions, conflicts and wars, and ecological crises (Hammar, 1992a). To a large degree, immigration is ultimately determined by a country's immigration policy, which in the case of Sweden, has been entirely unregulated between 1945 and 1966. Thereafter, it became regulated (for non-Nordic citizens) and increasingly restrictive. The changing nature of immigration in the 1980s also gave rise to a negative change in the ideological climate regarding immigration (Lange, 1995), and today much public concern is directed toward legal and illegal immigration.

The formal policy principle was adopted in the 1920s that immigrants should have salaries and working conditions on an equal footing with native Swedes. This led in the 1960s and 1970s to the political objective that immigrants should be able to enjoy living conditions and standards equal to these of the native population. The official goals of the Swedish immigrant and minorities policy are captured in the catchwords *equality—freedom of choice—cooperation.* Thus, the Swedish Constitution states (since 1976) that "ethnical, linguistic, and religious minorities' opportunities to preserve and develop their own culture and community shall be promoted." Sweden rejected the idea of "guest laborers," which characterized the policies of several other Western European countries (e.g., Germany) at that time. Immigration was not to be understood as a short period of residence, but rather as a permanent settlement (Hammar, 1992b). Therefore, the criteria

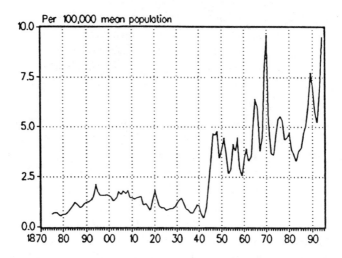

Figure 3.2. Immigration per 1,000 of the Mean Population, Sweden, 1875 to 1994

for obtaining Swedish citizenship are rather liberal: Nordic citizens can apply for Swedish citizenship after 3 years of permanent residency in Sweden, political refugees after 4 years, and other foreign citizens after 5 years. During the period from 1960 to 1993, about 577,000 immigrants received Swedish citizenship.

Since World War II, Sweden has become a multicultural society, in which more than 100 languages are spoken, but in which the Swedish language and culture usually prevail within one or two generations. For the time being, immigrant groups have not formed into ethnic minorities with claims for cultural autonomy. Naturally, the Swedish way of living has been influenced to a certain degree by the new immigrants, but actual cultural influences have been much stronger from the Anglo-Saxon (and to a lesser degree from other European) countries (Hammar, 1992a).

Surveys of living conditions in Sweden (Socialstyrelsen, 1995a) consistently reveal that some immigrant groups tend to report relatively inferior living conditions concerning health, housing, employment, personal economy, social relations, political resources, personal security and safety, and so on.

There is no systematic information on the number of immigrants who are employed as social workers, police, or as staff within the correctional services. This issue is, however, of current widespread interest. Scattered information is available only from the recruitment office of the Swedish

Police Board. Of about 1,000 recruits (Swedish citizenship is mandatory) admitted to the Swedish Police Academy between 1993 and 1995, about 11% had an immigrant background, which is somewhat less than the proportion of immigrants in this age group in general.

DESCRIPTIVE CRIME DATA

Immigrants and Foreign Citizens as Victims Of Crime

According to the yearly victim surveys conducted in Sweden since 1978, there are almost no differences between native Swedish and various immigrant groups in victimization by property crimes (theft and malicious damage), if gender, family type, geographical region, and type of housing are held constant. Only in the case of "theft or malicious damage in the respondent's home or store" do immigrants report a victimization rate about 1.3 times higher than that for native Swedes (Statistics Sweden, 1995, p. 158).

Immigrants report more often than Swedish citizens, however, that they have been victims of violence. If one controls for gender, age, geographical region, and family type, second-generation immigrants (that is, citizens born in Sweden with at least one parent born elsewhere) have a slightly higher risk (1.3 times) of being subjected to violence. Naturalized citizens experience a 1.5 times higher risk of being subjected to violence and threats than do citizens with Swedish parentage. For foreign citizens, however, there is almost no difference (Statistics Sweden, 1995, pp. 457-458). Other studies (Tham, 1983, p. 27; von Hofer, 1990, p. 34; Wikström, 1991, p. 63) show that a considerable amount of violence occurs within groups of immigrants. Consequently, immigrant women report in victim surveys a higher risk (1.5 to 1.8 times, standardized) for being exposed to domestic violence (Statistics Sweden, 1995, p. 118).

Since the latter part of the 1980s, Sweden has seen a growing number of crimes with racist or xenophobic motives (Björgo, 1994; Rikspolisstyrelsen, 1988). According to a survey among Africans, Arabs, Latin Americans, and Poles living in Sweden, a majority felt that xenophobia has increased in Sweden in recent years (Lange, 1995, p. 59). The fear of crime among foreign citizens is higher than among Swedish citizens (1.5 to 1.9 times, standardized; Statistics Sweden, 1995, p. 120), and this fear has in recent years increased at a faster rate among foreign citizens.

Self-Report Surveys, Cohort Studies, and Other Studies

Only a few self-report studies on offending and ethnicity have been conducted in Sweden. Suikkila (1983) studied young Finnish immigrants and found no differences in incidence rates compared with Swedish youth. About one half of the Finnish immigrants and of the Swedish control group claimed to have broken the law. Young Finnish immigrants reported, however, that on the average they had committed slightly more offenses than had Swedish pupils (Suikkila, 1983, p. 208).

According to a school survey among pupils in the ninth grade in Stockholm in 1990, pupils with immigrant backgrounds (i.e., with at least one parent born outside Sweden) reported (holding other things constant) no significantly different levels of crime participation compared with their Swedish counterparts (Martens, 1992, p. 46). Furthermore, juveniles living in public housing districts with high proportions of immigrants report no higher level of involvement in criminal behavior than their Swedish counterparts, except for violence, which is higher among the immigrants (Martens, 1992, p. 145).

Data, from a cohort study of Stockholmers born in 1953 and living in the Stockholm Metropolitan Area by the end of 1963 (Janson, 1995), were used to analyze officially registered criminality and other antisocial behavior of the cohort members, both native Swedes and immigrants, until they turned 30. Cohort members with an immigrant background showed only a slight overrepresentation; therefore, foreign background turned out to be a weak variable for predictions of criminal and other antisocial behavior (Martens, 1994, p. 104). The study further revealed no differences in total crime participation for those youths aged 15 to 30 years between the immigrant males born abroad and those born in Sweden.

Finally, according to a study on drug abusers, 19% of the reported cases concerned persons with an immigrant background (at least one parent born outside Sweden), which corresponds to an overrepresentation by a factor of 1.2. In about one half of such cases, the person had a Nordic background (Olsson, Byqvist, & Gomér, 1993, p. 27). No attempts for controlling other background variables was made in this study.

In sum, survey research on victims and young offenders indicates only a slight overrepresentation of immigrant populations; this overrepresentation tends to diminish or even disappear when controlling for background variables.

Data From Conviction Statistics

Official conviction statistics do not provide information on immigrant offenders, because the term *immigrant* has no legal meaning of its own. Instead, Swedish legislation and statistics distinguish between Swedish citizens and foreign citizens. The term *foreign citizen* encompasses non-Swedish citizens in Sweden, including those who are registered for domicile (domiciled) and those who are not (nondomiciled). A person may register for domicile if her or his stay in Sweden is intended to last for more than one year, and a residence permit is issued in those cases where it is required.

Due to the shortcomings of the official published conviction statistics, we conducted an inquiry—the first of its kind—with the help of Statistics Sweden, which establishes conviction rates for various immigrant groups, independent of their legal status as Swedish or foreign citizens. The data in Table 3.1 are based on 1993 conviction statistics. No attempt to control for background variables (other than age) is made.

Table 3.1 shows that all immigrant groups are overrepresented compared with indigenous Swedes. In most cases, these risks do not exceed a factor of 2. The differences among the age groups are small. The highest rates are displayed by foreign citizens. The difference between them and naturalized Swedish citizens, however, is small. So-called second-generation immigrants (born in Sweden with at least one parent born outside Sweden) do not exhibit the highest rates as is often maintained in the public debate.

The same data indicate, however, a high overrepresentation (by a factor of 3) for homicide, rape, and robbery (including attempts; not shown in Table 3.1). In total, more than one half of all rape cases (56%) involved immigrant and foreign offenders (including nondomiciled foreign citizens); the corresponding percentage for robbery was 53% and for homicide 50%.

High overrepresentations were also found in a study of all completed and attempted rapes reported to the police in Stockholm during the years 1986 to 1990 (Sarnecki, 1994). Foreign citizens were 4.3 times more likely to be suspected of these crimes than their proportion in the general population. Naturalized Swedes were overrepresented by a factor of 1.9. Among the

TABLE 3.1 Net Conviction Rates According to Individual's Status as Swedish, Naturalized, or Foreign Citizen, by Age and Type of Offense, Sweden, 1993

Age	Swedish Citizens		Naturalized Swedes		Domiciled Foreign Citizens	
Type of Offense	First	Second	First	Second	First	Second
15 to 20 years						
Penal code	1.0	1.5	2.0	1.9	2.2	2.1
Other	1.0	1.3	1.5	1.4	1.4	1.2
Total	1.0 (3,523)	1.4 (4,975)	1.8 (6,419)	1.7 (5,908)	1.9 (6,665)	1.7 (6,109)
21 to 29 years						
Penal code	1.0	1.4	2.2	2.1	2.6	2.1
Other	1.0	1.3	2.0	1.6	1.8	1.7
Total	1.0 (2,534)	1.3 (3,321)	2.1 (5,343)	1.8 (4,505)	2.1 (5,327)	1.8 (4,633)
30 to 49 years						
Penal code	1.0	1.3	2.3	2.1	3.1	3.2
Other	1.0	1.3	1.9	1.5	2.0	2.0
Total	1.0 (1,690)	1.3 (2,178)	2.0 (3,464)	1.7 (2,874)	2.4 (4,103)	2.4 (4,134)
50 to 69 years						
Penal code	1.0	1.1	2.0	—	2.5	—
Other	1.0	1.3	1.5	—	1.4	—
Total	1.0 (1,026)	1.2 (1,266)	1.7 (1,695)	—	1.8 (1,828)	—

NOTE: Numbers in parentheses: Number of convicted persons per 100,000 population. Base rate: Swedish citizens, with both parents born in Sweden = 1. Swedish citizen—first: Swedish citizen, both parents born in Sweden; Swedish citizen—second: Swedish citizen, at least one parent born outside Sweden; naturalized Swede—first: naturalized Swede, born outside Sweden; naturalized Swede—second: naturalized Swede, born in Sweden, at least one parent born outside Sweden; domiciled foreign citizen—first: domiciled foreign citizen, born outside Sweden; domiciled foreign citizen—second: domiciled foreign citizen, born in Sweden, at least one parent born outside Sweden.

victims of rape, immigrant women were only slightly overrepresented. Women from Finland, however, showed high victimization risks.

As mentioned earlier, conviction statistics only distinguish between Swedish and foreign citizens, and not between indigenous Swedes and immigrants (whether currently Swedish citizens or not). In 1994, a total of 153,000 convictions were entered for offenses both against the Penal Code and against special legislation. Of these 153,000 convictions, 82% involved Swedish citizens and 18% involved foreign citizens. Foreign citizens registered for domicile constitute two thirds of convicted persons of non-Swedish nationality.

Whereas 32% of Swedish citizens convicted in 1994 were 15 to 24 years old, the corresponding proportion for convicted foreign citizens was 26%. Therefore, convictions among foreign citizens appear to be an adult phenomenon to an even greater degree than among Swedish citizens.

Roughly three out of four convicted foreign citizens originate from Nordic countries or other European countries (including Turkey). A full 40% come from Sweden's neighboring countries of Denmark, Norway, Finland, Russia, Poland, and Germany; 28% come from non-European countries. High overrepresentations, but small numbers, are usually found among citizens from the African and the South American continents. Rates equal to those of Swedish citizens' are found among citizens from other Nordic countries (with the exception of Finland), Western Europe, North America, and Australia.

Traffic and property offenses (such as theft, receiving stolen goods, fraud, and malicious damage) are the most common offenses for which both Swedish and foreign citizens (74% and 64%, respectively) are convicted. Offenses against the person (that is, violent and sexual offenses) constitute a small proportion (6% and 5%, respectively). Drug offenses are numerically few. Roughly speaking, Swedes and foreign citizens are convicted for the same types of offenses. The greatest difference is found in traffic offenses, which are more common among Swedish citizens due to their greater participation in motor traffic.

The overall crime picture is very similar for Swedish and foreign citizens, and substantial differences in choices of criminal sanctions are not found. Foreign citizens are somewhat more often fined (70% vs. 66%) and receive less frequently waivers of prosecution or probation. In all, the differences are small and disappear almost entirely in comparisons of Swedish citizens and domiciled foreign citizens. The only difference that remains is that domiciled foreign citizens are slightly more often sentenced to imprisonment (12% vs. 10%), and less often to probation (4% vs. 5%). The average prison sentence imposed is longer for foreign citizens. These differences might first and foremost be explained by the fact that domiciled foreign citizens are sentenced more often for major crimes, such as homicide, rape, and robbery, and less often for traffic offenses, which in the case of drunk driving can render a short prison sentence. Finally, young people of recent foreign descent are clearly overrepresented among the inmates of reform schools in Stockholm (by a factor of 3.2 to 4; Bergström & Sarnecki, 1996).

In sum, the higher criminal involvement of immigrants compared to Swedes is almost nonexistent in self-report studies, about double according to conviction statistics, and threefold for serious crimes of violence. Possible explanations will be discussed next.

What Trends Do We See?

Trends in the gross convictions rate among Swedes and "non-Swedes" (that is, naturalized Swedes, domiciled foreign citizens, and nondomiciled foreign citizens) can be traced since the mid-1960s. Figure 3.3 indicates that the increase in adjudication of nontrivial offenses since the 1960s must be primarily attributed to the "non-Swedish" population. In 1966, 9% of all persons adjudicated for nontrivial offenses were immigrants/foreigners. By 1994, the percentage had increased to 28%. Roughly half of this increase is a function of the demographic growth of the immigrant/foreign population in Sweden; the other half is due to the previously discussed overrepresentation of the immigrant population with regard to crime. The overrepresentation of foreign citizens has remained more or less stable throughout the period. This stability has not been disrupted by the fact that the proportion of citizens from other Scandinavian and European countries in the total foreign population decreased from 91% in 1975 to 61% by 1993. Stable proportions, albeit high, are even found for the most serious crimes such as homicide, rape, and robbery. The statistics also show that convictions among Swedish and foreign young persons have not increased since the middle of the 1970s. Reconviction rates among young domiciled foreigners (age 15 to 24 years), however, are about 10 percentage points higher than among native Swedes in the same age group (53% vs. 44%, given a 3-year follow-up period, measured in the 1980s; von Hofer & Tham, 1991, p. 32).

RESEARCH AND THEORY ON CRIME, CRIMINAL JUSTICE, AND IMMIGRANTS

As the previous review of empirical research data indicates, there is no unambiguous evidence as to whether and to what extent foreign citizens/ immigrants in Sweden are in fact overrepresented with respect to crime. Most

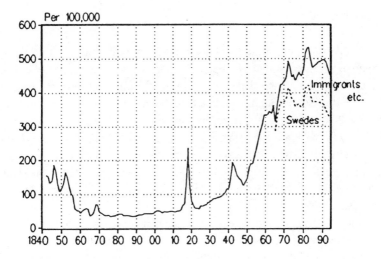

Figure 3.3. Number of Criminal Convictions per 100,000 of the Total Population (fines excluded), Swedes, and Immigrants/Foreigners (i.e., naturalized Swedes, domiciled foreign citizens, nondomiciled foreign citizens), 1841 to 1966

studies show small or no differences, especially when controlling for background variables. A more clear overrepresentation (by a factor of 2) is found in conviction statistics. The latter do not, however, control for social background variables. The highest rates are reported for young immigrants in institutional care, and serious crimes of violence (homicide, rape, and robbery, up to a factor of 3 to 4).

Such overrepresentation can be observed for a period of at least a quarter of a century. The risks have not been influenced to any great extent by the fact that the composition of the convicted foreign population has shifted (in terms of nationalities), or by the fact that immigration has shifted from labor migration to family and asylum-seeking migration. Given the higher risks discussed previously, the explanatory power of foreign citizenship is weak. Attempts to explain crimes by foreign citizens, and in particular serious crimes, are thus not much furthered by referring to the fact of foreign citizenship itself. Finally, the difference in offense rates between foreign and Swedish citizens has the about same dimensions as the difference between cities and rural areas, or upper and lower classes, and much less than that between young persons and their elders, or between men and women.

Given the varying higher rates that have been shown, however, how should they be explained?

Discrimination

It could be argued that the higher level of criminal registration of foreigners may be explained by selective reporting to the police, discrimination in the criminal justice system (with possible cumulative effects at each stage), or both. No systematic studies have been conducted in Sweden that illuminate this problem. Therefore, we cannot with certainty state whether foreign citizens face a different risk of being convicted than Swedes. Comparisons between statistics on persons suspected and convicted of offenses, however, indicate consistently that foreign citizens are convicted to the same degree as are Swedish citizens, once suspected of an offense (von Hofer & Tham, 1991, p. 25).

On the other hand, there is also evidence that supports the hypothesis of selective reporting. An experiment conducted by the Department of Psychology at Stockholm University (Lindholm & Christianson, 1995) indicated that witnesses might be biased against foreigners.

Bergström & Sarnecki (1996) have compared immigrant and Swedish young people in reform schools. The scenario of the groups' problems (criminality, substance abuse, mental problems) was on the whole identical. The only exception was that young Swedes had greater alcohol problems. No differences were found in family circumstances or other background factors; the majority of the young people came from very difficult social conditions. No differences were found with regard to recidivism into crime and other problems in a 2-year follow-up. These findings indicate that the social authorities treat Swedes and immigrant youths the same, and that both groups have similar problems and similar backgrounds. It should be noted, however, that there is a tradition of more often placing immigrant youths in institutions compared to Swedish youth, who are more often placed in family homes (Socialstyrelsen, 1995a, p. 25).

Ceteris Paribus

Another explanation for the different risk rates found in studies could be referred to as the ceteris paribus (i.e., holding everything else constant) argument. Self-report studies, both on offending and victimization, have shown no or only small differences between Swedes and foreigners. In these studies, it has been possible to control for a number of background variables. As discussed previously, conviction data indicate more substantial differences in criminal involvement between immigrants and native Swedes. It could be argued that the overrepresentation of foreigners would disappear or at least decrease in conviction statistics if controls (similar to those done in self-report surveys) could be made. There are, however, also problems associated with such controls. First, controlling for all differences between immigrants and natives, such as unemployment and command of (the Swedish) language, might explain away exactly the circumstances that characterize the situation of immigrants. Second, if a subpopulation de facto produces more offenders than its share of the total population, the public and the politicians might not be calmed by reference to the ceteris paribus argument.

Cultural Differences

An often used hypothesis for explaining crimes among immigrants is that of cultural differences, including both cultural conflict and deficient knowledge about prevailing norms. The fact that 70% of crime convictions involving foreign citizens concern quite mundane and culturally undisputed crimes, such as traffic and property crimes, is an indication that the cultural conflict hypothesis can only be considered valid for a low proportion of all crimes committed (such as some violence within the family, bribery/corruption, and gambling). To this can be added the fact that a majority of foreign citizens originate from societies rather similar to that in Sweden. Sarnecki (1994), in his study on rape, addresses the cultural argument and refutes the cultural misunderstanding hypothesis. He counters this notion with the fact that immigrants are also overrepresented in cases of stranger rapes where such misunderstanding could not feasibly arise.

Selective Immigration

If the differences found in conviction statistics (especially for serious crimes of violence) are accepted as real reflections of differential criminal involvement, selective immigration may be a plausible hypothesis to explain this phenomenon. It cannot be ruled out that a small number of people with personal problems or chaotic living circumstances are among the very large groups that have immigrated from different countries. Lenke (1983), for instance, has maintained that a group of immigrants who came to Sweden from Finland in the 1970s included persons with serious social problems. These people came to Sweden because the opportunities to "make it" were greater in Sweden than in Finland, even for people with serious problems. In this context, Lenke refers to "social political refugees." Olsson's (1986) findings lend support to Lenke's hypothesis; she showed that many of the

Finnish citizens who were deported from Sweden due to criminality or other asocial behavior had experienced serious problems in their land of origin.

Marginalization

An alternative explanation (not incompatible with the selective immigration theory) for the overrepresentation of foreigners involves the conditions in their adopted country. Regardless of the changing motives for immigration, there is, as previously pointed out, a remarkable similarity in overrepresentation in crime statistics for several large immigrant groups, as well as a stability over time in this overrepresentation. Thus, there may be some aspect of being a foreign citizen in Sweden that can be linked to a higher risk of committing crimes and being victimized.

Criminality is more common among individuals with poor living conditions. Immigrants tend to experience living conditions that are inferior to those of Swedes. A prediction based on living conditions would therefore yield a higher risk of offending in the immigrant population. This type of explanation can be referred to as the marginalization hypothesis.

Strain

Another central concept in criminology, relevant to the marginalization hypothesis, is that of strain (Merton, 1968). The life goals and aspirations of immigrant youth in their adopted country do not differ from those found in the majority population. Their opportunities, real, perceived, or both, of achieving these goals in a socially accepted manner, however, are less than those of the majority population (Killias, 1989). The manner in which immigrant youths deal with the strain (stress, frustration) that arises from the experience of this goals/means conflict may result in criminality, other social and psychological problems, or both. An experience of strain among persons of foreign descent is compatible with the results from the level-of-living surveys. Support for this hypothesis is also obtained in a recently published survey in which large proportions of the immigrant population claimed to feel discriminated against on the basis of their ethnic background. A considerable proportion of the respondents reported that as a result of their background, for example, their job applications were turned down, they were harassed on the job, landlords refused to rent or sell houses or apartments to them, they were threatened in public places, they were denied entry to restaurants, and so on (Lange, 1995).

A main point in Merton's (1968) theory is that deprivation is relative. True, immigrants might be better off in terms of absolute living conditions in their adopted country than in their country of origin, but entering a new country will also affect the relative position in society of both newcomers and natives. It has been hypothesized that, in Sweden in the postwar period, immigrants have taken jobs otherwise available to persons with criminal records, thereby contributing to the sharp increase in recidivism among Swedes (von Hofer & Tham, 1996). In general, however, the immigrants are worse off than the natives. In many cases, they enter Swedish society at the bottom and remain there. The other side of the coin is that this may mean that some native Swedes feel relatively less deprived (i.e., they are no longer at the bottom!), perceive less strain, and thus commit less crime. Can such a hypothesis receive support from the available data?

There has been a continuous rise in convictions for native Swedes from the 1920s until around 1970 (see Figure 3.3). Since then, there has been no increase in the rate of conviction among native Swedes. Meanwhile, the overall conviction rate has continued to rise, due to the overrepresentation of immigrants.

Two interpretations can be offered for the trends in convictions with regard to immigrants. First, immigration simply has added a number of crimes to the crime level in Sweden, crimes that would not have been committed if there had been no immigration. Support for this interpretation can be found in data on homicide. In the prewar period, almost all those convicted of homicide were Swedish citizens without prior record. At the end of the century, the number of convicted (for homicide) has tripled by the addition of two equally large groups, Swedish recidivists and foreign citizens (von Hofer, 1990, p. 33). Second, crimes by immigrants can be seen in part as a replacement phenomenon. The leveling off of convictions among native Swedes could be considered as too steep; historical trends would predict a future increase, even if not as steep as earlier ones. The leveling off among Swedes begins at the same time that immigrants start appearing in the conviction statistics. A similar development is observed for young lawbreakers in institutional care (Statistics Sweden, 1992, p. 27). This number has dropped by more than one half since the late 1960s. Young persons of foreign descent, however, constitute the majority of inhabitants of these institutions, at least in the Stockholm region (Bergström & Sarnecki, 1996). In relation to the situation in the late 1960s, the decrease of young Swedish lawbreakers in institutions has been quite drastic, perhaps even more drastic then could

reasonably have been predicted. "The worst of the worst," to use the vocabulary of the Swedish debate, were formerly young Swedes but are now young
immigrants.

Both trends (in total convictions and the institutionalized young lawbreakers) could be interpreted against the background of strain theory.
Groups at the bottom will feel more strain than others and will be more likely
to commit crimes. Given the overrepresentation of immigrants in the bottom
strata of society, they will be more likely to experience the most strain and
to show higher risks of offending than others. An important point is that, if
this is true, then the replacement of immigrants would not lead to a reduction
in crime equal to their present share.

DEBATE AND POLICY ISSUES

The case of immigrants and crime is a good illustration that developments
in criminality do not always coincide with the developments in public debate.
The debate in the Swedish media about the criminality of foreign citizens
was initiated in 1978. At that time, *Pockettidningen R* ("Sverige, Sverige
fosterhem," 1978), a magazine produced jointly by four organizations representing different categories of "deviants," published a volume about the
vulnerable situation of immigrants in Sweden. Data were presented that
revealed that foreign citizens were convicted for crimes more often than
Swedes, the idea being that this was a manifestation of poor living conditions. It was emphasized that the difference in criminality between Swedes
and foreign citizens was not particularly large, however, and that Swedes
committed the overwhelming majority of crimes. This statistical description
should not have been news to anyone. The fact that immigrants were
overrepresented among convicted persons was clear from the annual publications of Statistics Sweden. It had also been shown in various research
reports (e.g., Sveri, 1973). Nevertheless, the report seemed to make the issue
of "immigrants and crime" an item of great newsworthiness on radio,
television, and in newspapers.

Why did this not happen any earlier? One explanation may be that the
period ending in the late 1970s was characterized by a strong and expanding
economy, and to some degree by faith in the future, liberal ideas, and
tolerance toward rule- and normbreakers. During the 1960s, foreign labor
power was imported so that Swedish industry could push even further ahead.
Restrictions on labor immigration were introduced in 1967 as a response to

pressure from the trade unions, but immigrants were by and large received with goodwill by industry and public authorities alike. Possible problems linked to immigration were minimalized. Public authorities and the media responded to signs of negative attitudes toward immigrants, which at times did occur (Sveri, 1973, p. 284; Wadensjö, 1973, p. 49). The National Board of Immigration asserted in several local newspaper articles that immigrants did not commit more crimes than Swedes (Hedebro, 1977, p. 17), which was not really accurate according to the statistics. The Minister of Justice publicly criticized an article in the official journal *Svensk Polis* (Swedish Police), which suggested that some groups of gypsies were particularly criminal. During this period, the issue of higher crime rates among foreign citizens was taboo as a topic for open public debate.

In light of this, it was perhaps no coincidence that it was a leftist journal such as *Pockettidningen R* that took up the discussion. From that point on, crimes by foreigners were a legitimate topic of debate, and the media then swung toward the opposite extreme. Many of those who had previously accused the authorities of repressing the truth, now themselves started resorting to considerable exaggerations, and in several criminal cases involving foreign citizens, the media abandoned their former practice of not publishing the names and pictures of suspects. Furthermore, the perceived threat of drugs became increasingly linked to foreign countries. More open borders, a result of the development in Eastern Europe and in the European Union, gave rise to apprehension about the risk of heightened drug criminality. The media took the lead and the link between foreign citizens and drug crimes started appearing everywhere. In 1991, a new party entered Parliament on a platform of law-and-order and restrictive immigration policies (the party was not reelected to Parliament in 1994).

A reorientation of Swedish criminal policy in a more punitive direction during the 1980s undoubtedly contributed to the focus on foreign offenders (Tham, 1995b). The shift in sanctioning policies toward just deserts and "incapacitation" (i.e., a greater use of imprisonment), the emergence of debates about career criminals (i.e., a small group of offenders who commit a majority of the traditional crimes), and highlighting of "the worst juvenile delinquents" were components of the new orientation; criminality could be attributed, again, to specific groups of individuals with identifiable characteristics. The picture of criminality as being "foreign" to the average citizen was successfully reestablished.

In the autumn of 1989, the government introduced a more restrictive immigration policy. It was preceded by a debate about criminality by foreign citizens. This debate was triggered by a series of editorials in the leading liberal morning newspaper. Once more, the attention of the media was not caused by an upswing in crime trends, but rather by a heated discussion about the settlement of political refugees in certain municipalities.

In 1993, the government introduced a bill expanding the possibility of expelling foreign citizens who had committed less serious crimes. The background to the law was a government report on criminal violence (Statens Offentliga Utredningar, 1990, p. 92), that explicitly discussed the role of foreigners, and recommended increased deportation of foreign offenders and more careful screening of foreign citizens wishing to enter the country. The bill was based on the notion that criminality among foreign citizens had increased (Statens Offentliga Utredningar, 1993, p. 17, p. 54). The increase was, however, almost totally explained by the increase in the number of foreign citizens. The immediate build-up to the proposal, although not officially stated, was the alleged widespread shoplifting in 1992 by refugees from Kosovo in the former Yugoslavia. The government justified the new law in part by its wish to retain its otherwise humanitarian immigrant policies. The new law took effect in 1994. The problem of criminality among new immigrants had by then become a fairly academic question. With the introduction of a visa requirement in 1993 for persons from the former Yugoslavia, the flow of refugees started slowing considerably.

The public attention has in all likelihood increased the polarization of various groups of young people (mainly males), which have primarily emerged in the large metropolitan areas, but also to some degree now in mid-sized towns. Various militant groups of young people, such as Skinheads and antiracists, are intensifying the climate of confrontation. At present, the issue of ethnic origin is a central focus in the youth culture, and this fact compels many young people to take a stand for or against "racists" or "foreigners." There is the risk that this development will increase the level of violence in Swedish society, especially in and near the entertainment centers in the inner cities. In general, Sweden does not yet face the type of problem with crimes by immigrants and ethnic minorities that are observed in the large immigration countries of North America and Europe. In part, this may be related to the fact that in Sweden the relationship between ethnicity and class is still not very strong.

REFERENCES

Bergström, U., & Sarnecki, J. (1996). *Invandrarungdomar på särskilda ungdomshem i Stock-holms län* [Immigrant youth in reform schools in Stockholm county]. In B.-Å. Armelius,

S. Bengtzon, P.-A. Rydelius, J. Sarnecki, & K. S. Carpelan (Eds.), *Vård av ungdomar med sociala problem—En forskningsöversikt* (pp. 156-186). Falköping: Statens Institutionsstyrelse & Liber Utbildning.

Björgo, T. (1994). Terrorist violence against immigrants and refugees in Scandinavia: Patterns and motives. In T. Björgo & R. Witte (Eds.), *Racist violence in Europe* (pp. 29-45). New York: St. Martin's.

Council of Europe. (1992). *Penological information bulletin* (No. 17). Strasbourg, France: Author.

Erikson, R., & Fritzell, J. (1988). The effects of the social welfare system in Sweden on the well-being of children and the elderly. In J. Palmer, T. Smeeding, & B. B. Torey (Eds.), *The vulnerable* (pp. 309-330). Washington, DC: Urban Institute.

Fritzell, J. (1991). *Icke av marknaden allena: Inkomstfördelningen i Sverige* [Income distribution in Sweden]. Stockholm: Stockholm University, Swedish Institute for Social Research.

Hammar, T. (1992a). Invandring [Immigration]. In *Nationalencyklopedin* (Vol. 9, p. 533). Höganäs: Bra Böcker.

Hammar, T. (1992b). Invandringspolitik [Immigration policies]. In *Nationalencyklopedin* (Vol. 9, p. 534). Höganäs: Bra Böcker.

Hedebro, G. (1977). *Att informera om avvikande grupper. En genomgång av några olika samhällsområden* [How to inform of deviant groups]. Brottsförebyggande rådet, Rapport 1977:2. Stockholm: Liber.

Janson, C. G. (1995). *On project Metropolitan and the longitudinal perspective* (Project Metropolitan, Research Report No. 40). Stockholm: University of Stockholm.

Kangas, O. (1991). *The politics of social rights. Studies on the dimension of sickness insurance in Organization for Economic Cooperation and Development (OECD) countries.* Stockholm: Stockholm University, Swedish Institute for Social Research.

Killias, M. (1989). Criminality among second-generation immigrants in Western Europe: A review of the evidence. *Criminal Justice Review, 14*(1), 13-42.

Kühlhorn, E., Bejerot, C., Käll, K., Romelsjö, A., & Stenbacka, M. (1995). Legale und illegale Drogen. Wie gehen die Schweden mit Alkohol—Und anderen Drogenproblemen um? [Legal and illegal drugs in Sweden]. *Kriminologisches Bulletin, 21*(1), 67-106.

Lange, A. (1995). *Invandrare om diskriminering. En enkät—Och intervjuundersökning om etnisk diskriminering på uppdrag av Diskrimineringsombudsmannen (DO)* [Immigrants on discrimination]. Stockholm: Centrum för Invandraforskning [Center for Research in International Migration and Ethnic Relations]/Statistiska Centralbyrån.

Lenke, L. (1983). De "socialpolitiska flyktingarna"—Ett fall av "selektiv migration" [The "sociopolitical refugees"—A case of "selective migration"]. In U. B. Eriksson & H. Tham (Eds.), *Utlänningarna och brottsligheten* (pp. 215-224). Brottsförebyggande rådet, Rapport 1983:4. Stockholm: Liber.

Lindholm, T., & Christianson, S. Å. (1995). *Vittnesmål och våldsbrott: Effekter av etniska grupptillhörighet hos vittne, offer och gärningsman* [Evidence and violent crimes]. Polishögskolan Rapport 1995:1. Solna: Polishögskolan.

Marklund, S., & Svallfors, S. (1987). *Dual welfare-segmentation and work enforcement in the Swedish system.* Umeå: Umeå University, Department of Sociology.

Martens, P. L. (1992). *Familj, uppväxt, och brott* [Family, environment, and delinquency]. Brå-Rapport 1992:1. Stockholm: Allmänna Förlaget.

Martens, P. L. (1994). Criminal and other antisocial behavior among persons with immigrant and Swedish background—A research note. In B. Åkerman, C. Axelsson, D. P. Farrington, S. Fischbein, P. L. Martens, F. S. Pearson, W. R. Smith, S.-Å. Stenberg, M. Walldén, & P. -O. H. Wikströ (Eds.), *Studies of a Stockholm cohort* (pp. 83-108, Project Metropolitan, Research Report No. 39). Stockholm: University of Stockholm.

Merton, R. (1968). *Social theory and social structure.* New York: Free Press.

Nordic Statistical Secretariat. (1991). *Nordic criminal statistics 1950-1989* (Summary of a report, statistical reports of the Nordic countries). Copenhagen: Author.

Olsson, M. (1986). *Finland tur och retur—Om utvisning av finska medborgare* [Round trip to Finland. On deportation of Finnish citizens]. Brottsförebyggande rådet, Rapport 1986:1. Stockholm: Liber.

Olsson, O., Byqvist, S., & Gomér, G. (1993). *Det tunga narkotikamissbrukets omfattning i Sverige 1992* [Heavy drug use in Sweden 1992]. Stockholm: Centralförbundet för Alkohol—och Narkotikaupplysning [Swedish Council for Information on Alcohol and Other Drugs].

Organization for Economic Cooperation and Development—OECD. (1994). *The OECD Jobs Study. Facts, analysis, strategies.* Paris: Author.

Palme, J. (1990). *Pension rights in welfare capitalism. The development of old-age pensions in 18 OECD countries 1930 to 1985.* Stockholm: Stockholm University, Swedish Institute for Social Research.

Rikspolisstyrelsen [Swedish Police Board]—RPS. (1988). *Rasism och främlingsfientlighet* [Racism and xenophobia], RPS Rapport 1988:4. Stockholm: Rikspolisstyrelsen.

Sarnecki, J. (1994). *Våldtäkter i Stockholm: Polisanmälda våldtäkter i Stockholm 1986-1990* [Rape in Stockholm 1986-1990]. Stockholm: Kriminologiska Institutionen. Unpublished manuscript.

Socialstyrelsen. (1995a). *Invandrarbarn i familjehem* [Immigrant children in foster family homes], SoS-Rapport 1995:7. Stockholm: Socialstyrelsen/Epidemiologiskt Centrum.

Socialstyrelsen. (1995b). *Welfare and public health in Sweden 1994.* Stockholm: Author.

Statens Offentliga Utredningar [Government Official Reports]—SOU. (1990). *Våld och brottsoffer* [Violence and victims of crime] 1992:92. Stockholm: Justitiedepartementet.

Statens Offentliga Utredningar [Government Official Reports]—SOU. (1993). *Utvisning på grund av brott* [Deportation because of criminality] 1993:54. Stockholm: Kulturdepartementet.

Statistics Sweden. (1992). *Ungdomar och brott* [Youth and crime, 3rd ed., Rev.]. Örebro: Author.

Statistics Sweden. (1993). *Statistical yearbook of Sweden 1994* (Vol. 80). Stockholm: Author.

Statistics Sweden. (1995). *Offer for vålds—och egendomsbrott 1978-1993* [Victims of violence and of property crimes 1978-1993]. Levnadsförhållanden, Rapport 88. Stockholm: Author.

Statistics Sweden. (1996). *Statistical yearbook of Sweden 1996* (Vol. 82). Stockholm: Author.

Suikkila, J. (1983). Några synpunkter på alkoholmissbruk och brottslighet bland ungdomar i Sverige och Finland [Some comments on alcohol misuse and criminality among Swedish and Finnish youth]. In U. B. Eriksson & H. Tham (Eds.), *Utlänningarna och brottsligheten* (pp. 190-214). Brottsförebyggande rådet, Rapport 1983:4. Stockholm: Liber.

Svensson, B. (1995). *Criminal justice systems in Sweden* (Brå-rapport 1995:1). Stockholm: Fritzes.

Sveri, B. (1973). Utlänningars brottslighet. En kriminalstatistisk jämförelse mellan svenska och utländska medborgare [Foreigners' criminality]. *Svensk Juristtidning, 58,* 279-310.

Sverige, Sverige fosterhem [Sweden, Sweden foster home]. (1978). *Pockettidningen R., 8*(4), 99-121.

Tham, H. (1983). Utlänningar och brottsligheten—Forskningens läge [Foreigners and crime—A research review]. In U. B. Eriksson & H. Tham (Eds.), *Utlänningarna och brottsligheten* (pp. 11-30). Brottsförebyggande rådet, Rapport 1983:4. Stockholm: Liber.

Tham, H. (1995a). Drug control as a national project: The case of Sweden. *Journal of Drug Issues, 25*(1) 113-128.

Tham, H. (1995b). From treatment to just deserts in a changing welfare state. *Scandinavian Studies in Criminology, 14,* 89-122.

van Dijk, J. J. M., & Mayhew, P. (1993). Criminal victimization in the industrialized world: Key findings of the 1998 and 1992 international crime surveys. In A. Alvazzi del Frate, U. Zvekic, & J. J. M. van Dijk (Eds.), *Understanding experiences of crime and crime control* (pp. 1-49). Rome: United Nations Interregional Crime and Justice Research Institute.

von Hofer, H. (1990). Homicide in Swedish statistics, 1750-1988. *Scandinavian Studies in Criminology, 11,* 29-45.

von Hofer, H., & Tham, H. (1991). *Foreign citizens and crime: The Swedish case* (Promemoria 1991:1). Stockholm: Statistics Sweden.

von Hofer, H., & Tham, H. (1996). *Theft in Sweden 1831-1994.* Stockholm: Kriminologiska Institutionen.

Wadensjö, E. (1973). *Immigration and samhällsekonomi* [Immigrations and societal economy]. Lund: Studentlitteratur.

Wennemo, I. (1994). *Sharing the costs of children. Studies in the development of family support in the OECD countries.* Stockholm: Stockholm University, Swedish Institute for Social Research.

Wikström, P. -O. H. (1991). *Urban crime, criminals, and victims: The Swedish experience in an Anglo-American comparative perspective.* New York: Springer-Verlag.

Wikström, P. -O. H. (1994). "Brott, brottsprevention, och kriminalpolitik" [Crime, crime prevention, and criminal policy]. In P. -O. H. Wikström, J. Ahlberg, & L. Dolmén (Eds.), *Brott, brottsprevention, och kriminalpolitik* (pp. 7-49). Stockholm: Fritzes.

4

MINORITIES, CRIME, AND CRIMINAL JUSTICE IN THE FEDERAL REPUBLIC OF GERMANY

Hans-Joerg Albrecht

FROM "GUEST WORKERS" TO "IMMIGRANT" MINORITIES

In the Federal Republic of Germany (FRG), research on foreign and ethnic minorities has been stimulated mainly because of the so-called guest workers (*gastarbeiter*) who came to Germany in the early 1960s (Kaiser, 1974). Economic prosperity and a shortage of labor led to considerable governmental and private effort aimed at attracting workers from southern European countries (predominantly Italy, Spain, and Portugal) to Germany. Consequently, social science became interested in the topics of immigration and immigrant minorities. The focus of criminological research initially was on foreign "guest" workers; however, because the ethnic composition of immigrants, the motivation for migration, and the perception of migration changed significantly over the last 20 years (as described next), attention shifted to ethnic and racial "immigrant" minorities. What has changed over the last few decades?

First, the migrant work force no longer originates predominantly from southwestern European countries (Italy, Spain, Portugal), but rather from southeastern European countries (former Yugoslavia and Turkey). In the early 1960s, about 60% of the foreign population came from countries belonging to the European Union (EU); in the 1990s, the European Union share has dropped to a mere 27%. Turkish immigrants and immigrants from former Yugoslavia now account for almost half of the resident foreign population in Germany. Furthermore, since the mid-1980s, immigrants from African and Asian developing countries constitute substantial proportions of the immigrant population. More recently, after the breakdown of socialist regimes, migration has begun to include Eastern European countries, thus adding to the ethnic and cultural diversity of immigrant populations.

With this change in the ethnic composition of immigrants, a shift in the motives for migration and the legal aspects of immigration, as well as a change in the perception of ethnic and foreign minorities, occurred. With respect to motives for entering the FRG, the law essentially distinguishes between tourists (or short-term visitors), foreigners joining the labor force (or enrolling at schools or universities), and asylum seekers and refugees (to whom the Geneva Convention applies). In the 1980s, the complete abolition of programs to hire workers abroad, as well as the severe restrictions on granting permissions to non-EU foreigners to work in Germany, naturally resulted in larger numbers of foreigners asking for asylum (which until recent amendments to the German constitution and the immigration law that is in effect, provided automatic permission to stay on German territory awaiting the final decision on asylum).

Whereas in the 1960s foreign workers were attracted to Germany by the need of the German economy for (mainly unskilled) workers, the 1970s witnessed a process of structural change in the economic system with growing unemployment rates, as well as technological and organizational rationalization. Paralleling these processes, the public and political perceptions of migrant workers changed from viewing immigration as a positive solution to a labor shortage, to seeing immigration and immigrants as a social problem. These changes are visible in the concepts and categories used in describing and analyzing immigration and immigrants. In the 1960s and 1970s, the concept of the guest worker prevailed, pointing toward integration into the economic and labor system (as a guest, not a permanent immigrant). In the 1980s, notions such as immigration, illegal immigrants, and asylum seekers became focal concerns, highlighting the social problem view.

The proportion of foreigners approached 10% in the 1990s (from only 1% up to the 1950s). These figures underestimate the size of these ethnic minorities because, for instance, renaturalized Germans from the former Soviet Union, Afro Germans, German Sinti and Roma (gypsies), or naturalized immigrants, short-term visitors (on tourist visas), and illegal immigrants are not included. In 1992, approximately 39% of the resident foreign population had been in Germany for more than 15 years (down from more than 50% at the end of the 1980s). An increase in short-term residence (less than one year) took place reflecting the strong growth of immigration in the 1980s. Important regional differences in the density of foreign residents exist; metropolitan areas and the western part of Germany are the favorite places to which immigrants are attracted. In the 1990s, only approximately 2% of the foreign population live in the "new *Bundesländer,*" that is, in the eastern part of Germany (where approximately 20% of the population lives; Statistisches Bundesamt, 1993, p. 72).

Ethnic Germans

A rather unique phenomenon with respect to immigration concerns the population of ethnic Germans whose ancestors emigrated to Poland, Russia, and Rumania and who are entitled to be renaturalized (under the condition that evidence of German origins is provided). Slightly more than 2 million ethnic Germans have been renaturalized between 1968 and 1992, making them the most important ethnic minority in quantitative terms. The majority of these ethnic Germans have immigrated to Germany since the second half of the 1980s (Statistisches Bundesamt, 1993, p. 92). Although ethnic Germans from Eastern Europe certainly form a minority distinct from other foreign populations and distinct from the German majority, they have not attracted attention in terms of crime policy and criminological research. The reasons for this are obvious: Ethnic Germans do not become visible in police or other criminal justice statistics because they fall under the category of "Germans." Some social science research has dealt with ethnic Germans; however, the focus of these studies has been on the causes of migration as well as on the problems of integration and adaption of family structures (Bade, 1994; Riek, 1995; Wilkiewicz, 1989). Research shows that ethnic Germans from Russia experience ethnic isolation (two thirds feel that they are not welcome), which is underscored by a high rate of intraethnic marriages (75%; Wilkiewicz, 1989, p. 59). Recently, the Organization of German Police suggested that the increase in the crime rate among the German population, especially among German youth during the last few years, was due to the heavy immigration of ethnic Germans from Eastern Europe (see also Pfeiffer, 1995, p. 102, for some narrative information from several German cities). The number of German juvenile suspects (in the western part of Germany) has been on the increase since the beginning of the 1990s (Bundeskriminalamt, 1995, p. 88). Prison data from the central youth correctional facility in the state of Baden-Württemberg do indeed indicate that involvement of young ethnic Germans in crime and criminal justice contributes significantly to this increase. The rate of prison admissions of young German offenders born abroad has increased during the first 5 years of the 1990s (from 2% in the late 1980s to approximately 5% in 1994[1]).

THE ROLE OF MEDIA, PUBLIC POLICY, AND SCIENCE

Powerful belief patterns concerning the potential of conflicts and instability associated with immigration and the "stranger" link migration or minority status, crime, and deviance. The joining of the topics "ethnicity" and "crime" facilitate polarization and political exploitation. Indeed, the issue of ethnic minorities' and—especially—asylum seekers' potential for threatening safety has become a rallying point for authoritarian sentiments in German society as well as for new right-wing political parties and extremist groups. A recent content analysis of print media in Germany revealed that two fifths of the articles related to foreigners highlighted the topic of "crimes committed by foreign minorities" (Kubink, 1993, p. 87; see also Delgado, 1972). Among the topics covered by these articles, drug trafficking and organized crime dominated with a share of approximately 60%, outweighing other types of crimes.

New dimensions have been added to the debate on ethnicity, migration, and crime in the 1980s with the process of European integration and abolition of border controls between several European Union countries. This put the focus on control of immigration and cross-border crime and shifted public concerns toward organized crime. The discussion of ethnicity and organized crime replaced the earlier public focus on foreign terrorism and politically motivated violence among ethnic minorities. Asylum seekers and illegal immigrants especially have become focal concerns with perceived problems of deviance, crime, and economic burdens. Control of borders with neighboring non-EU countries has been upgraded to hitherto unknown extents. The effects of stiffer border controls are visible in the sheer numbers of illegals intercepted at borders. Although illegal immigration was not seen as a problem until 1989, in 1995 as many as 29,000 (in 1994—31,000) illegals have been arrested while trying to enter the territory of the FRG, most of them (24,000) at the East-German/Tcheque and Polish border.

International organized crime has become a major point of concern of the EU's internal policy (Kühne, 1991). From the perspective of organized crime policies and research, migration and ethnic minorities receive twofold attention. First, organized crime is still conceived as a threat posed by alien groups, for example, the Sicilian mafia (or the Polish, Russian, Chinese mafia), which according to most official statements is supposed to extend its scope of criminal activities to central European countries (Boge, 1989). Official accounts of organized crime in Germany suggest that a majority of the people suspected of belonging to organized crime groups are foreigners (Bundeskriminalamt, 1991/1992). Second, ethnic and foreign communities in central European countries are thought to provide logistical support for organized criminals (Bovenkerk, 1993). Of course, it is also possible that within ethnic minority communities organized crime may have flourished from the very beginning (e.g., drug trafficking and supply of local drug markets), and new immigrants may be pulled into organized crime as a promising way to make a living if other legitimate opportunities are barred (e.g., "ethnic ladders"; Korf, 1993). The dramatic increase in mobility has also been associated with changes in general criminal opportunity structures and with the development of black markets (illegal drugs, cars) linking various countries and regions with each other (Pilgram, 1993) and serving thus as push-pull factors in migration.

After German reunification (1990), increasing numbers of police-recorded incidents of violence against ethnic minorities have contributed in redirecting scientific attention to another facet of the problem of ethnicity and criminal justice (Willems, 1993). Violence against minorities may be a consequence of rapid sociopolitical transition resulting in social disintegration, cultural disintegration, or cultural segregation. Moreover, these "hate crimes" may also be viewed as reflecting feelings of prejudice in the general population. Recently, there is new sociological concern for these phenomena that were thought to belong to the past (see Brock, 1993; Möller, 1993).

The danger of polarization exists in scientific research also. One can, in fact, observe such polarization in parts of German criminology (Mansel, 1994; Reichertz & Schröer, 1994). Some analyses focus on assumptions of disproportional criminal involvement of foreign minorities, whereas others favor hypotheses on discriminatory treatment within the justice system. During the last three decades, the bulk of criminological research has emphasized criminal involvement of foreign and ethnic minorities and has sought answers to the question of how to explain this higher involvement. Fewer resources were invested in research on the relationship between minorities and criminal justice agencies, especially the police. Few studies have dealt with victimization, although there is some evidence that members of ethnic minorities are disproportionally affected by victimizing events, both in terms of criminal victimization (including violence in the family), as well as other types of victimization (e.g., workplace accidents or traffic accidents; Albrecht, 1987; Pitsela, 1986). Vulnerability of minority women and children is likely to be reinforced by their weak legal position as foreigners, by language problems, and by their culturally determined inferior role.

THE ROLE OF CRIMINAL JUSTICE INFORMATION SYSTEMS

Focusing on Particular Minorities

Among the most important forces shaping the public perception of crime are police statistics, which in the FRG are broken down by the nationality ("citizenship") of suspects. Information on the race or ethnicity of the suspect is not available. Although some are currently challenging the notion that such variables (i.e., nationality) should be included in criminal justice statistics, it seems unlikely that citizenship will be omitted from official statistics (Kerner, 1994).

Focusing on minorities in police information systems has an extensive history. For example, police authorities traditionally have kept special files on certain groups of suspects among whom the Sinti and Roma (gypsies) have played a rather prominent role. Special police attention devoted to these ethnic minorities is rooted in the historical preoccupation with these minorities, producing numerous myths ultimately culminating in the systematic terror against them in Nazi Germany. After 1945, police continued to keep special files on gypsies to collect data on the group at large without special reference to criminal behavior (Feuerhelm, 1988). This practice came to an end in the 1970s when political organizations of gypsies started to exert pressure, backed up by an emerging general policy pursuing better protection of privacy and personal data. Today, instead of direct information on Sinti and Roma, the police use another variable, "numerous changes of place of residence," which may be assumed to be a synonym for "gypsies."

Research on Crime Involvement
on the Basis of Police Statistics

Most research on the criminal involvement of minorities in the FRG is based on police data. One main limitation of relying on police statistics is their use of "foreign citizenship," which does not validly measure the concepts of ethnicity or (visible) minority. Police statistics divide foreign suspects into subcategories based on their legal status: illegals, guest workers, and tourists. Official federal prison statistics use the category foreign citizenship (yes/no) without, however, providing additional breakdown by nationality, age, or type of sentences. Self-report studies and victimization surveys have only rarely included foreign minorities. Because of these data constraints, most German research on minorities and crime employs the very broad category of "foreign inhabitants."

A Snapshot of Police Data
on Criminality by Foreigners

Research demonstrates that encounters between police and immigrant populations do affect major parts of the young male immigrant population (Karger & Sutterer, 1988). In some metropolitan areas, contacts with the criminal justice system are considered "normal" for some immigrant populations. For example, in the city of Frankfurt in 1994 three fifths of all suspects were foreigners. For 6 of the 43 cities with more than 200,000 inhabitants, the share of foreign suspects is above 40%, and for 16 the proportion amounts to between 30% and 40%. (The eight metropolitan areas with a proportion of foreign suspects below 20% are all located in the east of Germany.)[2]

Police figures on criminal involvement of foreign minorities show that foreign suspects in 1993 accounted for 33.6% of all arrests (including the new Bundesländer), although the proportion of foreigners in the German population is well below 10%. If immigration offenses are not counted, the share of foreign suspects is reduced to 26.7%. In 1953, when police statistics were published for the first time after the Second World War, the rate of foreign suspects was as low as 1.7%.

Thus, police statistics suggest offending rates among certain groups of minorities that are two- to fourfold higher than the rates observed in society at large (Albrecht, 1988). But of course, some minorities have less-than-average offender rates, for example, Spanish and Portuguese (Geißler & Marißen, 1990). Indeed, analysis of police crime statistics shows that enormous differences exist in crime rates among various foreign minorities. Such interethnic differences in criminal involvement suggest that ethnicity and minority status do not have a uniform and consistent effect on crime rates (whether these are used as indicators of actual criminal involvement or as an indicator of law enforcement activities; Junger, 1990). These differences suggest also that a simplistic analysis may mask underlying processes. Comparative analyses of different regions in Germany also show that rather large differences can be observed with respect to the size of offender rates among the same minority groups (Mansel, 1986).

Police Trend Data for
Different Nationalities

Police data also allow for a longitudinal analysis of crime data. Figure 4.1 presents the number of foreigners arrested by the police from 1973 to 1993 in North Rhine-Westphalia. Although the trend in the numbers of Turkish suspects corresponds to those found for other ethnic groups such as Germans or Western Europeans (not shown on the graph; corresponds on a somewhat higher level), trends in the figures related to other nations (Yugoslavia, Morocco, and Poland) demonstrate a marked leap in the second half of the 1980s. This marked increase coincides with an increase in migration activities from Poland, ex-Yugoslavia (due to the civil war), and Morocco.

Research findings point to significant differences in the degree of criminal involvement among generations of immigrants, with the second or third generations born or raised in the FRG displaying considerably higher offending rates than did the first generation of immigrant workers who did not differ (in terms of crime rates) from the corresponding group of German citizens (Kaiser, 1974). Trends in foreign offender rates may be interpreted as reflecting the combined impact of changes in behavior patterns of second- and third-generation immigrants, as well as of changes in migration patterns (percentage of people living in the FRG who are foreign, as well as nationality composition of the foreign population; see Figure 4.2). In the 1960s, the proportion of foreign suspects was rather close to the proportion of foreign population; however, the gap widens during the 1970s and the trends then take completely different courses. Disproportionate involvement of

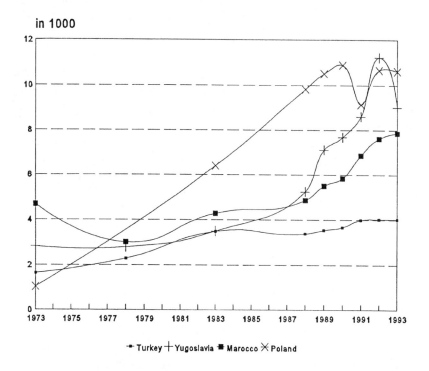

Figure 4.1. Number of Suspects in Selected Foreign Groups, 1973 to 1993 (North Rhine-Westphalia)
SOURCE: Police statistics, North Rhine-Westphalia.

foreigners can be observed especially in the 18- to 20-years-of-age bracket: In 1993, almost half of the suspects aged 18 to 20 years (46.5%) were foreign. (34% of all juvenile offenders aged 14 to 17 years and 30.7% of children aged 7 to 13 years). A tentative explanation may be that first-generation immigrants coming as guest workers to the FRG did experience improved conditions of living, housing, medical care, and so on, outweighing existing differences between minority and majority groups (Kunz, 1989). Moreover, migration of foreign immigrants in the 1960s was triggered exclusively by the demands of German economy (i.e., labor shortage), and therefore, the context of migration was the positive prospect of secure employment and labor contracts. Immigrant selection took place through hiring schemes; interaction patterns of first generations remained largely limited to the ethnic group itself, with contacts with the majority group confined to the place of work.

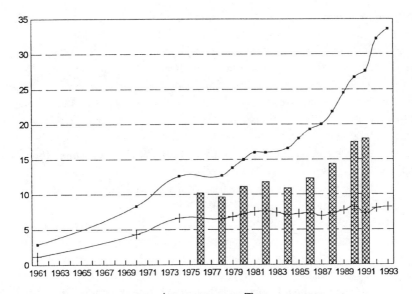

Figure 4.2. Foreign Population, Foreign Suspects, and Foreigners Found Guilty and Sentenced (in percentages)
SOURCE: Bundeskriminalamt: Polizeiliche Kriminalstatistik, 1961-1993; Statistisches Bundesamt: *Statistisches Jahrbuch 1994,* Statistisches Bundesamt: Strafverfolgungsstatistik 1976-1991.

Both police and court statistics show that the significant increase in the numbers of foreign suspects since the second half of the 1980s is not the result of increased criminal involvement of foreigners who are employed (between 4 and 5 per 100,000). The rate of foreign offenders found guilty and sentenced remained fairly stable between 1980 and 1991 in the older (over 30) age group, comparable to the corresponding German age group. Differences in trends are found among juveniles and young adults. Perhaps second or third generations are more likely to become conscious of deprivation and socioeconomic inequality; they also may suffer from conflicting expectations from their traditional parents and modern society. Moreover, the rate of interactions with native Germans increases for the second and third generations, and thus increases the risk of conflicts. Research shows that the marginal position of Turkish and other minorities with respect to income, general socioeconomic status, housing conditions, and so on did not improve over the last decade and over different generations (Seifert, 1991); differences between native Germans and immigrants in average income, housing, and unemployment remain rather substantial (Seifert, 1991, p. 40). Furthermore, although approximately half of young immigrants (18 to 24 years old) express the desire to live permanently in Germany, the vast majority (73%) felt strong bonds to the home culture and deny a "German identity."

Although most crimes committed by minorities are property crimes, their disproportional criminal involvement is especially marked for violent offenses such as assault, rape, robbery, and homicide. Findings from a longitudinal study on criminal offending in a birth cohort show that prevalence rates of all types of offenses combined amount to 29% among 18-year-old foreign males—about twice that of their German counterparts (14%). For violent offenses, the rates are 7% (foreign males) and 2% (German males), respectively (Karger & Sutterer, 1990).

The composition of the foreign offender population has changed over time; the relative sizes of the various ethnic subgroups are subject to significant changes. Although proportions of Turkish, Italian, and Greek suspects decreased dramatically over the last 10 years, the proportions of suspects from former Yugoslavia, Rumania, Poland, the former Soviet Union, as well as from some African countries, did increase considerably. These changes reflect a significant shift in immigration patterns that has occurred during the last three decades with the replacing of former guest worker nationalities (e.g., Italians and Spanish) by immigrants from southeastern Europe as well as Africa and Asia. In addition, considerable changes have also occurred with respect to the legal position (or the stated motive for presence in the FRG) of foreigners suspected of having committed a crime. Whereas in the mid-1980s, about one third of foreign suspects belonged to the group of guest workers, the share of this group has dropped to 18% in 1993. In 1993, one third of foreign suspects belong to the group of foreigners seeking asylum in Germany (up from less than 10% in 1984).

Distinct patterns of offending emerge when categorizing criminal offenses by immigration motives. Illegals are primarily involved in immigration offenses. The fact that other crimes are rare among illegals may be explained by their attempts to avoid all types of confrontation with public authorities. Asylum seekers, on the other hand, seem to be mainly involved with property and immigration offenses. Thus, those groups that rank rather high on the public immigration problem agenda show only minor crime problems. Moreover, changes in the German constitution with regard to asylum took effect in July 1993, which had immediate and strong effects on the total number of people applying for asylum; this, in turn, had immediate effects on the number of crimes recorded for asylum seekers. (Between 1993 and 1994 the absolute number of asylum seekers suspected of having committed any criminal offense dropped again from 225,501 to 134,348.)

Analysis of offending patterns observed in the groups of illegal immigrants, tourists, and foreigners seeking asylum reveals that among these groups petty offending prevails. It is especially shoplifting that drives their crime rate up (Ahlf, 1994). Significantly, their contribution to serious crime is almost negligible. In fact, it is the rate of serious crime involvement that separates illegals, tourists, and asylum seekers from the foreign resident population: Among those moving to the FRG for education or employment, violent offenses are relatively more important than for illegals, tourists, and asylum seekers.

How to Interpret Police Statistics

Police crime data may provide a distorted picture of criminal involvement of minorities. For instance, some foreign minority populations differ sharply from the majority in terms of composition with regard to age, sex, and other variables that are associated strongly with officially recorded crime. The findings from a recently published comparative study on foreigners' crime illustrate the effects of controlling for the effect of demographic and other variables on rates of police recorded crime (Steffen, 1992). The general offending rate found in the immigrant population in Germany is 5.6-fold the offending rate in the German population. If the variable "place of residence" is controlled (and therefore only those foreigners are included who have a permanent place of residence in Germany), then the offender rate is reduced to 2.8-fold that of the German population. If offenses against immigration laws are excluded, then the offender rate is further reduced to 2.5 times that of the German population. If age and gender are controlled, then crime involvement of the male immigrant population aged 18 to 24 years drops to 2.2 times the crime involvement observed in the comparable age/gender segment in the German population.

Most self-report and victimization surveys do not include foreign minorities. Evidence from those surveys that did include groups of foreign juveniles is not conclusive. In the early 1980s, self-report research in the city of Bremen showed that foreign juveniles were not more involved in delinquency than their German counterparts, but also that those foreign juveniles seemed remarkably conformist (Schumann, 1987). A small-scale study of self-reported delinquent behavior among youth in a large city in the south of Germany (Mannheim) recently came to similar conclusions. This survey demonstrated that the rates of offending behavior reported by German youth matched those reported by foreign youth (Sutterer & Karger, 1993). On the other hand, a self-report survey based on a larger sample of German and foreign youth discovered recently a significantly larger proportion of foreign juveniles reporting violent behavior (Heitmeyer, 1995).

LAW ENFORCEMENT AND DISCRIMINATION: FOREIGN MINORITIES IN THE JUSTICE SYSTEM

Are Foreign Minorities More Likely to Be Reported?

Little evidence can be provided with respect to the role of ethnic variables in reporting criminal behavior by the public or the victims of crime (Killias, 1989, p. 17). The few studies that have included the nationality or race of the offender did not come up with unambiguous results (Donner, 1986; Kubink, 1993, p. 56). The much greater involvement of young foreigners in acts of shoplifting and fare dodging, which are reported exclusively by private police in department stores and public transportation, may explain their lower likelihood of being reported by the police themselves (see Donner, 1986; Kubink, 1993). Ethnic minority offenders run a somewhat higher risk of being reported in cases of shoplifting or offenses at the place of work (Blankenburg, 1973; Kaiser & Metzger-Pregizer, 1976; Killias, 1988). On the other hand, minority victims of crime seem to be slightly more reluctant to report an offense if the offender had the same national or ethnic background (Pitsela, 1986, p. 340). This latter observation supports the assumption of underreporting of ethnic minorities' crimes (especially when taking into account that substantial proportions of crimes—particularly personal crimes—committed by members of ethnic minorities are within-group crimes; Sessar, 1981).

Police, Public Prosecution, and Discriminatory Decision Making

The probability of being arrested is extremely low for most offenses, and the police decision to arrest seems to be primarily guided by characteristics of the offense, especially seriousness of the offense (Steffen, 1977). The probability of being processed as a criminal suspect, given a certain number of offenses committed, is about the same for minority and majority offenders. It has been hypothesized that overarresting could be the consequence of ethnic minority suspects confronting police more negatively during encounters than majority members do (Smith, Fisher, & Davidson, 1984). But preliminary research based on an experimental design does not lend support to this assumption: Ethnic minority suspects seem to be even more cooperative while being questioned (Vrij & Winkel, 1991). Furthermore, there is no empirical support for the assumption that there is a larger risk of minority suspects being charged with a criminal offense (Kubink, 1993, p. 60).

Obviously, decisive criteria for taking suspects to criminal court include prior record, offense seriousness, and a guilty plea (Blankenburg, Sessar, & Steffen, 1978). On the other hand, there is considerable evidence that minority offenders are less often brought to court in Germany than their majority counterparts (Reichertz, 1994; Villmow, 1993). Possibly, these dismissals result from the petty nature of criminal acts, as well as from a larger proportion of cases having weak evidence that involve minorities. Similar findings are available for rape cases (Steinhilper, 1986). Recent research demonstrates, however, that the rates of adjudicated juvenile offenders are rather similar for foreign and German juvenile suspects if illegal immigrants, tourists, and asylum seekers are excluded from analysis (Sutterer & Karger, 1993, p. 23). These findings clearly point to rather consistent prosecution patterns that are not biased by race, ethnicity, or citizenship. Even the higher rate of dismissals for tourists, illegal immigrants, and so forth does not challenge this noted consistency in decision making by the public prosecutor; indeed, these groups of suspects are difficult to trace, which make dismissal a reasonable and frequent occurrence.

Sentencing the Foreign Offender

Sentencing research approaches the discrimination issue by way of introducing the variable citizenship into the range of "extralegal" variables, which are controlled in comparison to "legal" variables for their power in explaining sentencing variation. Rather small discrimination effects can be found. Minority defendants run a somewhat higher risk of receiving prison or custodial sentences and are somewhat less likely to receive suspended sentences or probation (Steinhilper, 1986). But in general, ethnic and minority variables, as well as citizenship, add only very modestly to the explanation of sentencing variation (Albrecht, 1994; Greger, 1987). This holds true not only for adult criminal sentencing but also for dispositions in juvenile criminal cases (Albrecht, 1994; Albrecht & Pfeiffer, 1979; Geißler & Marißen, 1990, p. 683; Oppermann, 1987). The slight difference in likelihood of receiving a prison sentence between young German offenders and young foreigners (respectively 2.4% vs. 3.4% of all offenders sentenced) found by Geißler and Marißen (1990) is mostly explained by the type of illegal behavior. When controlling for drug trafficking, the difference fades away. It is especially noteworthy that differences in dispositions are virtually nonexistent in case of violent crimes and sexual offenses; similar results have been obtained by Oppermann (1987).

The relatively small effects of ethnic variables on sentencing outcomes might be due to the fact that many serious personal crimes committed by minority offenders involve a minority victim; effects might turn out to be larger for crimes involving minority offenders victimizing members of the majority group. Effects of ethnicity might also be larger for those crimes in which severe penalties are given and in which foreign minority offenders are greatly overrepresented (e.g., drug trafficking and drug distribution).

Superior court rulings have dealt with the legal question whether ethnicity and the status of being a foreigner may legitimately be used as an aggravating factor in sentencing. The Supreme Court has emphasized that these status variables in principle may not be used to justify increases in the severity of sentences because the constitution precludes differential treatment based on citizenship or ethnicity alone (Bundesgerichtshof [Supreme Court] Beschluß vom 29.11.1990, 1 StR 618/90). The Supreme Court regularly sets aside verdicts that seem to be influenced by the opinion that asylum seekers or other foreigners are especially obliged to comply with the laws of the host country (Bundesgerichtshof [Supreme Court] Strafverteidiger 1987, p. 20; Bundesgerichtshof Strafverteidiger 1991, p. 557; Oberlandesgericht [High Court/High District Court] Bremen Strafverteidiger 1994, p. 130). Voices have been raised in favor of adapting sentencing to the level of sanctions in those countries from which foreign offenders originate (Grundmann, 1985; Schroeder, 1983). The Supreme Court has accepted the view that a need for deterrence (i.e., harsher sentences) may be established in case of a sharp increase of violent acts that are associated with interethnic or national conflicts (Bundesgerichtshof, Beschluß vom 29.11.1990, 1 StR 618/90), or if drug traffickers move their business because of milder penalties meted out in Germany (Bundesgerichtshof 1982, p. 112; Wolfslast, 1982).

A prison sentence received by a foreign offender is among the most important legal grounds justifying (or even requiring) deportation of a foreigner, and thus may add to the punishment. Therefore, decision making within the administrative bodies implementing immigration laws becomes of paramount importance for minority offenders with the legal status of an "alien." Because statutes regulating deportation and expulsion in Germany grant large discretionary powers to these agencies, it is not surprising that research demonstrates large variation in criteria adopted in administrative decision making, as well as in decision outcomes (Otte, 1994).

Foreign Offenders in the Prison System

The proportion of immigrant prisoners in Germany did rise considerably in the last decade, amounting now to approximately 25% of the prison population (including pretrial detainees and sentenced prisoners, youth and adult prisoners). Significant differences in imprisonment rates between various foreign minorities exist. Substantial differences also exist with respect to certain types of incarceration. By far the most significant development is noticed in the area of pretrial detention. In the state of Hesse, the number of foreigners detained prior to their criminal trial amounts to approximately one half of the entire pretrial detention population. This is consistent with the trend observed in other German states. In juvenile pretrial detention, the proportion of foreigners is even more pronounced. In Hessian youth correctional facilities, foreign youth made up 57% of the population in 1994.[3] In the states of *Niedersachsen* (Lower Saxony) and Berlin, the proportion of foreign pretrial detainees rose to approximately two thirds in 1992 (Abgeordnetenhaus Berlin Drucksache 12/3597; Schütze, 1993). The data for the state of Baden-Württemberg show a sharp decrease in the number of German youth prison inmates (during the 1980s and early 1990s), whereas the number of foreign youth prison inmates continuously increased. This trend is consistent with the rising rate of foreign juveniles and young adults in the police statistics. Moreover, detention of foreigners awaiting deportation has recently increased considerably. Every sixth foreigner detained in prisons of North Rhine-Westphalia (January 31, 1994) simply awaits deportation and is not serving time because of criminal offending.

Drug offenses play a crucial role in the sharp increase in the use of imprisonment for foreign offenders since the second half of the 1980s. Property offenses also contributed considerably to the rise in incarceration rates. In the state of Hamburg, 62% of the increase in the number of prisoners between 1982 and 1994 was due to drug offenses and theft.

Foreign prisoners are participating less in furlough programs and prison leave programs (Albrecht, 1989; Janetzky, 1993, p. 114). Differential treatment (e.g., education and training) exists also within the group of foreign prisoners. Prisoners from South America, often sentenced to long prison sentences because of drug trafficking (couriers), are extremely isolated. Foreign offenders create particular problems within prison facilities (i.e., access to television, newspapers, books; Janetzky, 1993. p. 112; Schütze, 1993). Furthermore, reports on interethnic conflicts between various groups (e.g., from former Yugoslavia or Turkey) point to the need for reliable information on such conflicts to reduce the risk of inter- and intraethnic violence within prison facilities (Janetzky, 1993, p. 116).

Under the condition that deportation takes place immediately after release, foreign nationals sentenced to imprisonment can be granted parole after having served half of the prison sentence. Drug couriers usually are paroled and deported to their home country some 3 to 4 months before two thirds of their prison sentence has been served (Kraushaar, 1992).

EXPLAINING CRIMINAL INVOLVEMENT OF ETHNIC MINORITIES

German-Born Resident Ethnic Groups and Crime

The concept of culture conflict has played a central role in research that can be traced back to the mid-1960s when migrant workers became a subject of concern in German criminology and in social sciences at large (Kurz, 1965). Throughout the 1970s and 1980s, the concept of cultural conflict was challenged as not providing sufficient explanatory power (Kaiser, 1974, p. 228; Kubink, 1993, p. 69; Sack, 1974, p. 211; Schüler-Springorum, 1983, p. 532; Villmow, 1993, p. 44). For the first generations of immigrant workers, neither the extent of crime involvement nor the types of crime committed pointed to cultural conflicts (Kubink, 1993, p. 70; Schöch & Gebauer, 1991, p. 56).

The apparent overrepresentation of various ethnic minorities as offenders and victims may, to some extent, be explained by deprivation and control theory (Aronowitz, 1989; Bielefeld, 1982; Kaiser, 1988, p. 599; Villmow, 1993, p. 45). But criminology has to go beyond these types of theories. Immigrants have slipped into the role that the German working class occupied during the 1960s and 1970s (in terms of overrepresentation in police, court, and prison statistics). As we observe today's segmentation in society along ethnic lines, we see that immigrant groups continue to be most likely to be affected by unemployment, bad housing, and poverty as well as insufficient education and vocational training, and these groups are likely to remain in this situation for a considerable time to come. The research questions, which in the 1960s and 1970s highlighted social class, will in the decades to come be replaced by ethnicity.

Foreign-Born Aliens and Crime

The explanation of crime by foreign born in the FRG requires a different strategy. Police statistics show that crime trends of foreigners vary significantly for different national groups. Using as an example the state of Hessen, at least four groups of foreign offenders may be distinguished—each group exhibiting distinct offense patterns. These patterns suggest that explanations of criminality among foreign-born minorities should be distinct from those used to explain criminality among resident ethnic minority groups. First, for the Indian offender population, immigration offenses, fraud, and forgery prevail, offenses typically associated with attempts to enter the country without proper permission (forgery refers here mainly to the use of false documents or passports). Traditional crime, especially property crime, is marginal only. People from Afghanistan, Pakistan, and Ceylon display the same offense patterns.

A second group of foreign offenders (Rumanian suspects; similar trends can be observed for Polish, Bulgarian, and Russian offenders) is characterized by an extremely high proportion of property offenses and immigration offenses. Other crime (especially violent crimes and drug offenses) is negligible.

A third group of foreign offenders consists of nationalities that belong to traditional guest worker countries (characterized by a rather stable and large resident population in Germany). In this group, represented by the Turkish offender population, more or less "ordinary" offense patterns can be observed, with a large share of property offenses and a somewhat elevated level of violent offenses. Immigration offenses are rather marginal in this group.

A fourth distinct group includes nationalities with a significant involvement in drug offenses (Figure 4.3). Here, several subgroups may be distinguished. The Senegalese and Gambian offenders showed up at the beginning of the 1980s in several German states as suspects almost exclusively because of drug offenses (and immigration offenses). These groups were engaged in

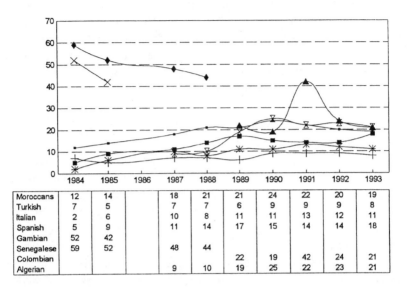

	1984	1985	1986	1987	1988	1989	1990	1991	1992	1993
Moroccans	12	14		18	21	21	24	22	20	19
Turkish	7	5		7	7	6	9	9	9	8
Italian	2	6		10	8	11	11	13	12	11
Spanish	5	9		11	14	17	15	14	14	18
Gambian	52	42								
Senegalese	59	52		48	44					
Colombian						22	19	42	24	21
Algerian				9	10	19	25	22	23	21

-•- Moroccans + Turkish ✳ Italian -■- Spanish ✕ Gambian ◆ Senegalese ▲ Colombian ⊠ Algerian

Figure 4.3. Proportions of Drug Offenses in Selected Groups of Foreign Suspects, 1984 to 1993 (Hesse)
SOURCE: Police statistics, Hesse.

drug (heroin) distribution in some metropolitan areas. In the second half of the 1980s, Senegalese and Gambians faded out of police statistics as police pressure on drug distribution schemes became very tough (there is no significant resident Senegalese or Gambian population in the state of Hesse). Colombians, too, were (in 1990) mainly registered because of cocaine trafficking (plus immigration offenses). A second subgroup concerns nationalities in which the share of drug offenses is rather high, yet not dominant. Here, Moroccans should be mentioned, because some of them are heavily involved in cannabis trafficking and distribution. In addition to the Moroccan drug trafficking group, however, there exists a rather small community of resident Moroccans (which contributes to the adjustment of the structure of offenses toward normal distribution). A third subgroup concerns Spaniards, Italians, and Turks in which drug offenses are somewhat above the average, suggesting that—next to the substantial resident (Spanish, Italian, and Turkish) populations in Hessen—some Spaniards, Turks, and Italians presently are significantly involved in all types of drug offenses.

In sum, the data available on foreign minorities and police-recorded crime display different trends. On the one hand, opening of the borders after the breakdown of communist regimes in the east of Europe has resulted in a sharp rise in property offenses, mainly of a petty nature committed by short-term visitors, tourists or asylum-seekers respectively (representing overlapping categories as tourists may ask for asylum during their stay). The wealth on display, for instance, in department stores in near-border cities clearly serves as an important pull factor attracting large numbers of short-term visitors. This is underscored by the huge increase in shoplifting, that was experienced by some cities in the eastern part of Germany located near the border to East European countries (Ahlf, 1994). Furthermore, huge black markets in the east of Europe have popped up with a growing demand for all types of those goods not available in East European countries (e.g., cars, communication technology). On the other hand, immigrant youth and other groups of the resident foreign population heavily contribute to all types of ordinary criminal offenses. Finally, black markets (especially drug markets) in Germany provide opportunities for various ethnic and foreign groups to make money (e.g., South American groups in cocaine; North Africans and black Africans, Kurdish and Arab groups in heroin and cannabis). Black markets are based on international networks and require participation of residents from other countries. Trafficking routes change, adjusting to continuing police pressure; consequently, the nationalities of offenders involved in drug trafficking (and arrested in Germany) change, too. The same type of processes take place in other black markets, for example, in the trafficking of human beings (be it prostitutes, children, or clandestine workers).

SUMMARY AND CONCLUSIONS

Ethnic and foreign minorities do not cause exceptional crime problems and do not pose dangers for safety in society. Crime among ethnic minorities reflects marginalization and structural problems in society. Theories of crime among resident foreign or ethnic minorities should rely on the same set of variables that are used in explaining crime in general. There is no evidence that variables referring to ethnicity or nationality are useful in etiological research.

There should be more research on victimization among ethnic minorities. Victimization rates are higher in these groups, and effects of victimization are reinforced by their marginal position, which hinder adequate access to relevant institutions. In this context especially, trafficking in women and children has to be considered.

A sharp distinction must be made between resident minority populations versus migrating groups (or individuals) and black market participants. The latter two should not be analyzed from a minority view but rather from a perspective of migration (and push-pull factors affecting migration and offending patterns), or from an economic perspective. Police and judicial statistics do not provide adequate data to study these phenomena. It is grossly misleading to study the phenomena of black markets, migration, and immigration under the heading of "foreigners and crime." In terms of theory, black markets and migration with push-pull factors are far more important than categories such as citizenship, or ethnicity.

NOTES

1. Unpublished data provided by the prison administration of the state Baden-Württemberg.

2. In the case of juveniles and young adults this trend is even more pronounced—in the city of Frankfurt, some 70% of young adults (aged 18 to 20 years) suspected of having committed a criminal offense belong to foreign minorities.

3. Unpublished prison data from the Hessian Ministry of Justice as of March 31, 1994.

REFERENCES

Ahlf, E. (1994). Ausländerkriminalität in der Bundesrepublik Deutschland nach Öffnung der Grenzen. *Zeitschrift für Ausländerrecht, 14,* 132-138.

Albrecht, G. (1988). Neue Ergebnisse zum Dunkelfeld der Jugenddelinquenz: Selbstberichtete Delinquenz von Jugendlichen in zwei westdeutschen Gro städten. In G. Kaiser (Ed.), *Kriminologische Forschung in den 80er Jahren. Projektberichte aus der Bundesrepublik Deutschland* (pp. 661-696). Freiburg: Max-Planck-Institut für Auslaendisches und Internationales Strafrecht.

Albrecht, H. (1987). Foreign minorities and the criminal justice system in the Federal Republic of Germany. *Howard Journal of Criminal Justice, 26,* 272-288.

Albrecht, H. (1988). Ausländerkriminalität. In H. Jung (Ed.), *Fälle zum Wahlfach Kriminologie, Jugendstrafrecht, Strafvollzug* (2nd ed., pp. 183-204). München: Beck.

Albrecht, H. (1989). Ethnic minorities, crime, and public policy. In R. Hood (Ed.), *Crime and criminal policy in Europe* (pp. 174-181). Oxford, UK: Center for Criminological Research.

Albrecht, H. (1994). *Strafzumessung bei schwerer Kriminalität.* Berlin: Duncker und Humblot.

Albrecht, P., & Pfeiffer, C. (1979). *Die Kriminalisierung junger Ausländer. Befunde und Reaktionen sozialer Kontrollinstanzen.* München: Juventa.

Aronowitz, A. A. (1989). *Assimilation, acculturation, and juvenile delinquency among second-generation Turkish youth in Berlin, West Germany.* Unpublished doctoral dissertation, State University of New York, Albany.

Bade, K. (1994). *Ausländer, Aussiedler, Asyl. Eine Bestandsaufnahme.* München: Beck.

Bielefeld, U. (1982). *Junge Ausländer im Konflikt. Lebenssituationen und Überlebensformen.* München: Juventa.

Blankenburg, E. (1973). Die Selektivität strafrechtlicher Sanktionierung. In J. Friedrichs (Ed.), *Teilnehmende Beobachtung abweichenden Verhaltens* (pp. 5-32). Stuttgart: Enke.

Blankenburg, E., Sessar, K., & Steffen, W. (1978). *Die Staatsanwaltschaft im Proze strafrechtlicher Sozialkontrolle.* Berlin: Duncker und Humblot.

Boge, H. (1989). Einflüsse nichtdeutscher Straftäter auf die organisierte Kriminalität. In Bundeskriminalamt Wiesbaden (Ed.), *Ausländerkriminalität in der Bundesrepublik Deutschland* (pp. 101-110). Wiesbaden: Bundeskriminalamt.

Bovenkerk, F. (1993). Crime and the multiethnic society: A view from Europe. *Crime, Law, and Social Change, 19,* 271-280.

Brock, D. (1993). Wiederkehr der Klassen? Über Mechanismen der Integration und Ausgrenzung in entwickelten Industriegesellschaften. *Soziale Welt, 44,* 177-198.

Bundesgerichtshof. (1982). Neue Zeitschrift für Strafrecht, p. 112.

Bundesgerichtshof. (1987). Strafverteidiger, p. 20.

Bundesgerichtshof. (1991). Strafverteidiger, p. 557.

Bundeskriminalamt. (1991/1992). *Lagebild Organisierte Kriminalität, Bundesrepublik Deutschland.* Wiesbaden: Bundeskriminalamt.

Bundeskriminalamt. (1995). *Polizeiliche Kriminalstatistik 1994.* Wiesbaden: Bundeskriminalamt.

Delgado, M. (1972). *Die Gastarbeiter in der Presse. Eine inhaltsanalytische Untersuchung.* Opladen: Leske.

Donner, O. (1986). Junge Ausländer im polizeilichen Ermittlungsverfahren. *Recht der Jugend und des Bildungswesens, 34,* 128-136.

Feuerhelm, W. (1988). Die fortgesetzte Bekämpfung des Landfahrerunwesens. *Monatsschrift für Kriminologie und Strafrechtsreform, 71,* 299-314.

Geißler, R., & Marißen, N. (1990). Kriminalität und Kriminalisierung junger Ausländer. Die tickende soziale Zeitbombe—Ein Artefakt der Kriminalstatistik. *Kölner Zeitschrift für Soziologie und Sozialpsychologie, 42,* 663-687.

Greger, R. (1987). Strafzumessung bei Vergewaltigung. *Monatsschrift für Kriminologie und Strafrechtsreform, 70,* 261-277.

Grundmann, S. (1985). Beruecksichtigung auslaendischer Rechtsvorstellungen im Strafrecht. *Neue Juristische Wochenschrift, 38,* 1251-1255.

Heitmeyer, W. (1995). *Gewalt. Schattenseiten der Individualisierung Jugendlicher aus unterschiedlichen Milieus.* München: Juventa.

Janetzky, K. (1993). Ausländer im Strafvollzug. In Der Generalstaatsanwalt von Schleswig Holstein Kiel (Ed.), *Gewalt gegen Ausländer—Gewalt von Ausländern* (pp.109-125.). Schleswig Holstein Kiel: Generalstaatsanwalt.

Junger, M. (1990). *Delinquency and ethnicity.* The Netherlands, Deventer: Kluwer.

Kaiser, G. (1974). Gastarbeiterkriminalität und ihre Erklärung als Kulturkonflikt. In T. Ansay & V. Gessner (Eds.), *Gastarbeiter in Gesellschaft und Recht* (pp. 208-240). München: Beck.

Kaiser, G. (1988). *Kriminologie* (2nd ed.). Karlsruhe: C. F. Müller.

Kaiser, G., & Metzger-Pregizer, G. (1976). *Betriebsjustiz.* Berlin: Duncker und Humblot.

Karger, T., & Sutterer, P. (1988). Cohort study on the development of police-recorded criminality and criminal sanctioning. In G. Kaiser & I. Geissler (Eds.), *Crime and criminal justice* (pp. 89-114). Freiburg: Max-Planck-Institut für Auslaendisches und Internationales Strafrecht.

Karger, T., & Sutterer, P. (1990). Polizeilich registrierte Gewaltdelinquenz bei jungen Ausländern. *Monatsschrift für Kriminologie und Strafrechtsreform, 73,* 369-383.

Kerner, S. R. (1994). Nichtdeutsche Tatverdächtige in der polizeilichen Kriminalstatistik. *Die Polizei, 85*(2), 105-109.

Killias, M. (1988). Diskriminierendes Anzeigeverhalten von Opfern gegenüber Ausländern? *Monatsschrift für Kriminologie und Strafrechtsreform, 71,* 156-165.

Killias, M. (1989). Criminality among second-generation immigrants in Western Europe: A review of the evidence. *Criminal Justice Review, 14*(2), 13-42.

Korf, D. J. (1993). Neue Grenzen—Neue Szenen? Die Bedeutung von Entwicklungen in Mittel- und Osteuropa für den illegalen Drogenhandel in Deutschland. *Sucht, 39*(2), 105-110.

Kraushaar, H. (1992). *Der Körperschmuggel von Kokain.* Giessen: Giessen Universität.

Kubink, M. (1993). *Verständnis und Bedeutung von Ausländerkriminalität. Eine Analyse der Konstitution sozialer Probleme.* Pfaffenweiler: Centaurus.

Kühne, H. (1991). *Kriminalitätsbekämpfung durch innereuropäische Grenzkontrollen? Auswirkungen der Schengener Abkommen auf die innere Sicherheit.* Berlin: Duncker und Humblot.

Kunz, K. (1989). Ausländerkriminalität in der Schweiz—Umfang, Struktur, und Erklärungsversuch. *Schweizerische Zeitschrift für Strafrecht, 106,* 373-392.

Kurz, U. (1965). Partielle Anpassung und Kulturkonflikt. Gruppenstruktur und Anpassungsdispositionen in einem italienischen Gastarbeiter-Lager. *Kölner Zeitschrift für Soziologie und Sozialpsychologie, 17,* 814-832.

Mansel, J. (1986). Die unterschiedliche Selektion von jungen Deutschen, Türken, und Italienern auf dem Weg vom polizeilich Tatverdächtigen zum gerichtlich Verurteilten. *Monatsschrift für Kriminologie und Strafrechtsreform, 69,* 309-325.

Mansel, J. (1990, October). *Kriminalisierung als Instrument der Ausgrenzung und Disziplinierung.* Paper presented at the 25th Meeting of the German Association of Sociology, Frankfurt.

Mansel, J. (1994). Schweigsame "kriminelle" Ausländer? Eine Replik auf Jo Reichertz und Norbert Schröer. *Kölner Zeitschrift für Soziologie und Sozialpsychologie, 46,* 299-307.

Möller, K. (1993). Rechtsextremismus und Gewalt. Empirische Befunde und individualisierungstheoretische Erklärungen. In W. Breyvogel (Ed.), *Lust auf Randale. Jugendliche Gewalt gegen Fremde* (pp. 35-64). Bonn: Dietz.

Oberlandesgericht (OLG) Bremen. (1994). Strafverteidiger, p. 130.

Oppermann, A. (1987). Straffällige junge Ausländer: Kriminalitätsbelastung und soziale Bedingungen. *Bewährungshilfe, 34*(2), 83-95.

Otte, W. (1994). Die Ausweisung nach dem Ausländergesetz. *Zeitschrift für Ausländerrecht, 14,* 67-76.

Pfeiffer, C. (1995). *Kriminalität junger Menschen im vereinigten Deutschland. Eine Analyse auf der Basis der polizeilichen Kriminalstatistik 1984-1994.* Hannover: Kriminologisches Forschungsinstitut Niedersachsen.

Pilgram, A. (1993). Mobilität, Migration, und Kriminalität—Gegen die Vordergründigkeit kriminologischer Studien über Ausländer. In A. Pilgram (Ed.), *Grenzöffnung, Migration, Kriminalität* (pp. 17-36). Baden-Baden: Nomos.

Pitsela, A. (1986). *Straffälligkeit und kriminelle Viktimisierung ausländischer Minderheiten in der BRD.* Freiburg: Max-Planck-Institut für Ausländisches und Internationales Strafrecht.

Reichertz, J. (1994). Zur Definitionsmacht der Polizei. *Kriminalistik, 48,* 610-616.

Reichertz, J., & Schröer, N. (1994). Gute Gesinnung oder Prüfende Forschung? Eine Erwiderung zu Jürgen Mansels Replik. *Kölner Zeitschrift für Soziologie und Sozialpsychologie, 46,* 308-311.

Riek, G. (1995). *Die neue Ost-West-Migration. Am Beispiel der Ruß landdeutschen in der Russischen Föderation.* Neuried: ars una.

Sack, F. (1974). Kulturkonflikt. In G. Kaiser, H.-J. Kerner, F. Sack, & H. Schellhoss (Eds.), *Kleines Kriminologisches Woerterbuch* (pp. 207-211). Freiburg: Herderverlag.

Schöch, H., & Gebauer, M. (1991). *Ausländerkriminalität in der Bundesrepublik Deutschland. Kriminologische, rechtliche und soziale Aspekte eines gesellschaftlichen Problems.* Baden-Baden: Nomos.

Schroeder, F. C. (1983, October 13). Strafen zum Heimattarif. *Frankfurter Allgemeine Zeitung,* p. 23.

Schüler-Springorum, H. (1983). Ausländerkriminalität. Ursachen, Umfang, und Entwicklung. *Neue Zeitschrift für Strafrecht, 3,* 529-536.

Schumann, K. F. (1987). *Jugendkriminalität und die Grenzen der Generalprävention.* Neuwied: Luchterhand.

Schütze, H. (1993). Junge Ausländer im Vollzug der Straf- und Untersuchungshaft. In T. Trenczek (Ed.), *Freiheitsentzug bei jungen Straffälligen* (pp. 137-144). Bonn: Forum.

Seifert, W. (1991). *Ausländer in der Bundesrepublik—Soziale und ökonomische Mobilität.* Berlin: Arbeitsgruppe Sozialberichterstattung, WBZ.

Sessar, K. (1981). *Rechtliche und soziale Prozesse einer Definition der Tötungskriminalität.* Freiburg: Max-Planck-Institut für Ausländisches und Internationales Strafrecht.

Smith, D. A., Fisher, C. A., & Davidson, L. A. (1984). Equity and discretionary justice: The influence of race on police arrest decisions. *Journal of Criminal Law and Criminology, 75,* 234-250.

Statistisches Bundesamt. (1993). *Statistisches Jahrbuch 1993.* Wiesbaden: Kohlhammer.

Steffen, W. (1977). *Die Effizienz des polizeilichen Ermittlungsverfahrens aus der Sicht des spaeteren Strafverfahrens.* Wiesbaden: Bundeskriminalamt.

Steffen, W. (1992). *Ausländerkriminalität in Bayern. Eine Analyse der von 1983 bis 1990 polizeilich registrierten Kriminalität deutscher und ausländischer Tatverdächtiger.* München: Bayerisches Landeskriminalamt.

Steinhilper, U. (1986). *Definitions und Entscheidungsprozesse bei sexuell motivierten Gewaltdelikten.* Konstanz: Universitätsverlag.

Sutterer, P., & Karger, T. (1993). *Taetigkeitsbericht 1993.* Freiburg: Max-Planck-Institut für Auslaendisches und Internationales Strafrecht.

Villmow, B. (1993). Ausländerkriminalität. In G. Kaiser (Ed.), *Kleines Kriminologisches Wörterbuch* (3rd ed., pp. 39-47). Heidelberg: C. F. Müller.

Vrij, A., & Winkel, F. W. (1991). Encounters between the Dutch police and minorities: Testing the noncooperation hypothesis of differential treatment. *Police Studies, 14*(1), 17-21.

Wilkiewicz, L. (1989). *Aussiedlerschicksal: Migration und familialer Wandel.* Pfaffenweiler: Centaurus.

Willems, H. (1993). *Fremdenfeindliche Gewalt. Einstellungen, Täter, Konflikteskalation.* Opladen: Leske und Budrich.

Wolfslast, G. (1982). Anmerkung zu BGH Urteil vom 16.9.1981. *Neue Zeitschrift für Strafrecht, 2*(2), 112-113.

5

MINORITIES, CRIME, AND CRIMINAL JUSTICE IN ITALY

Uberto Gatti
Daniela Malfatti
Alfredo Verde

INTRODUCTION

Italy is a country of about 56 million inhabitants; it is divided into 20 regions, and there are remarkable differences between the south and the north: The north can be compared to the most advanced European regions, whereas the south is less industrialized, with a very high unemployment rate. After World War II, a remarkable economic boom took place, causing a widespread internal migration from the southern regions to the north, and from rural areas to urban areas.

During the 1970s, terrorism and drug-related problems started to attract the attention of the population and of social control agencies. Presently, however, concern has shifted to the influence and the consequences of organized crime and political corruption. Since 1993, political corruption has been the target of numerous judicial actions, resulting in tremendous political

AUTHORS' NOTE: This chapter was translated by Maria Teresa VanderBoegh, University of Illinois at Urbana-Champaign.

and social changes as well as the establishment of new social movements and political parties.

Changes have also taken place in the Italian judicial system, which has Roman origins and appears very formal when compared to Anglo-Saxon models of judicial tradition. These gradual changes are related to recent modifications in the criminal trial process (which in 1988 was transformed from inquisitorial to predominantly accusatory), and in civil proceedings, which are now conducted more quickly. Many negative characteristics continue to define the criminal justice system, such as the overuse of preventive detention, slowness of legal procedures, overcrowded jails, and a generally inefficient administration.

ETHNIC MINORITY GROUPS IN ITALY

Traditionally, in Italy the relationship between minorities and crime has been seen through the analysis of the phenomenon of "internal migration" (i.e., from the south to the north of Italy), which characterized this country from the second half of the 1950s to the end of the 1960s. A large proportion of research carried out during those years deals with the relationship among socioeconomic deprivation, cultural diversity, and the criminality of these internal immigrants; crime was interpreted both as the outcome of sociocultural imbalance, and as the expression of processes of marginalization and stigmatization (Bandini, Gatti, Marugo, & Verde, 1991). More recently, however, a radical change has taken place; now most immigration originates from other countries, whereas internal migration has basically stopped. Italy, which for decades has sent large numbers of the poor population to economically better-developed countries, has now become a desirable country for immigrants coming from abroad (for a bibliography related to this problem, see Melchionda, 1993).

At the present time, many immigrants in Italy are facing a variety of difficult problems related to integration. In a Censis (1990) survey, more than half of the immigrants mention the following major problems: finding food and a place to live, finding a job, and dealing with language-related problems. About one half of the people interviewed want to go back to their country of origin; they consider their stay in Italy as a temporary solution. This precarious situation has had two major consequences: a considerable social degeneration of the immigrants and increased intolerance toward immigrants on the part of Italian people (Istituto di studi politici economici e sociali, 1992).

A number of movements and groups (some linked to political parties) have developed whose aim it is to send foreign immigrants out of Italy. The occurrence of acts of intolerance against foreigners (i.e., hate crimes) has prompted the Italian Parliament to promulgate a bill (D.P.R. No. 122/93) that provides for the increase of penalties for those who participate in violence caused by xenophobia, or those who spread ideas of racial superiority, and ethnic and racial hatred.

Foreigners are also poorly protected from the standpoint of health care (which is a right for all Italian citizens). Even those who have been living in Italy for a long time do not have the right to vote (both at the national and local level). A recent decision by the Ministry of Public Education, however, declared that all minors who are illegal immigrants (i.e., without a residence permit) have the right to attend school at all levels.

Some Statistics on the Number of Immigrants

Because of the questionable quality of public statistics, it is difficult to assess the actual number of foreigners living in Italy; available data must be viewed as estimates only. Perhaps the most appropriate statistical estimate is based on data provided by the Ministry of the Interior, to whom police departments send data on the number of legal residence permits issued foreigners. Based on these data, it is estimated that on December 31, 1992, 923,626 foreigners were living in Italy (Istituto Nazionale de Statistica [ISTAT], 1993); this number had increased to 987,405 by December 1993 (data from the Centro Elaborazione Dati, Ministry of the Interior, 1994). One year later (December 31, 1994), a decrease was recorded, however, showing 922,706 foreigners legally living in Italy (data from the Centro Elaborazione Dati, Ministry of the Interior, 1995). The interpretation of these data remains controversial, because they do not include all those who have entered the country illegally, or who continue to live in Italy after their residence permit has expired (the so-called clandestine or irregular foreigners). Based on data on the birthrate of foreigners, Natale (1990), for instance, assessed that in 1990 the number of foreigners residing in Italy could be anywhere between a minimum of 849,000 and a maximum of 1,201,000. He also estimated the number of foreigners who had entered the country illegally or who had an expired residence permit to be somewhere between 100,000 and 400,000. Other available estimates fluctuate between the highest figures (Consiglio Nazionale per l'economia e il lavora, 1991) and the lowest figures of the research quoted here (ISTAT, 1993). Palidda (1994b), however, thinks that the number of legal residence permits overestimates the actual number of foreigners by some 30%; some foreigners, when moving from one province to another, may register at more than one police department. Another source of overestimation could derive from the fact that expired permits are not subtracted from the total number of permits.

With these cautions in mind, using information about residence permits and data from the registry of births, marriages, and deaths (from the Vital Statistics Office), we arrive at the estimate that 501,921 (ISTAT, 1993) immigrants are living permanently in Italy. (Some of them have residence permits, some have no such permit, but are registered at the commune where they live.) According to the latest available statistics (December 31, 1992), the largest number of immigrants come from African, in particular, North African, countries (Morocco and Tunisia). Immigrants from European Union (EU) countries constitute the second largest group (most immigrants come from Germany, France, and the United Kingdom). Third is the group of immigrants from Asia (the Phillipines), followed by the immigrants from other (non-EU) European countries (immigrants from Albania and ex-Yugoslavia prevail). The fifth and last group of immigrants comes from America (mostly Latin America).

It is possible to describe the demographic composition of those immigrants who have a residence permit. Overall, immigrants are most likely to be young adults; however, there are some differences in the proportion of males relative to females. Among the Asian immigrants, the number of females is almost identical to that of males, but the number of females is definitely larger among South American immigrants. Both sexes are almost equally represented among the immigrants from European countries (ISTAT, 1993). According to an estimate by the Caritas (1993) agency in Rome, 54.1% of the immigrants are Christians (32.1% are Catholics), and 33.5% are Muslims. There is an increase in the number of residence permits requested to obtain a job: At the end of 1992, 70% of the requests for a residence permit cited employment as the main reason for their request (ISTAT, 1993; Laboratorio per le politiche sociali, 1990).

Gypsies

Separate consideration needs to be given to the gypsies, who have been a consistent presence in Italy. (For example, Robotti, 1995 speaks of about 100,000 gypsies living in 100 camps.) The gypsies are characterized by a particular culture and identity, grounded in nomadism and a clear separation from the surrounding community. The gypsies have maintained their cultural identity for centuries; in the past, they never integrated with the population near which they temporarily settled. As Calabrò (1992) points out, gypsies have frequently been the object of prejudice, hostility, and persecution.

Gypsies have always had very little sense of solidarity and identification with other ethnic groups, partly because they traditionally never entrusted their traditions to writing. Their fundamental social unit is the strongly bonded family, but the bond is less strong among the various groups of families *(kumpania)*. In Italy, different family groups, varying in degrees of assimilation and integration into Italian society, are currently present: the Sinti, who work in carnivals, and live in the Piedmont region; and the Rom, who are definitely nomadic. The latter group is subdivided in several smaller groups: the strongly cohesive Lovara, originally horse breeders and nowadays knife sharpeners, who practice a Pentecostal religion; two other groups, the Kanjiarija and the Khorakhane, come from Yugoslavia and are Muslims—their immigration is quite recent, a consequence of the recent war. They constitute about one third of the total gypsy population in Italy. Sociological analyses have discussed the crisis situation in which the gypsies find themselves in postmodern society; the central element of gypsy culture (i.e., nomadism) is more suited to rural, preindustrial and early industrial societies. Crafts, horse sales, and repair jobs, the most typical activities of the gypsy culture, have no equivalent within modern economic society. The gypsy camps situated at urban peripheries are bound to limit their autonomy; they live in ghetto-like environments under anomic conditions that encourage behaviors (such as involvement in criminal activities) that are otherwise not traditionally practiced (Calabrò, 1994). The breakup of Yugoslavia and the war in Bosnia further complicate the situation, because several groups of gypsies (mostly Rom Khorakhane, of Muslim religion) are now definitely staying in Italy, although previously they were used to moving periodically from one country to another. There is now a sizable number of Rom, who can no longer return to Yugoslavia because of the war and who live in particularly precarious conditions, with little social support and with virtually no chance of obtaining war refugee status. Their situation is even more problematic because native Italians have shown themselves to be nonaccepting of the Rom and extremely intolerant. The Rom are rather deviant and poorly integrated; unfortunately, Calabrò (1994) lists this group as one that could not be included in his research. Indeed, because of methodological problems, research on gypsies is very difficult. For example, some gypsies are of Italian nationality, which makes it hard to identify them as gypsies in national or local statistics.

CRIMINAL INVOLVEMENT OF ETHNIC MINORITIES

Attempts to estimate the criminal involvement of ethnic minorities (see Bandini et al., 1991; Bandini, Gatti, & Traverso, 1995) are seriously hampered by a series of methodological problems, with no easy solutions. We previously discussed the problem of the lack of certainty about the number of foreigners living in Italy. Also, the problem of "clandestinity" is not the same for each ethnic group. Furthermore, even official crime statistics do not represent "real" crime, but rather a filtered "image" of it.

Still, crime statistics are one very valuable source of information, because they provide information on the social adaptation and integration of foreigners, as well as on how social control is exerted on this group.

Table 5.1 represents the total number of people admitted to prison between 1971 and 1993, as well as the proportion of foreigners in all people admitted. The involvement of foreigners in officially recorded criminality is a relatively new phenomenon in Italy; the growth in involvement parallels the growth of the number of immigrants living in Italy. The statistics on prison admissions (the only long-term judicial statistics showing data relative to foreigners) show that the percentage of foreigners among total admissions was 3.25% in 1971, 6.91% in 1976, 9.71% in 1981, 9.04% in 1986, 16.24% in 1991, and 21.44% in 1993, the last year for which data are available (see Table 5.1).

Table 5.2 represents the percentage of foreign inmates in Italian jails on December 31 for the years 1985 through 1992.

Table 5.2 shows that about 9.83% of the prison population in 1988 consisted of foreigners, 15.36% in 1990, and 13.97% in 1992. If we compare this information to the admission data (Table 5.1), we may conclude that foreigners spend less time in prison than Italian citizens. Other sources support our conclusion. If we examine data on the nationality of foreigners admitted to prison, we find that 29.7% are from Tunisia, 20.04% from Morocco, and 19.36% from former Yugoslavia. Many other nationalities are present, but only in very small numbers (Marotta, 1995).

The statistics regarding charges (or accusations) also show a remarkable increase of foreigners (see Table 5.3). In 1988, foreigners represented 2.76% of all accused people, but in only 6 years, the percentage doubled (to 5.66% in 1993). Table 5.4 shows that foreigners are not equally represented in all crime types; the percentages vary from crime to crime. For example, for-

TABLE 5.1 Foreign Prison Admissions Between 1971 and 1993 (Italy)

Years	Total Admission	Foreign Admission (N)	Foreign Admission (%)
1971	52,736	1,716	3.25
1972	64,443	2,355	3.65
1973	72,061	2,987	4.15
1974	83,540	5,000	5.99
1975	91,369	8,772	9.60
1976	91,662	6,337	6.91
1977	92,176	7,266	7.88
1978	89,164	7,718	8.66
1979	84,607	8,613	10.18
1980	92,576	9,160	9.89
1981	101,143	9,817	9.71
1982	102,925	10,827	10.52
1983	107,868	10,690	9.47
1984	112,834	11,433	10.13
1985	95,329	9,859	10.34
1986	95,026	8,587	9.04
1987	85,875	11,652	13.57
1988	89,741	10,233	11.40
1989	83,600	13,904	16.63
1990	57,738	9,363	16.22
1991	80,234	13,033	16.24
1992	93,774	16,115	17.18
1993	99,072	21,239	21.44

NOTE: Data from ISTAT, 1971-1993.

eigners are highly represented among those charged with crimes committed against property (11.08% in 1993 for the combined category; 16.60% for burglary, and 13.52% for robbery); they are overrepresented among those charged with the exploitation of prostitution (22.74%) and in drug crimes (16.10%). The figures for crimes against the person remain low; however, 8.73% of the homicide suspects were foreigners, and 14.04% of the rape suspects were foreigners in 1993 (see Table 5.4).

Regarding the geographical distribution of charges against foreigners, reports against foreigners are not randomly distributed across Italy. Accusations against foreigners are concentrated in the northern regions of Italy and in the Lazio region. Southern regions are sparsely represented. Information

TABLE 5.2   Foreign Inmates in Prison on December 31 (from 1985 to 1992, Italy)

Years	Total Number of Inmates	Foreign Inmates (N)	Foreign Inmates (%)
1985	41,536	3,945	9.50
1986	33,609	3,513	10.45
1987	31,773	3,377	10.63
1988	31,382	3,084	9.83
1989	30,680	3,302	10.76
1990	26,150	4,017	15.36
1991	35,485	5,365	15.12
1992	47,588	6,650	13.97

NOTE: Data from ISTAT, 1985-1992.

on the nationality of people charged (ISTAT data for 1993) indicates that a global analysis (combining all non-Italian citizens into one category of "foreigners") would be extremely misleading. The different groups vary tremendously with regard to the quantity of charges in general, and there is also a remarkable lack of homogeneity in the different types of crimes with which different nationalities are charged. Not surprising in view of their total numbers, African immigrants are most involved in crime (15,328 reports in 1993, which is about 49% of all foreigners charged), followed by Europeans from non-EU countries (10,135 reports, about 33% of all foreigners criminally charged), immigrants from South America (2,027 reports, 6.5% of all charges involving foreigners), and North Americans (267 reports, less than 1% of all foreigners accused). The specific countries with the highest volume of criminal charges are the former Yugoslavia (6,761 reports); followed by Morocco (with 6,146 reports); and finally, Tunisia (3,180), Algeria (2,370), and Senegal (1,316). Furthermore, burglary reports are most likely to involve immigrants from former Yugoslavia (who are mostly gypsies, as we have seen); drug crimes are related mostly to immigrants from Tunisia and Morocco; crimes of prostitution are mostly committed by immigrants from Albania and the former Yugoslavia.

Not much research has been done on the victimization of foreigners and minorities. What little research there is, however, suggests a growing victimization of ethnic minorities by criminality; a survey of homicide victims in Milan shows, for example, that the number of victims coming from developing countries or from non-EU European countries, has steadily risen during the past years (from 8.6% in 1989 to 20.9% in 1992; Merzagora, Zoja, & Gigli, 1995).

TABLE 5.3 Foreigners Charged With a Crime Between 1988 and 1993
(Italy)

Year	Total Number of Charged Individuals	Foreign Charged (N)	Foreign Charged (%)
1988	764,610	21,136	2.76
1989	744,421	19,996	2.69
1990	348,127	12,441	3.57
1991	506,280	21,307	4.21
1992	561,230	25,030	4.46
1993	550,354	31,174	5.66

NOTE: Data from ISTAT, 1988-1993.

Thus, all three statistical sources (prison admissions, convictions, and charges) support the notion that there has been a remarkable rise in the number of foreigners involved in the criminal justice system. Each of the three statistics, however, emphasizes a different aspect of the involvement of foreigners in the criminal justice circuit; specifically, in 1993, 5.66% of individuals charged with a crime were foreigners, 8.27% of individuals convicted of a crime were foreigners, and 21.44% of individuals admitted to prison were foreigners. Without entering into a detailed analysis of the data relative to every single crime, an explanation of this phenomenon may be offered through the results of empirical research on the situation of foreigners' experience during judicial procedures. This research (Centro Informazione Detenuti Stranieri in Italia [CIDSI], 1991, 1994; Gennaro, 1990) shows that lawyers do a poor job defending foreigners during trials. Even the most recent research points out that there are many deficiencies in the defense of foreigners. CIDSI (1991), an association started through the initiative of foreign convicts at the Roma Rebibbia prison, conducted a survey in 1988 and found that of 909 convicts, 44.4% had never had a personal consultation with a lawyer (although 79% of them did have a personal lawyer). In a subsequent survey, done in 1993 by the same association (CIDSI, 1994), it was found that of a total of 1,476 convicts, only 62.3% had a personal lawyer, and that in general the defendants had real difficulties in the relationship with their lawyers and communication problems with the judges who tried them.

One of the factors that may influence the high percentage of convictions and incarcerations of foreigners is the substantial weakness of their defense during the trial and the preventive custody. There is no further research in this area, except for some studies limited to specific crimes, such as those

TABLE 5.4 Charges Against Foreigners, Against Whom Judicial Action Was Initiated, by Type of Offense (Italy)

Offense	Total Charged	Foreigners Charged (N)	Foreigners Charged (%)
Against the person	64,702	2,415	3.73
Intentional homicide	1,959	171	8.73
Assault	1,806	40	2.21
Intentional personal injury	17,834	628	3.52
Other offenses against persons	43,103	1,576	3.66
Against the family and public morality	9,807	667	6.80
Rape	1,226	172	14.03
Other violent sex offenses	728	47	6.46
Instigation and exploitation of prostitution	752	171	22.74
Other offenses against family and public morality	6,041	277	4.59
Against property	130,423	14,447	11.08
Theft	61,409	10,196	16.60
Robbery	10,065	1,361	13.52
Extortion	5,191	194	3.74
Other offenses against property	53,758	2,696	5.02
Against the economy and public trust	241,043	7,489	3.11
Fraud	940	22	2.34
Manufacture and sale of drugs	25,105	4,041	16.10
Counterfeiting	14,080	1,845	13.10
Other offenses against the economy and public trust	200,918	1,581	0.79
Against the state, other social institutions, and public order	48,292	2,152	4.46
Violence, resistance, insult against public officials	14,331	1,512	10.55
Participation in criminal organization	2,931	157	5.36
Other offenses against the state, other social institutions, and public order	31,030	483	1.56
Other offenses	56,087	4,004	7.14
Total	550,354	31,174	5.66

NOTE: Data from ISTAT, 1993.

linked to drugs. From these studies, it may be concluded that, other legal factors being equal, foreign drug dealers are prosecuted with greater severity than Italian drug dealers (Gatti & Marugo, 1987; Lagazzi, Malfatti, Palestrini, & Rossoni, 1995).

Even during the execution of the punishment, foreign convicts suffer as a consequence of the general conditions in jails, which in Italy are particularly poor. The problem is exacerbated by the fact that a high proportion of foreign inmates are drug dependent (28.82% of foreigners admitted to prison in 1992, and 22.17% in 1993; CIDSI, 1994; ISTAT, 1994). Drug-dependent foreigners and foreigners who are not drug dependent but who are involved in drug crimes in 1992 made up 58.3% of the entire non-Italian prison population (Marotta, 1995). Moreover, alternative sentences (other than detention) can rarely be used for foreigners, because these require the existence of some type of external support, such as family, work, and a social network that would help reintegration. All this, in fact, is almost never available (Camera dei Deputati, 1988; CIDSI, 1991, 1994).

Methodological Problems

Judicial and prison data provide only partial and indirect information about the real criminality of foreigners compared to the criminality of natives; this estimate remains the object of research and debate, and is vulnerable to certain methodological errors. A primary error consists of comparing the different crime rates without considering the varying demographic compositions of the Italian population and the immigrants, in particular with regard to age and sex (which are strongly correlated to the probability of delinquency). For this purpose, Puggioni and Peddes (1992) worked on a sophisticated theoretical analysis of the population in the province of Cagliari. The study's aim was to verify the expected specific crime rates for particular crimes, assuming the age composition of the native population to be equal to that of the immigrants. The results showed that, if the age distribution of the native population was comparable to that of the immigrant population, the crime rates of the former should be significantly higher.

Crime statistics are, in fact, a product of the repressive actions of state agencies. Thus, one cannot but wonder whether foreigners, by virtue of their social and cultural situation, are highly visible and vulnerable, more so than native Italians, which may account for their overrepresentation in formal crime statistics. For both property crimes and the crime of rape, the "dark number" (i.e., the not-reported offenses) is very high; furthermore, there is a high proportion of unsolved crimes (i.e., unknown criminals) among reported crimes. It would be necessary, therefore, to examine the relationship between immigration and criminality further by using other indicators, which are, unfortunately, rarely available in Italy. Barbagli (1994) carried out one of the few meaningful pieces of research related to crimes committed against public property. In a survey on theft in department stores, he estimated that every year undercover surveillance catches about 300,000 people while they are stealing; however, only 3% of these thieves are reported. The fact that natives are reported in 2.6% of the cases and foreigners twice as often (in 5.2% of the cases) is significant.

One possible method of reaching better-founded conclusions would be to use homicide data, a crime for which the dark number is extremely small, which makes it easier to consider it as a real index of crime, especially of interpersonal violence. Nevertheless, when comparing homicide rates of foreigners and natives, we still confront several problems. First, the judicial statistics provided by ISTAT indicate that in about two thirds of the completed homicides and in half of the attempted homicides, the perpetrator of the crime is not discovered. This fact could seriously distort conclusions about nationality and violence. We do not know if the nationality of the perpetrator may influence the likelihood that the police can solve the crime; for instance, it is possible that homicides that are not cleared by arrest are more frequently the work of "mafiosi" groups, or are committed by individuals belonging to organized crime, or subcultures into which foreign immigrants are unable to penetrate. Moreover, in the ISTAT statistics, even when the perpetrator's identity (and nationality) is known, it is not possible to distinguish between completed and attempted homicide. Obviously, this distinction is crucial if one wants to draw valid conclusions about the homicide rates of foreigners relative to those of native Italians. A survey done in Genoa of all homicides processed by the court during a period of 15 years, concluded that attempted homicide is quite different from completed homicide, and that social characteristics of the offender, including low social class, have a significant influence on the decision to charge a suspect with attempted homicide rather than assault (Bandini et al., 1983). Based on these data, we speculate that foreign immigrants will be more easily charged with attempted homicide (rather than assault) than their Italian counterparts.

From a methodological perspective, one must also consider the distorting impact of the different sociodemographic composition (i.e., age and sex) of the immigrant groups compared to native Italians: Homicide is usually carried out by males (in 1993, of 933 people charged with completed homicide, only 5.25%—or 49—were women). Also, most of the homicides are committed by adults (in 1993, 79.95% of the people charged with completed homicide ranged between 18 and 44 years of age; ISTAT, 1994). It is clear, then, that the sociodemographic categories most strongly correlated to homicide are typically found among immigrants: Among them, young adults prevail (71% of the foreigners with a residency permit are in the age range between 18 and 40), and 57.0% of the immigrants are males (Caritas, 1994). One must further consider that immigrants with a higher incidence of homicide also tend to have a relative high proportion of males: Of all immigrants charged with completed and attempted homicide in 1993, 49.12% involved an African perpetrator (about 88.95% of Tunisian immigrants are males, as are 88.95% of Moroccan immigrants and 74.53% of Egyptian immigrants). Thus there are several indications to suggest that the overrepresentation of immigrants among those charged with homicide might disappear once we control for the effects of age and gender.

Criminality of Immigrant Youth

Of particular importance is the fact that the mass media and public opinion have recently stressed the involvement in street crime of foreign minors. Actually, foreign minors are only a very small part of the immigrants in Italy (on December 31, 1993, they constituted only 2.7% of the foreigners with a residence permit). In recent years, however, foreign minors have become a growing presence in juvenile jails: In the early 1980s they made up 15% of the inmates (Verde & Bagnara, 1989), but the percentage has risen considerably in the following years, to 38.47% in 1993 (see Table 5.5).

Because there are no statistics related to charges and convictions of foreign minors, this category can only be analyzed by using statistics of juvenile penal institutions and receiving centers. (Receiving centers are small institutions to which arrested minors are sent; they are less harsh than the juvenile penal institutions.) These statistics indicate that receiving centers for juveniles have a very high proportion of foreigners: Of all juveniles admitted to such an institution in 1993, 42.08% was classified as non-Italian (28.27% of the males and 92.57% of the females respectively). When looking at juvenile penal institutions, it is obvious once again that the number of foreign minors detained in these institutions is also out of proportion with respect to the size of the foreign juvenile population in Italy. That is, 943 foreign minors were admitted to prison in 1993 (ISTAT, 1994); that figure is over one tenth of the total number of minors between the ages of 15 and 18 with a residency permit (8,843; Caritas, 1994).

Table 5.5 Foreign Minors Admitted to Juvenile Detention Facilities, From 1984 to 1993 (Italy)

Year	Total Admission to Juvenile Institutions	Foreigners Admitted to Juvenile Institutions (N)	Foreigners Admitted to Institutions (%)
1984	10,067	1,064	10.57
1985	9,412	1,679	17.84
1986	8,709	1,287	14.78
1987	4,907	733	14.94
1988	5,462	1,420	26.00
1989	4,335	1,634	37.69
1990	597	238	39.87
1991	735	250	34.01
1992	1,632	588	36.03
1993	2,551	943	38.47

NOTE: Data from ISTAT, 1984-1993.

It is interesting to compare the types of offenses for which foreign minors were incarcerated with those of Italian minors. The most striking observation is that delinquency of foreign minors is relatively less serious than that of Italian minors. In fact, foreign minors commit fewer violent crimes against the person, but they commit property crimes more often, particularly theft. Offenses related to drug possession and drug sales appear to be a distinct category: More and more foreign minors are getting involved with drug-related crimes. This is shown in extensive research conducted in Turin (Buffa, 1990), which also documented that foreign youth deal predominantly in marijuana and hashish.

There are two main categories of foreign youth involved: Europeans from countries that do not belong to the European community (i.e., nomads from the former Yugoslavia who represent 60% of foreigners entering juvenile prisons in Italy), and North African minors, especially Moroccans and Tunisians (who represent about 30% of the total number of foreigners entering prisons in Italy). It also should be noted here that female minors represent a very special case: They are predominantly non-Italian (90.4%), and they are most likely to belong to the gypsy culture (ISTAT, 1994).

There is no question that the prison data discussed here reflect a high level of social reaction to foreign minors, but it remains very difficult to draw any conclusions about the actual criminal involvement of foreign minors. Analysis of formal statistics on the outcome of penal proceedings shows that foreign minors (whose crimes are usually less serious than those of the Italians) receive disciplinary measures that are often more severe and penalizing than those applied to Italian minors (Verde & Bagnara, 1989). To be more specific: In 1986, 45.1% of the incarcerated foreign minors had received a sentence without any benefits (or leniency), whereas the percentage of sentences without any benefits (or leniency) relating to Italian minors was 30.9%.

RESEARCH AND THEORY ON CRIME, CRIMINAL JUSTICE, AND MINORITIES

For several years now, Italy has been concerned with the problems of crime and the criminalization of immigrants. A minority opinion is reflected in the conclusions of research done by Segre (1993) who, based on analysis of data related to prison admissions and convictions of foreigners, stated that a particular "disposition to commit a crime" exists in immigrants. According to Segre, such a criminal disposition does not exist in the female counterpart of the immigrants, except for female gypsies; also, this disposition to commit a crime is rather weak within certain ethnic groups. Segre argues that these data may be interpreted by integrating a series of theories, among which the "relative deprivation" theory has particular importance.

Segre (1993) is exceptional in his conclusions. Indeed, in Italy almost all scholars who have studied the relationship between immigration and deviance come to an opposite conclusion. Palidda (1994a, 1994b, 1995), in particular, strongly argues that data related to imprisonment and convictions do not constitute a reliable and valid measure of foreigners' deviant behavior; rather, they reflect the activity of social control organizations, which operate in a selective and discriminatory fashion. Palidda uses the results of a qualitative field survey regarding the behavior of police squads to support his argument.

Drawing from this perspective, many Italian scholars are engaged in demystifying the stereotype of immigrants as criminals. This stereotype is based on laws regarding immigrants, which tend to discriminate against them (Pastore, 1995), and is largely supported by the mass media (Maneri, 1995). Also, the agencies that collect statistics produce them in a very noncritical manner (Barbesino, 1995). Authors such as Chinnici (1983), Fiasco (1991), Puggioni and Peddes (1992), and Marotta (1995), for example, use their research and analysis of the complexity of official statistical data to reject the assumption that immigrants commit more crime than native Italians.

Many scholars support the notion that the immigration phenomenon brings attention to a new "public enemy"—the immigrant. It is easy to focus, through the typical mechanisms that create a scapegoat, collective aggressiveness on this individual (Ceretti, 1995; Quirico, 1993). This theory draws from the following sources: Christie's (1984) work, the general literature on the function of the scapegoat in the evolution of society (see Girard, 1987), and a psychosocial interpretation of social problems, inspired by psychoanalysis (Verde, 1995). According to these perspectives, the foreigner constitutes a metaphor for the "internal enemy," and represents the obscure and intolerable part of the collectivity that is alternatively expelled and reintegrated, depending on the point of penal enforcement (see, for example, the dialectic between the process of expulsion and the reparative penalty). In this sense, the processes of xenophobia and the criminalization of foreigners, that have started to emerge in Italy and that are common to all nations of the European community represent a reaction to a situation of crisis and disorganization and a loss of national identity characteristic of our time, now that the borders of Europe are changing in an effort to overcome the barriers among nations (Melossi, 1993).

Some Italian scholars support the position that, to adequately analyze the complex relationships between immigration, deviance, and criminalization, conducting ethnographic research is indispensable. Ethnographic research is more important than statistical analysis, they argue—ethnographic studies allow us to understand more deeply the social dynamics of the foreigners' inclusion and exclusion through participatory observation (Dal Lago, 1990; Dal Lago & Moscati, 1992).

In general in Italy, social research on immigrant problems and other related aspects cannot yet provide satisfactory answers. We do think, however, that statistical data do not confirm the hypothesis that foreigners commit more crimes than native Italians. Instead, qualitative research suggests that in Italy there exist undeniable processes of both social and judicial discrimination against immigrants.

LEGAL AND POLICY ISSUES

Until a few years ago, there was virtually no developed debate regarding immigration policies in Italy. Only in recent times, and in a rather confused way, differentiated positions about legal and social initiatives to regulate immigration have emerged.

From the legislative point of view, until 1986, regulations with respect to foreigners were included in the penal code and in the public safety law (both date from 1931). The entry and residence of foreigners in Italy was regulated, and some suggestions regarding the expulsion of foreigners convicted of a crime in Italy were provided, including the types of punishment.

By the end of 1986, Law No. 943 was promulgated. This law regulated access to work by foreigners, equality of wages, and rights relative to Italian workers, and, most importantly, granted the possibility to legalize—through an "act of indemnity"—the position of a large number of illegal immigrants. The intent of the legislators to obtain full legalization of the situation was realized later, when a new act of indemnity was put into effect, Decree-Law No. 416/1989 (later converted into Law No. 39 of February 28, 1990, the so-called Martelli law). This law contained a series of norms regarding the admission, residence, and expulsion of foreigners, and established for the first time a document called the "residence permit," which formalizes the position of the immigrant in Italy. This law also established a plan for the migratory flow for employment reasons, and controlled self-employment of foreigners. From the penal point of view, the law also included different circumstances under which convicted foreigners may be expelled. More recently, some new penal regulations have been established; these aim to increase control over foreigners who have committed a crime. One of these laws refers to "voluntary expulsion by request of the foreigner or his or her defense attorney" (this regulation was introduced with Decree-Law No. 187/1993, and later converted into Law No. 296/1993).

In conclusion, Italy's justice system (not only criminal law, but also administrative law) is a much more structured system than before, and it recognizes a series of rights for foreigners. Full equality with Italian citizens, however, is quite far from being realized and, moreover, appears at the present time difficult to attain (Pastore, 1995).

At the time of this writing, legislation concerning foreigners is the object of criticism and debate by all political forces, each of which appear to propose different types of reforms. In substance, there are three different positions with regard to immigrants in Italy. The first position, defined by Cotesta (1992) as "refusal and expulsion," wants to send foreigners away, out of Italy. The second position, called "subordinated inclusion," is inspired by criteria of economic opportunity and proposes to accept foreigners only when necessary; that is, as indispensable labor for the smooth functioning of the economy. The third strategy, defined as "cooperation and citizenship," considers the foreigner as an opportunity for growth, not only economic growth but also cultural and human growth, as part of a multiethnic society.

With regard to legislation dealing with the problem of immigrants' deviance, the government has recently issued a series of temporary and urgent regulations aimed at increasing social control over foreigners. These include the possibility of expulsion if the person is caught in the act of committing a crime; they also include a first-degree conviction for crimes of moderate seriousness and if there is reason to believe that the immigrant makes his or her living from illegal activities. As one can see, this is legislation with discriminatory implications. Such legislation could lead to widespread injustice toward foreigners, and for this reason this legislation has been criticized by groups of people more sensitive to the problems faced by immigrants.

The topic of immigrants and criminality is a very sensitive one. We agree with Palidda (1994a)—the way a country deals with foreigners indicates its level of civilization.

REFERENCES

Bandini, T., Gatti, U., Marugo, M. I., & Verde, A. (1991). *Criminologia. Il contributo della ricerca alla conoscenza del crimine e della reazione sociale.* Milano: Giuffrè.

Bandini, T., Gatti U., & Traverso, G. B. (1995). *Omicidio e controllo sociale.* Milano: Franco Angeli.

Barbagli, M. (1994). *L'occasione e l'uomo ladro. Furti e rapine in Italia.* Bologna: Il Mulino.

Barbesino, P. (1995, October). *A coffehouse observation of those observing migration and other funny things.* Paper presented at the COST Deviance and Criminality Among Migrants in Europe workshop, Milan.

Buffa, P. (1990). La criminalità minorile straniera: L'esperienza torinese, 1980-1989. In G. Cocchi (Ed.), *Stranieri in Italia* (pp. 437-499). Bologna: Misure, Materiali di Ricerca dell'Istituto Cattaneo.

Calabrò, R. (1992). *Il vento non soffia più. Gli zingari ai margini di una grande città.* Venezia: Marsilio.

Calabrò, R. (1994). Gli zingari tra tradizione e cambiamento: Un percorso difficile. *Dei Delitti e delle Pene, 4*(1), 95-126.

Camera dei Deputati: Centro Studi. (Eds.). (1988, September). *La condizione dello straniero in Italia* (Atti, 178/1 e 178/II, X Legislatura).

Caritas. (1993). *Immigrazione. Dossier statistico 1993.* Roma: Sinnos.

Caritas. (1994): *Immigrazione. Dossier statistico 1994.* Roma: Anterem Ed. Ricerca.

Censis. (1990). *XXVI rapporto sulla situazione sociale nel paese.* Milano: Franco Angeli.

Centro informazione detenuti stranieri in Italia—CIDSI. (1991). *Detenuti stranieri in Italia: La loro condizione.* Roma: Consiglio Regionale del Lazio e Comune di Roma.

Centro informazione detenuti stranieri in Italia—CIDSI. (1994). *Gli stranieri in carcere. Dossier 94.* Roma: Sinnos.

Ceretti, A. (1995). Dal sacrificio al giudizio. Da Girard a Chapman. In A. Francia (Ed.), *Il capro espiatorio* (pp. 56-78). Milano: Angeli.

Chinnici, G. (1983). La criminalità tra migranti in Italia e immigrati stranieri. *Rassegna di Criminologia, 20,* 277-286.

Christie, N. (1984). *Suitable enemies.* Paper presented at the Howard League 2nd Annual Conference of the Individual and the State: The Impact of Criminal Justice, Oxford, United Kingdom.

Consiglio Nazionale per l'economia e il lavora—CNEL. (1991). *Immigrati e società italiana.* Roma: Author.

Cotesta, V. (1992). *La cittadella assediata. Immigrazione e conflitti etnici in Italia.* Roma: Riuniti.

Dal Lago, A. (1990). *Descrizione di una battaglia. I rituali del calcio.* Bologna: Il Mulino.

Dal Lago, A., & Moscati, R. (1992). *Regalateci un sogno. Mito e realtà del tifo calcistico in Italia.* Milano: Bompiani.

Fiasco, M. (1991). *La criminalità degli anni 1990.* Roma: Consiglio regionale del Lazio.

Gatti, U., & Marugo, M. I. (1987). La devianza degli stranieri in Italia. Una ricerca sullo spaccio di sostanze stupefacenti nella città di Genova. *Rassegna di Criminologia, 18,* 167-182.

Gennaro, G. (1990). La devianza degli stranieri in Italia. Risultati di una ricerca. In G. Cocchi (Ed.), *Stranieri in Italia* (pp. 451-468). Bologna: Misure, Materiali di Ricerca dell'-Istituto Cattaneo.

Girard, R. (1987). *Il capro espiatorio.* Milano: Adelphi.

Istituto di studi politici economici e sociali—ISPES. (1992). *Rapporto Italia 1992.* Roma: Koinè.

Istituto Nazionale de Statistica—ISTAT. (1993). *Gli stranieri in Italia. Fonti statistiche* (Note e relazioni no. 4). Roma: Author.

Istituto Nazionale de Statistica—ISTAT. (1994). *Statistiche giudiziarie penali. Anno 1993* (Annuario no. 2). Roma: Istat.

Laboratorio per le politiche sociali—LABOS. (1990). *La presenza straniera in Italia.* Roma: Tipografia editrice romana.

Lagazzi, M., Malfatti, D., Pallestrini, E., & Rossoni, N. (1996). Immigrazione, comportamento criminale e sanzione penale. Riflessioni sulla figura dell' 'immigrato spacciatore' nella città di Genova. *Rassegna Italiana di Criminologia, 7*(1), 145.

Maneri, M. (1995). *Stampa quotidiana e senso comune nella costruzione sociale dell'immigrato.* Tesi di dottorato in Sociologia e ricerca sociale, Università di Trento, Trento, Italy.

Marotta, G. (1995). *Immigrati. Devianza e controllo sociale.* Padova: Cedam.

Melchionda, U. (1993). *L'immigrazione straniera in Italia. Repertorio Bibliografico.* Roma: Lavoro.

Melossi, D. (1993). Punishment and social action. Changing vocabularies of punitive motive within a political business cycle. *Current Perspectives in Social Theory, 6,* 169-197.

Merzagora, I., Zoja, R., & Gigli, F. (1995). *Vittime di omicidio. Fattori di predisposizione alla vittimizzazione, caratteristiche delle vittime, scenari di omicidio a Milano.* Milano: Giuffrè.

Natale, M. (1990). L'immigrazione in Italia. Consistenza, caratteristiche, prospettive. *Polis, IV,* 5-40.

Palidda, S. (1994a). Devianza e criminalità tra gli immigrati. Ipotesi per una ricerca sociologica. *Inchiesta, 24*(123), 25-38.

Palidda, S. (1994b). *Devianza e criminalità tra gli immigrati.* Milano: Fondazione Cariplo-Ismu.

Palidda, S. (1995, October). *La construction sociale de la dèviance parmi les immigrès. Le cas italien.* Paper presented at the COST Deviance and Criminality Among Migrants in Europe Workshop, Milan.

Pastore, M. (1995). *Produzione normativa e costruzione sociale della devianza e criminalità tra gli immigrati.* Milano: Quaderni I.S.M.U., Fondazione Cariplo-I.S.M.U.

Puggioni, G., & Peddes, S. (1992, May). *The influence of age structure on crime rates. An application to immigrants of Cagliari province.* Paper presented at the National Conference of the Italian Society on Forensic Psychiatry, Cagliari-Chia Laguna, Italy.

Quirico, M. (1993). Capro espiatorio, politiche penali, egemonia. *Dei Delitti e delle Pene, 3*(1), 115-130.

Robotti, E. (1995). Mutazioni e migrazione. *Socialismo e Barbarie, 13*(13), 58-60.

Segre, S. (1993). Immigrazione extracomunitaria e delinquenza giovanile. Un'analisi sociologica. *Studi Emigrazione, 30*(111), 384-414.

Verde, A. (1995). Délit, procès et peine dans "l'Étranger" d'Albert Camus. *Déviance et Société, 19*(1), 23-33.

Verde, A., & Bagnara, F. (1989). L'utilizzazione delle strutture penitenziarie minorili in Italia nel triennio 1984-1986. *Rassegn a di Criminologia, 20,* 317-330.

6

MINORITIES, CRIME, AND CRIMINAL JUSTICE IN FRANCE

Pamela Irving Jackson

INTRODUCTION

In the spring of 1990, the Prime Minister of France convened an advisory council on integration, the Haut Conseil à l'intégration, specifically to dispel the "fantasies surrounding the presence of *étrangers* in France" (as translated, Haut Conseil, 1991, p. 7)—to replace the fragmented, dispersed, and sometimes incoherent knowledge about immigrants with a longitudinal perspective on both the flow of immigration and the social and judicial situation of *étrangers*—non-French citizens living in France. In its first report, published in 1991, the group indicated its intention to "recover the notion of integration" so that immigrants could "play a positive and enriching" role even in the face of the transformation of French society and its international environment (quotations translated from Haut Conseil, 1991, pp. 7, 8).

AUTHOR'S NOTES: The Groupe Européen de Recherche sur les Normativités (GERN), Madam Lopez at GERN, the Centre de Recherches Sociologiques sur le Droit et les Institutions Pénales (CESDIP), and the Faculty Research Committee of Rhode Island College all provided invaluable assistance that enabled the completion of this project.

The term *Département* has been retained throughout this chapter. It refers to France's administrative units.

The creation of the Haut Conseil signaled France's recognition of the segmentation of French society socially, religiously, and in terms of class; it also represented an effort to develop a *modèle français d'intégration,* based on a *fusion individuelle,* rather than on recognizing, as the *modèle américain* does, *groupes minoritaires* (Haut Conseil, 1991, p. 12).

Long-term assimilation, the report points out (Haut Conseil, 1991, p. 11) was characteristic of French society, from the beginnings of its *phénomène de l'immigration* in the early 19th century until the last third of the 20th century. A significant and persistent drop in its birthrate (a century before other European nations), its involvement in war, and the industrial revolution necessitated reliance on workers of foreign origin to provide for economic growth. Toward the end of the 20th century, however, several changes led to an overflow of immigrants into the "prosperous economic zones, beyond the capacity of their absorption." Chief among these transitions were *la crise économique* (p. 12) posed by the deindustrialization of Western economies, and "demographic pressure from countries south of the Mediterranean," (p. 13) including North African nations, sub-Saharan nations, and Turkey. These conditions combined with rapid change in the east as Soviet influence waned and communist economies collapsed, providing the push triggering massive immigration. The report notes (p. 13) that through "the quality of their work, their competence, and their energy" *étrangers* have made a "precious contribution to French society . . . economically . . . demographically . . . and culturally," but warns that their position in French society is now endangered.

During the last 15 years, unemployment rates reaching 11% of the French labor force—20% for young people (15 to 24 years), and near 30% for *étrangers* in this age group—have created a new proletariat living in degrading conditions, with high levels of illiteracy, generating racism, xenophobia, delinquency, and violence (Haut Conseil, 1991, p. 14). This chapter will delineate the threads linking minorities, crime, and criminal justice in France by examining the characteristics of the *étranger* population, its proximity to areas of high unemployment and crime, and its involvement with the criminal justice system.

FRANÇAIS/ÉTRANGERS DIVISION

Étranger is the term used in the French census (Institut National de la Statistique et des Etudes Économiques [INSEE]) for those individuals who are foreign workers (similar to the *Gastarbeiter* of Germany), not French citizens, but who are living in France. The distinction between French nationals and *étrangers*, as limited as it is, has been the primary official majority/minority division in France. In its report, the Haut Conseil à l'intégration notes the need for the creation of a category that provides for recognition of the fact that not all citizens of France have fully assimilated, and taken on its language, religion, and culture. Efforts toward a broader statistical conceptualization of minorities, developed by Tribalat, a researcher at l'Institut National d'Etudes Démographiques (INED), are described by the Haut Conseil (1991, p. 14).

Tribalat has added a third category to the national/*étranger* dichotomy based in the law: those individuals born in France who have a parent or grandparent who immigrated to France. The importance of gathering data on this group cannot be underestimated, the Haut Conseil (1991, p. 16) notes, in terms of understanding the processes of integration over time. Officially, France does not recognize the existence of minority groups among its citizens; the size of such groups is not statistically tabulated. Sociological study of their situation would illuminate the difficulties of their integration into French society. Awareness of these problems, the Conseil (1991, p. 16) emphasizes, would be preferable to the current assumption, fostered by the official *français/étranger* division, that nationality does not divide the nation.

The Conseil emphasizes (1991, p. 17) that the marginality faced by Algerians and those of other North African groups and their children is "one of the gravest problems" of French society. Without serious attention, the future will not bring an improvement in their situation; a pattern of "integration-exclusion" will be established, rather than a form of "integration-participation."

At the present time, the French census, gathered and published by the INSEE, regularly provides comparative counts of those who are French by birth *(français par naissance)*, those who have become French citizens *(français par acquisition)*, and noncitizens *(étrangers)*. INSEE gathers the most detailed data available regarding the characteristics of the French population, and is also the official picture of the population used by French government officials and accepted by the public. The analysis below rests on INSEE data, despite the limitations in France's count of its minority population.

Size and Distribution of *Étranger* Population

Census data from INSEE yield a figure of 6.3% *étrangers* in the French population (see Table 6.1). Most official estimates of the proportion of *étrangers* in the population in 1990, however, were larger, at 7.9% (cf. Direction Générale de la Police Nationale, 1991, p. 125). As noted previously, even this figure is a vast underrepresentation of France's minority population, because it ignores the children of *étrangers* and those who do not assimilate, those who retain their native language and culture beyond one generation. According to a 1990 survey of mayors of 73 cities (40 of whom responded), this number also fails to communicate an important dimension of the immigration problem as they perceive it: its geographic origin. In those municipalities with the largest proportion of *étrangers* (ranging between 9% and 47% of the total population), the principal nationalities, in decreasing order, are Algerian, Moroccan, Portuguese, Spanish, Tunisian, Turkish, and Italian. In the mayors' estimation, the vast Maghreb (North African), southern European, and recently, Turkish presence creates an urban management nightmare with several facets: a high level of unemployment among the young, hostility engendered by the impression that many are in France illegally, the failure of these groups in school, and their juvenile delinquency (cf. Haut Conseil, 1991, pp. 20-22).

As Table 6.1 indicates, excluding *étrangers* from common market countries (2.3% of the total French population), the largest groups of immigrants nationally are from Algeria and Morocco, each constituting about 1% of the French population. They are the most visible groups of *étrangers*, respectively comprising roughly 17% and 16% of the total. Tunisians, Turks, and sub-Saharan Africans are each about 5% of the total.These groups are overwhelmingly Muslim and may be dark-skinned, providing a notable contrast to the white, largely Catholic native French.

In those *départements* whose étranger population is greater than the national average (6.3%), the Muslim and black preponderance within the minority population is clear. Indeed, there is not one such département in which the Algerian and Moroccan groups combined do not constitute at least 20% of *étrangers* (see Table 6.1.) In some southern or Mediterranean *départements*, such as Gard (30), Bouches-du-Rhône (13) and Vaucluse (84), these groups combined are 50% or more of the *étranger* population (see Figure 6.1).

The island of Corsica, considered part of metropolitan France (the term used for continental France and Corsica, not urban locations only), contains only two *départements* (2A and 2B), one whose *étrangers* are 47% Moroccan, and the other 57%. In Hauts-de-Seine (92), Seine Saint-Denis (93), Val-de- Marne (94), and Val d'Oise (95), all of which surround Paris (75), at least 19% of the *étranger* population is Algerian, while between 7% and 17% is Moroccan. Rhône (69), in the east central part of the nation, has an *étranger* population that is close to 31% Algerian, as do its bordering *départements*

TABLE 6.1 Population (P) and *Étranger* (E) Composition in 1990: France and Départements at or Above National Étranger Average (6.3%)

Number	Administrative Unit Name	E (%)	Algerian %P	Algerian %E	Moroccan %P	Moroccan %E	Tunisian %P	Tunisian %E	African/ Sub-Saharan %P	African/ Sub-Saharan %E	Turks %P	Turks %E	Total Unemployed (%) %E	Crime (per 1,000) 0.00
Nation	France	6.3	1.1	17.1	1.0	15.9	0.4	5.7	0.3	4.9	0.4	5.4	11	61.7
01	Ain	9.4	0.9	9.4	1.7	18.0	0.6	6.2	0.1	1.1	1.4	14.3	6.6	39.0
06	Alpes-Maritimes	9.1	1.0	11.3	0.8	9.1	2.1	22.5	0.1	1.2	0.05	0.5	11.6	124.3
13	Bouches-du-Rhône	6.4	2.3	36.3	0.8	13.0	0.8	12.2	0.3	4.5	0.1	1.5	16.4	97.4
2A	Corse-du-Sud	10.4	0.3	2.9	4.9	47.0	1.2	11.8	0.09	0.9	0.00	0.00	14.5	110.0
2B	Haute-Corse	9.5	0.2	2.6	5.4	57.3	0.6	6.6	0.04	0.5	0.06	0.6	15.3	69.5
25	Doubs	7.2	1.4	19.6	1.5	21.8	0.2	2.5	0.2	2.3	0.9	12.5	8.9	46.3
30	Gard	6.5	1.1	17.0	2.4	38.2	0.2	3.2	0.06	1.0	0.08	1.3	15.4	82.3
34	Hérault	6.3	0.7	10.6	2.3	37.3	0.1	2.0	0.2	3.0	0.07	1.2	15.9	93.4
38	Isère	8.0	1.8	22.5	0.6	7.7	0.7	9.2	0.2	2.3	0.7	8.6	9.1	65.3
42	Loire	7.0	2.2	30.9	1.1	15.6	0.4	5.9	0.08	1.1	0.8	11.0	11.6	56.5
45	Loiret	7.4	0.5	6.4	1.8	24.7	0.2	2.5	0.3	4.5	0.8	10.6	9.0	49.4
57	Moselle	8.6	1.8	21.0	1.1	12.3	0.1	1.5	0.04	0.5	1.1	12.2	11.2	37.9
66	Pyrénées-Orientales	7.1	1.0	14.5	0.9	12.3	0.07	1.0	0.03	0.4	0.2	2.2	16.7	96.6

67	Bas-Rhin	7.0	0.6	8.3	1.2	16.6	0.2	2.9	0.2	2.2	1.8	25.1	7.4	57.4
68	Haut-Rin	8.9	1.6	17.8	1.1	12.7	0.2	2.7	0.1	1.5	1.4	15.4	7.0	50.3
69	Rhône	9.5	3.0	30.8	0.6	6.1	1.3	13.7	0.3	3.0	0.6	5.8	8.7	83.3
73	Savoie	6.4	1.1	16.6	0.8	12.5	0.2	3.7	0.04	0.6	0.6	9.3	7.2	70.2
74	Haute-Savoie	8.4	1.3	14.8	0.8	9.4	0.6	7.0	0.1	1.6	1.0	12.1	6.2	61.0
75	Paris	15.9	2.0	12.7	1.2	7.8	1.2	7.6	1.3	8.3	0.4	2.3	9.4	140.0
77	Seine-et-Marne	8.6	1.1	13.3	0.7	7.7	0.3	3.5	0.5	13.4	0.3	3.9	7.7	61.6
78	Yvelines	10.2	1.4	13.1	2.0	19.5	0.3	2.7	0.8	7.5	0.2	2.3	6.5	65.5
83	Var	6.3	1.1		17.9	1.1	18.0	1.5	23.6	0.09	1.4	0.06	1.0	15.7
84	Vaucluse	7.8	1.0	12.7	3.4	43.7	0.3	4.3	0.04	0.5	0.2	2.0	13.7	75.4
90	Territoire-de-Belfort	7.6	2.3	30.7	1.4	18.6	0.2	2.5	0.1	1.6	1.2	15.5	11.0	43.1
91	Essone	8.7	1.4	15.2	0.9	9.6	0.4	4.3	0.7	7.4	0.3	3.3	6.8	69.7
92	Hauts-de-Seine	13.1	2.5	19.4	2.2	17.3	0.6	4.9	0.8	6.1	0.1	1.0	7.9	69.8
93	Seine-Saint-Denis	18.9	4.6	24.6	2.1	11.3	1.2	6.5	2.0	10.8	0.7	3.9	11.5	73.1
94	Val-de-Marne	12.6	2.5	19.3	0.9	7.4	0.6	5.9	1.0	7.8	0.3	2.3	8.6	80.5
95	Val-d'Oise	11.1	2.1	19.0	1.3	12.2	0.5	4.9	1.0	9.3	0.7	6.6	8.4	75.3

SOURCE: Direction Générale de la Police Nationale, 1991; Institut National de la Statistique et des Etudes Economiques, 1992a.

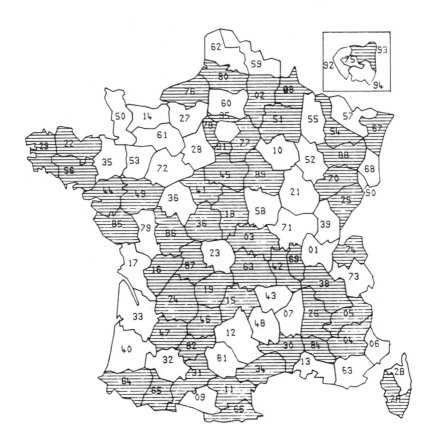

Figure 6.1. Growth in Major and Moderately Serious Offenses in the *Départements* (administrative units) of France, 1989 to 1990
SOURCE: Direction Générale de la Police Nationale, 1991, p. 187.
NOTE: Rate of growth less than the national average (+6.93%). Rate of growth greater than the national average. Numbers appearing on the map above are codes for the various *départements.*

of Loire (42) and the *département,* Territoire-de-Belfort (90). Also notable are the northeast *département* of Haut-Rhin (68), whose *étranger* population is almost 18% Algerian and 13% Moroccan; the eastern *département* of Doubs (25), whose foreign population is over 19% Algerian and about 22% Morrocan; Moselle (57) in the northeast with an *étranger* population that is 21% Algerian and 12% Moroccan, and Loiret (45) below the Paris region, with an *étranger* population of about 25% Moroccan.

Visibility and Unemployment

Because they include only those born outside of France, not their children born in France and those who do not assimilate culturally, the figures in Table 6.1 considerably underestimate the visibility of Algerians and Moroccans in these *départements* in particular, and in France in general. These groups are singled out by native French as the source of the nation's problems. Originally invited by the French government, which once had colonial ties with Algeria, Morocco, and Tunisia, North Africans continued to arrive in large numbers as France headed into the downturn in the unskilled labor market that is part of the deindustrialization process. Limitations were imposed on Algerian immigration between 1968 and 1974, with final efforts working toward ending the flow.

For the *étranger* population nationally, the rate of unemployment in 1990 was over 19.5% (INSEE, 1992a, p. 60). Those who had taken French citizenship *(français par acquisition)*, 3% of the population, had a slightly lower level at 14.3%. France's overall 1990 unemployment rate of 11% underscored the unemployment problem of the North African groups, especially where their population was greatest; unemployment levels varied tremendously throughout the nation and among *départements* with high minority populations (INSEE, 1992b, pp. 18, 54, see Table 6.1.)

In the Marseilles area, for example, unemployment in the *département* of Bouches-du-Rhône (13) was 16.4%. Also on the Mediterranean coast, Pyrénées-Orientales' (66) unemployment level was 16.+%. Similarly, the southern Mediterranean *départements* of Gard (30), Vaucluse (84), and Alpes-Maritimes (6) had 1990 unemployment rates of 15.4%, 13.7%, and 11.6%, respectively. The *départements* of the island of Corsica, Corse-du-Sud (2A) and Haute-Corse (2B), also have high unemployment levels at 14.5% and 15.3%, respectively. The northeastern *département* of Territoire-de-Belfort (90) is just at the national average of 11% in unemployment, while Loire (42), in the central part of France, and Moselle (57) in the northeast, have levels that are only slightly higher at 11.6% and 11.2%, respectively. Hérault (34) and Var (83), both bordering Bouches-du-Rhône, have high unemployment rates of 15.9% and 15.7%, respectively.

Although officially the *étranger* population of these *départements* ranges from 6% to over 9%, it is, even by these official figures, from 20% to almost 60% Algerian and Moroccan. Combined with the high *départemental* unemployment rate, the relative size of these groups among the *étranger* residents has triggered claims by the political group, the Front National, that France is being irreparably changed in both demographic character and in level of prosperity by immigrants from the Maghreb.

———————————

CRIME

Crime statistics in France, records of notifiable offenses, are recorded by the National Police force and the National Gendarmerie (cf. Direction Générale de la Police Nationale, 1991). They include several categories of theft (among them robberies, burglaries, automobile and motorcycle theft, and larcenies such as shoplifting); fraud, economic and financial crimes (including forgeries, counterfitting, contract fraud, tax fraud, bankruptcy offenses, and check fraud); offenses against the person (including actual and attempted homicide, assault, sexual offenses, and offenses against family and children); and in the last category, drug, public order, and gambling offenses. Even at first glance it is clear that any comparisons to recorded crime rates in the United States require careful scrutiny, because many more categories of offenses are included in the French total than are included in the Federal Bureau of Investigation's total of Part I Index Offenses. The French totals are presented for the whole population of continental France (which is referred to as France Métropolitaine and includes the island of Corsica), and for the individual *départements* (administrative units) within the nation. These totals include major offenses *(crimes),* which require a jury trial, and moderately serious offenses *(délits),* which are normally judged by a correctional tribunal. The third category of offenses in France, minor offenses (contraventions), are normally judged by a police tribunal, are not considered recordable, and are not included in these totals (cf. Direction Générale de la Police Nationale, 1991, p. 19; Robert, 1995, p. 4).

Overall, the official total 1990 crime rate in France was 61.7 crimes per 1,000 population (see Table 6.1). As is the case in the United States, the total rate masks stark variations in the likelihood of crime throughout the nation. In reviewing the list of *départements* with a higher than average official level of *étrangers*, the southern Mediterranean *département* of Alpes-Maritimes (06), for example, is over twice the national average at 124.3 crimes per 1,000. Because this *département* includes Nice and the famous Côte d'Azur, its crime rate may, in part, be a result of the juxtaposition of the grandeur of its tourist attractions and vacation visitors with its 11.6% unemployment rate. Although the role of the minority population in crime is not clear from these statistics, it is true that most of the *départements* with noticeably high crime rates are on Table 6.1's list of *départements* with *étranger* levels that are higher than the national average. They are also in tourist areas in which routine activities would make crime both accessible and profitable (cf. Cohen & Felson, 1979). In the area of the Côte D'Azur, for example, besides Alpes-Maritimes (06), Bouches-du- Rhône (13) and Var (83) have overall crime rates of 97.4 and 101.5, respectively. Hérault (34), also on the southern Mediterranean coast, stands out with a crime rate of 93.4 crimes per 1,000 population. Bordering Bouches-du-Rhône on the north, Vaucluse (84) has a crime rate of 75.4, 22.5% higher than the national average; and Pyrénées-Orientales (66), on the southern border with Spain and with a Mediterranean coast, has a high crime rate of 96.6 crimes per 1,000.

In addition to the southern *départements* near or bordering the Mediterranean, there is another pocket of crime in Paris and its surroundings. At 140 crimes per 1,000, Paris (75) has the highest rate of crime in the entire 1990 listing of 95 administrative *départements* (Direction Générale de la Police Nationale, 1991, p. 32), not only in Table 6.1's list of *départements* with *étranger* levels greater than or equal to the national average. The *départements* surrounding Paris (75), Hauts-de-Seine (92), Seine-Saint-Denis (93), Val-De-Marne (94), and Val d'Oise (95), have crime rates ranging from 13% to 30% above the national rate of 61.7 crimes per 1,000. The *départements* in this area, as noted previously, have official *étranger* levels from 76% (Val d'Oise (95)) to 200% (Seine-Saint-Denis (93)) greater than the national average of 6.3%. Except for Seine-Saint-Denis (93), with an unemployment rate of 11.5%, unemployment in these *départements* is lower than the national average of 11%. Finally, Rhône (69), the *département* containing Lyon, has a crime rate of 83.3 per 1,000, 35% greater than the national average; its official *étranger* population, at 9.5% was about 51% higher than the national average.

Overall, it is apparent, then, that official crime rates in France are highest in those *départements* with the largest official counts of *étrangers*. Although this link says little about the sources of criminality in these *départements* (especially because the official crime rate includes some categories of white-collar crime that are likely to be committed by those with higher levels of education who understand and can manipulate bureaucratic regulations), it does help to explain French perceptions of trouble in those locations with the largest minority populations. In the United States, the transitional areas, in which poor minority populations, especially immigrants, settle, have been found to have the highest crime rates not only because their social disorganization destabilizes conventional normative structures allowing deviant norms to prevail, but also because those outside of these areas recognize that these are places where residents are less likely to initiate contact with police to report drug sales or other criminal behavior (cf. Shaw & McKay, 1942; Warner & Pierce, 1993; Wievorka, 1992).

Infractions Committed by *Étrangers*

According to official statistics published by the police, gendarmerie, and the police judiciaire, 16.96% of those suspected of a criminal offense in 1990 were *étrangers*, foreign nationals (Direction Générale de la Police Nationale, 1991, p. 27). When immigration-related offenses are removed, this figure is reduced to 13.1% *étrangers*, roughly twice the official incidence of *étrangers* in the population (Direction Générale de la Police Nationale, 1991, p. 27). These figures are not provided on a départemental level.

Information regarding the nationality of the prison population is reported in the aggregate as well. Tournier and Robert (1991, p. 14) explain that useful information on the nationality of the incarcerated is not routinely provided by each penal institution in its quarterly reports, and that the information on nationality that they do provide is aggregated at the regional and then the national level. Data from la Statistique Informatisée de la Population Pénale (SIPP), 1984 do provide nationality, but are only available in useful form for the 1982 to 1985 period (Tournier & Robert, 1991, p. 14). The only statistics regarding the nationality of those whose sentences for criminal offenses did not involve imprisonment is the total of *étrangers* among those convicted, provided by the Travail d'interet general since 1984 (Travail d'intérét général [TIG], 1984; cf. Tournier & Robert, 1991, p. 13).

Working within these limitations, however, several pertinent characteristics of the incarcerated population are evident. First, in 1990, 29.7% of those who were incarcerated were *étrangers* (Tournier & Robert, 1991, p. 103). About 18% of the incarcerated *étrangers* were from European nations including Belgium, Spain, Italy, Poland, Portugal, the United Kingdom, and Yugoslavia. Just under 70% were from African nations (i.e, 23% were from Algeria, 15% from Morocco, 9% from Tunisia, and 21% from other African nations). The group from other African nations (21% of incarcerated *étrangers*), was composed of *étrangers* from several nations including Zaire (21%), Senegal (19%), Mali (12.5%), Angola (7%), Nigeria (5.5%), and the Ivory Coast (5%; Tournier & Robert, 1991, p. 23). The remaining 13% of *étrangers* detained were from several locations: the American continent (3.4%, over half of whom are from Colombia), Asian nations (8.1%), Oceania (.1%), or unknown (.7%; cf. Tournier & Robert, 1991, pp. 107-113).

Comparison of the pattern of criminality characteristic of French nationals and of *étrangers* shows clear differences between the two groups. Unfortunately, as indicated earlier, data on those entering penal institutions provided by SIPP are only available in useful form for the 1982 to 1985 period. For both groups, moderately serious offenses *(délits)* constitute the majority of infractions (92% for French and 96% for *étrangers*). Only 8% of French and 4% of *étranger* entrants to penal institutions were imprisoned for major crimes (cf. Tournier & Robert, 1991, pp. 138-139). These figures do not vary much during the 4-year period for which the data are available (see Table 6.2). In addition, Tournier and Robert (1991, p. 25) point out, "the proportion of *étrangers* among those admitted to prison is greater for moderately serious crimes *(délits)* than for major crimes (29% vs. 18%, respectively); the difference is greatest for women (28% for moderately serious offenses vs. 8% for major crimes)." These statistics fit with the immigration advisory council's 1991 conclusion and that of the mayors it surveyed: The criminal involvement of *étrangers* consists primarily of less serious, nonviolent incidents, often related to drugs and undertaken by youths (Haut Conseil, 1991, p. 22).

Further consideration of the pattern of moderately serious offenses (délits) characteristic of the native and *étranger* population indicates that in 1985, 24% of *étranger* entrants to penal institutions had committed as their primary offense a public order violation. Only 1.7% of French inmates entering prison in 1985 were there for such an offense. Although there was little change over the 4-year period in the proportion of French entrants each year who were in prison for public order violations, there was a noticeable increase for *étranger* entrants between 1982, when 10% of entrants were picked up for public order violations, and 1983, when the figure was 24%. The majority of these violations (80% to 97%) involved *étrangers* picked up in police efforts to control illegal immigration (Tournier & Robert, 1991, pp. 26, 57). French nationals, Tournier and Robert point out, are practically absent from this category. When these offenses are removed from the tally of *étranger* infractions, the number of *étranger* criminal suspects appears to have dropped noticeably between 1985 and 1986. Removing, in addition, the offenses of bad check writing and the small category of offenses labeled "other," yields an even greater 1985 to 1986 drop in *étranger* suspects for moderately serious offenses (Tournier & Robert, 1991, pp. 57-61).

The other change that stands out in Table 6.2 is the increase in the number of *étrangers* entering prison for whom the principal offense was categorized as a moderately serious offense *(délit)* against the person, from 17.6% in 1982 to 22.1% in 1985. According to Tournier and Robert (1991, p. 26), in

TABLE 6.2 Admission to Penal Institutions for Major and Moderately Serious Offenses: *Étranger* and French, 1982 to 1985

	French		Étranger	
	Nature of the Infraction[a]		Nature of the Infraction[a]	
	Délit (moderate)	Crime (major)	Délit (moderate)	Crime (major)
1982	90.9	9.1	94.0	6.0
1983	91.0	9.0	94.6	5.4
1984	92.1	7.9	95.1	4.9
1985	92.1	7.9	95.7	4.3
	Nature of Délit[b]		Nature of Délit[b]	
	Against Persons	Against Public Order	Against Persons	Against Public Order
1982	14.8	1.8	17.6	10.1
1983	16.0	1.9	19.0	24.0
1984	15.3	1.8	21.8	22.3
1985	16.8	1.7	22.1	23.9
	Nature of Crime[c]		Nature of Crime[c]	
	Against Persons	Against Morals	Against Persons	Against Morals
1982	30.5	33.8	32.2	35.1
1983	30.0	32.2	31.7	37.2
1984	31.0	32.2	30.5	36.8
1985	31.1	28.4	32.8	35.9

SOURCE: Tournier & Robert, 1991, pp. 138, 142-153.
NOTES: a. Percentage of total French or *étrangers* admitted for moderate or serious offense.
b. Percentage of total French or *étrangers* admitted for specified category of moderately serious offense. Entrants into penal institutions are grouped according to the most serious offense. Those categories of offenses that are not central to this analysis (theft, vandalism, traffic, fraud/bad checks, military violations, offenses against children) have not been included. As a result, the figures do not total to 100%. Over 50% of *délits,* moderately serious offenses, against persons are violations of laws regarding illegal drug use or dealing (Tournier & Robert, 1991, p. 26). Over 80% of public order *délits,* moderately serious offenses, involve *étrangers* picked up in police efforts to control illegal immigration (Tournier & Robert, 1991, pp. 26, 57).
c. Percentage of total French or *étrangers* admitted for specified category of major offense. Entrants into penal institutions are grouped according to the most serious crime. Those categories of crimes that are not central to this analysis (theft, fraud and economic crimes, offenses against children, destruction of private property and criminal damage) have not been included. As a result, the figures to not total to 100%. Crimes against persons include homicide, assault, and rape. Morals crimes include serious violations of laws regarding controlled substances, public order, (e.g., bombings), and regulations.

over half of these cases of moderately serious offenses *(délits)* against the person, drug infractions were involved, although it is not possible to distinguish between infractions involving drug usage and those related to drug trafficking. Efforts to closely monitor the *étranger* population and to forestall illegal immigration may be reflected in the growth in *étrangers* incarcerated for both categories of moderately serious offenses (délits), public order and against persons violations, without a corresponding growth among French nationals.

THE CRIMINAL JUSTICE RESPONSE

Of the *étrangers* who were imprisoned in 1985, 90% were held in pretrial detention; the figure was 75% for French nationals (Tournier & Robert, 1991, pp. 147; 26), and had risen to 77.2% by 1993 (Robert, 1995, p. 4). Of all cases of provisional detention in 1985, 60% resulted from the decision of an examining magistrate, while 31% involved direct seizure. Among French nationals, direct seizure accounted for only 25% of provisional detentions, while 66% involved a magistrate. For *étrangers*, this rapid procedure (direct seizure) accounted for 43% of provisional detentions, while 48% resulted from the decision of a magistrate (Tournier & Robert, 1991, pp. 26- 29; 150-152). (The figures do not total to 100% because other rarely invoked mechanisms for placing a person in provisional detention are not presented here.)

The use of provisional detention, "punishment without the determination of guilt" (Robert, 1992, p. 12), with *étrangers* particularly, has fueled the debate about the violation of liberty involved in what is seen by many as a "necessary evil" (Robert, 1992, p. 10). Although most of France's neighbors use this technique of prejudgment detention sparingly, France is not as conservative in its application, despite numerous regulative reforms since the end of the 18th century. The prevailing view is that despite the problems it creates for liberty, "and possibly also for the coherence of the law," it is indispensable for maintaining public order (Robert, 1992, p. 11). In his most recent analysis of the subject, Robert (1995, p. 5) concludes that, "Pretrial detention serves as a way of getting around the delays and uncertainties of a criminal justice system that is terribly overloaded [and] lacks resources." It is most likely to be used, he points out, during periods of employment uncertainty, with increases in "the number of individuals who apparently do not offer the necessary guarantees against failure to appear, because they cumulate several of the customary traits of marginality, such as lack of an occupation, unemployment, no fixed address, no solid family ties, or in the case of foreigners, the fact of illegal entry" (Robert, 1995, p. 5). France has the highest rate of pretrial detention in Western Europe (36.2 per 100,000, followed closely only by Belgium at 33.9 per 100,000 inhabitants; Robert, 1992, p. 8). This deprivation of liberty without conviction is seen as a threat to justice in France; it has also seriously overcrowded its prisons (Robert, 1995, p. 5).

Commitments to provisional detention grew to a peak of over 72,000 annually in 1984, dropping off somewhat to 64,000 by 1989. The increased length of the period of detention, however, reaching its highest average (3.9 months) in 1985, reducing to 3.7 months on average by 1989, and rising to 3.9 months again by 1993, kept the average number of individuals in pretrial detention high (Robert, 1992, p. 9; 1995, p. 5). Because only about one in six incarcerations involves an individual already sentenced, provisional detention has become the most common mechanism for entry into prison. "Globally rare, it has become . . . current practice in official channels" (Robert, 1992, p. 264). The reasons dominating the police decision to pick up a person and take them to the public prosecutor, and the prosecutor's subsequent consideration of prison before judgment and without complete proof include "*étranger* nationality, homelessness, lack of work or profession." All of these problems make it likely that the person will not be well represented legally (Robert, 1992, p. 264). Those who are held in provisional detention, Robert (1995, p. 5) points out, are ultimately more likely to receive a prison sentence than a suspended sentence or acquittal. For some, Robert (1995, p. 3) indicates, it may be that "detention at the time of the court decision is an encouragement to pronounce a sentence to prison, if only to cover the time spent in pretrial detention and not disavow the examining judge."

In their analysis of incarceration patterns of *étrangers*, Tournier and Robert (1991, p. 91) suggest that efforts to reduce illegal immigration in France during the 1980s have heightened the visibility of minorities as "potential suspects" attracting police curiosity. That, in addition to efforts to repress illegal drug use and distribution, they point out, has led to the rapid growth in the presence of *étrangers* in French prisons. Whether the figures reflect increased drug addiction among migrants, greater vigilance by authorities regarding drug infractions, or stricter control of migrants is the final question posed, but not answered, by Tournier and Robert in their volume, *Étrangers et Délinquants"* (1991, pp. 91- 92).

Other French scholars have considered the question of the extent to which *changements économiques* have led in France to *répression pénale*. In the subtitle to their study (*plus de chômage, plus d'emprisonnement?*), Godefroy and Laffargue (1991) raise the question of a relationship between unemployment levels and imprisonment rates. They also note (p. 79) that *étrangers* are overrepresented in the prison population, having doubled over 20 years to 30% of the prison population in 1990, up from 15% 20 years earlier. The number of *étrangers* detained was 2.8 times higher by the most recent statistics available than it was 15 years earlier, while the figure for French nationals was only 1.4 times higher. Using a historical, statistically based analysis, Godefroy and Laffargue investigate directly whether periods of growth in incarceration coincide with periods of economic recession. They describe their research as investigating the relationship between economic conditions and delinquency, and conclude that unemployment influences imprisonment rates even after the official delinquency rate is controlled.

The fact that Godefroy and Laffargue's (1991) volume was published by the Centre De Recherches Sociologiques Sur Le Droit et Les Institutions Pénales (CESDIP), a research group loosely organized by the Ministry of Justice, suggests that the possibility of such links is not being ignored in France. Godefroy and Laffargue cite Melossi's (1985, 1989) proposition that periods of recession are periods of repression, and they discuss the possibility that although penal law in its application does not have much practical effect on the rate of delinquency, it has a pedagogical effect, in "contributing to the general climate of submission to authority" (Godefroy & Laffargue, 1991, p. 72). They also consider the question of the extent to which the modern manifestation of this trend involves a growth in the number of prison admissions or an increase in sentence length (p. 72). They end with a discussion of the boundaries between penal and social separation, noting that both are political processes directed at the same population (p. 108).

Michel Wieviorka (1992, p. 29) in *La France Raciste,* considers the problem of the dualization of French society with the passing of the industrial era and the demise of labor unions. Xenophobia and racism, he stresses, are not the only consequences of the decline of industrial society. An equally serious division is developing between those who have decent jobs and who, along with their families, can participate in modern, postindustrial society, and those who, on the other hand, are excluded from the new economy by unemployment or precarious employment, surrounded by misery, plagued by family breakup, and whose children are being poorly educated. This, he argues, is the division that will have the most dire long-term consequences for society. It will prevent the integration of Maghrebians and Turks.

The dualization of French society, Wievorka (1992) argues, has led to a sorting or classifying process on the basis of economic mobility. Those who are moving up economically are gentrifying urban centers or moving to pleasant suburban locations. Those who are not, he notes, are forming "ghettos á l'américaine." Their social and spatial exclusion has received media attention, become the subject of political concerns and the focus of police attention; and, it has led to violence and riots. Such spatial dualization of the population, he argues, will prolong the social exclusion of France's minority populations. In response to their separation, minority groups have established their own networks of mutual aid, reaffirming their solidarity based on their shared, Islamic religious identity.

On the basis of his study of focus groups, Wievorka (1992, p. 249) notes that these new patterns of social and spatial segregation, combined with the economic dualization of the population, have led to problems in defining the police role and in controlling police behavior. Wievorka elaborates on the problem of police racism that emerged in his research. Its roots lie, he assesses, in both societal conditions and in the structure and operations of the police (Wievorka, 1992, p. 262). In some areas of high minority concentration and significant unemployment, police/minority relationships are characterized by hostility and fear. In Marseille, for example, a police station was closed because of the work involved in removing trash and debris from its front door each morning, unfastening the door welded shut, or, four or five times a night, responding to attempts to break down the door. One police officer noted that tacit agreements were often made with local toughs, to overlook stolen car operations in return for their not threatening or trashing police cars patrolling the area (Wievorka, 1992, p. 228).

When interviewed, police complained of having become racist (Wievorka, 1992, p. 264) as a result of dealing with Maghrebian communities (p. 255). Police reported acceptance of the ideal of equality in the policing of all groups, and in general rejected the idea of community policing wherein the ethnic background of officers in a community would reflect its population composition.Nonetheless, they did not deny their own developing verbal and behavioral racism on the job (pp. 266-267). As surmised from these reflections, their work situation appears to have much in common with that described by a U.S. policeman from Miami, Florida, who, in 1979 affirmed,

> No doubt about it, the job makes you more racist. Not in a one-on-one situation. But when I'm having to deal with a crowd of blacks, they're the enemy. I'm not the good guy to them. I'm the white establishment. (Jackson, 1989, pp. 119-120)

Police resentment of the judicial system for what they see as its inefficiency and lack of meaningful punishment standards again mirrors what is heard in the United States, with police complaining about the release of the minority youths that they bring into the system (Wievorka, 1992, pp. 231-232). The emerging role of the police in what is becoming a bifurcated French society has been considered by other French authors, including the journalist Jean-Marie Ancien (1988, pp. 193-194), in his book, *La Police des policiers,* in which he ultimately poses the question that must be answered even as police chase illegal immigrants or those without their papers: What kind of police do the French want, and what do they want them to do? A similar question was the subject of intense consideration in the United States during the early part of the 1980s, and led to the creation of a new role for urban police. In 1980, Philadelphia's new Police Commissioner Solomon held up a new standard for policing, in which every police officer should be "a community relations officer." He elaborated on this new standard, pointing out that

> The police department . . . is one of the agencies in the City of Philadelphia that works 24 hours a day, 7 days a week . . . I want to start building up a mutual respect between the people of Philadelphia and the police department . . . the best way to do it is to let everyone know that policemen are their friends. (Jackson, 1989, p. 118)

If a similar conceptualization of the police officer's role develops in France, it will require greater official recognition of the cultural and socioeconomic differences between France's minority population and its police professionals, as well as efforts to bridge these gaps through either greater communication or greater inclusion of minorities of *étranger* extraction in police agencies.

CONCLUSIONS AND IMPLICATIONS

The visibility of *étrangers* in France no doubt contributes to their scrutiny by police agencies, to their provisional detention, and to their longer term incarceration in French prisons. The deterioration of France's economic situation in the 1980s, part of Western nations' transformation from industrial to service-based economies, led by 1990 to an overall unemployment rate of 11% for the nation; noticeably higher unemployment levels (17%) existed in some of the *départements* with the greatest proportion of *étrangers*. These *départements* also had the most "visible" *étrangers*, with at least a quarter and sometimes over half from the northern African nations of Algeria and Morocco. The presence of people of color with a Muslim heritage, in the midst of high unemployment accentuated both the *étrangers'* problems of adjustment and assimilation and the problems of economic scarcity, especially for those with the lowest skill levels. The size of these minority populations, combined with their poverty, have emphasized the problems of inequality, triggering ethnic antagonism and contributing to criminal justice efforts and exclusion movements to reduce their visibility and protect the cultural heritage of the majority. Questions of economic interests, ethnic antagonism, and cultural identity are central to the new political landscape in France as established institutions, including criminal justice agencies, address the presence of significant minority populations in the midst of economic change (cf. Jackson, 1992a, pp. 218-219, 1995).

No longer useful in the French economy, *étrangers*, once the mainstay of French industry, had by the mid-1980s become a target of both political campaigns (such as the Front National) and of criminal justice authorities. Tolerance for infractions by *étrangers* (or by those who appeared to be *étrangers*) lessened. Because drug offenses typically symbolize societal erosion, these groups were carefully scrutinized for such offenses, then held (in pretrial detention) if there was any question of their involvement in a drug-related or other offense, or because of the legality of their status in France. The fact that most *étrangers* who are incarcerated are being held for lesser offenses *(délits)* often related to immigration problems or illegal drugs, and that the proportion of *étrangers* entering prison for public order crimes more than doubled between 1982 and 1983, lends support to this interpretation. It also suggests that criminal justice processes have been part of French efforts to reduce *étranger* visibility and to control their impact on French society (cf. Jackson, 1995). Research in the United States has supported Blalock's (1967) proposition that social control resources, including those of corrections and the police, are mobilized in time periods and locations in which the minority population is perceived to be threatening to the dominant culture or to the dominant group's economic position (cf. Inverarity, 1992; Jackson, 1985, 1986, 1989, 1992b; Tolnay & Beck, 1992). The evidence presented in this chapter suggests that criminal justice resources are being directed toward France's effort to reduce the visibility of its *étranger* population and protect the French way of life.

The integration of minority populations is deemed so important in France that there is no routinized, official statistical effort to enumerate minority populations in ways more complicated than the *étranger/français* distinction. It remains to be seen whether such distinctions will have to be made to better incorporate these populations into French life, especially in the face of the problems of economic transition that deindustrialization has imposed. Despite the marginalization of *étrangers*, their general lack of involvement in serious crime has been confirmed by the survey of urban mayors (Haut Conseil, 1991, p. 22), by the work of French researchers (Tournier & Robert, 1991, p. 25), and by official statistics (Direction Générale de la Police Nationale, 1992). These findings augur well for the integration advisory council's conclusion that under the right circumstances *étrangers* can play a positive and enriching role in France (*Haut Conseil,* 1991, p. 8). They also fuel the advisory council's work to reduce their marginalization in French society.

REFERENCES

Ancian, J.-M. (1988). *La Police des polices.* Paris: Ballard.

Blalock, H. (1967). *Toward a theory of minority group relations.* New York: John Wiley.

Cohen, L. E., & Felson, M. (1979). Social change and crime rate trends. *American Sociological Review, 44,* 588-607.

Direction Generale de la Police Nationale (1991). *Aspects de la Criminalité et de la Délinquance Constatés en France en 1990.* Paris: Documentation Française.

Godefroy, T., & Laffargue, B. (1991). *Changements Economiques et Répression Pénale: Plus de chômage, plus d'emprisonnement?* Paris: Centre de Recherches Sociologiques Sur Le Droit et Les Institutions Pénales (CESDIP).

Haut Conseil à l'intégration. (1991). *Pour un modèle français d'intégration* (Rapport au Premier Ministre). Paris: Documentation Française.

Institut National de la Statistique et des Etudes Economiques—INSEE. (1992a). *Recensement de la Population de 1990: Nationalités* (Résultats du sondage au quart). Paris: Author.

Institut National de la Statistique et des Etudes Economiques—INSEE. (1992b). *Recensement de la Population de 1990: Nationalités* (Résultats du sondage au vingtième). Paris: Author.

Inverarity, J. (1992). Extralegal influences on imprisonment: Explaining the direct effects of socioeconomic variables. In A. E. Liska (Ed.), *Social threat and social control* (pp. 113-130). Albany: State University of New York Press.

Jackson, P. I. (1985). Ethnicity, region, and public fiscal commitment to policing. *Justice Quarterly, 2*(2), 167-199.

Jackson, P. I. (1986). Black visibility, city size, and social control. *Sociological Quarterly, 27*(2), 185-203.

Jackson, P. I. (1989). *Minority group threat, crime, and policing: Social context and social control.* New York: Praeger.

Jackson, P. I. (1992a). Minority group threat and social control: Twenty years of investigation. In M. Dobkowski & I. Wallimann (Eds.), *Research in inequality and social conflict* (Vol. 2, pp. 209-222). Greenwich, CT: JAI.

Jackson, P. I. (1992b). Minority group threat, social context, and policing. In A. E. Liska (Ed.), *Social threat and social control* (pp. 89-102). Albany: State University of New York Press.

Jackson, P. I. (1995). Minority group threat, crime, and the mobilization of law in France. In D. F. Hawkins (Ed.), *Ethnicity, race, and crime: Perspectives across time and place* (pp. 341-359). Albany: State University of New York Press.

Melossi, D. (1985). Punishment and social action: Changing vocabularies of punitive motive within a political business cycle. *Current Perspectives of Social Theory, 6,* 169-187.

Melossi, D. (1989). An introduction: Fifty years later, "punishment and social structure." *Comparative Analysis, Contemporary Crisis, 13,* 311-326.

Robert, P. (Ed.). (1992). *Entre L'ordre Et La Liberté, La Détention Provisoire: Deux Siècles De Débats.* Paris: l'Harmattan.

Robert, P. (1995, March). A lawmaker's headache: Pretrial detention. *Penal Issues: Research on Crime and Justice in France, 6,* 3-5.

Shaw, C. R., & McKay, H. D. (1942). *Juvenile delinquency and urban areas 1969.* Chicago: University of Chicago Press.

Statistique Informatisée de la Population Pénale—SIPP. (1984). Structure socio-démographique et pénale de la cohorte des personnes incarcérées en 1982. Paris: Direction de l'administration pénitentaire.

Tolnay, S. E., & Beck, E. M. (1992). Toward a threat model of Southern black lynchings. In A. E. Liska (Ed.), *Social threat and social control* (pp. 33-52). Albany: State University of New York Press.

Tournier, P., & Robert, P. (1991). *Etrangers et Délinquances.* Paris: l'Harmattan.

Travail d'intérêt général—TIG. (1984). Paris: Direction de L'administration pénitentaires.

Warner, B., & Pierce, G. L. (1993). Reexamining social disorganization theory using calls to the police as a measure of crime. *Criminology, 31,* 493-517.

Wieviorka, M. (1992). *La France Raciste.* Paris: Seuil.

7

MINORITIES, CRIME, AND CRIMINAL JUSTICE IN BELGIUM

Patrick Hebberecht

IMMIGRANTS AND ETHNIC MINORITIES IN BELGIUM

Belgium shares borders with The Netherlands, France, and Germany; it has approximately 10 million inhabitants. Three languages are spoken in Belgium: Dutch in Flanders (60% of the Belgian population), French in Wallonia (39%), and German (less than 1% of the population; Bruyssinck, Boudart, & Boudart, 1990). Brussels, the capital of Belgium, is the seat of the European parliament, the European Union Commission, as well as NATO, which gives Brussels an important position internationally.

From the mid-1900s until the beginning of the 20th century, about 3% of the population in Belgium were immigrants. This small group was primarily of French, German, or Dutch origin (i.e., from neighboring countries). Mostly, these immigrants lived near borders and in urban areas. Since the beginning of the 20th century, people moving into Belgium (i.e., immigration) outnumbered the Belgians who left the country (i.e., emigration).

AUTHOR'S NOTE: I would like to thank Peter Colle, Jimmy Feys, Ronnie Lippens, and Bart Van Hoorebeeck of the Criminological Research Group at Ghent University for their assistance with this chapter.

After the First World War, immigration became less spontaneous; special campaigns were set up to recruit foreign labor (Grimmeau, 1992). Periods of intense immigration, from that moment on, converged with periods of economic boom and with a tight labor force market. It should be noted that immigration in Belgium differs from that in other European countries; it is not related to its colonial and postcolonial history in the former Belgian Congo (now Zaire). Between the two World Wars, a significant immigration wave originated from neighboring countries such as France, The Netherlands, and Germany, but also for the first time from Italy and from some Eastern European countries (Poland, Czechoslovakia, and former Yugoslavia). These immigrants were employed in the coal mining industry. During the postwar economic recovery, a sharp shortage on the local labor force market emerged. Belgium's heavy industries attracted foreign labor mostly from Italy. With the closing of the Eastern European borders, immigration from these countries stopped. When, in 1955, many Italian miners died in a mining disaster, the Italian government slowed down emigration of its citizens to Belgium. Thereafter, workers were also recruited from Spain and Greece.

With the economic expansion and the establishment of a European Market at the end of the 1950s, the need for unskilled, mobile, and flexible labor became a structural trait of the Belgian economy. Belgium was now also recruiting Maghrebians and Turkish citizens, mostly as unskilled rural workers. In contrast to the previous foreign workers from European countries, these newly recruited Turkish and Maghreb workers were not employed in the mining industry and heavy industries, but in various industrial sectors in and around the large metropolitan areas and in the Limburg Campine region. Belgian authorities tried to win the international competition with other Western European countries for foreign labor by allowing immigrants' families to join them and settle in Belgium. This caused, mostly during the 1960s, a feminization and an expansion of the foreign population. With the Maghrebian (especially the Moroccan) and Turkish workers, immigration obtained a Muslim component that has had a considerable impact on Belgian society, not because of its size, but rather because of obvious differences in cultural and social values (Martens, Bastenier, & Dassetto, 1990).

The economic crisis caused the Belgian authorities to issue, in 1974, an immigration stop. The presence of the "guest workers" was to become, then, of a permanent character. Throughout the 1970s and 1980s, the economic crisis intensified; older industries disappeared, whereas others were purged or reorganized. New industries emerged, production became strongly automated and in less need of unskilled workers. The traditional industrial infrastructure in the urban regions disintegrated, especially in the Brussels area. This economic crisis resulted in a spectacular increase in unemployment. North African and Turkish (mostly unskilled) workers and their families were hit especially hard by these economic and social developments. Moreover, these immigrants lived mostly in the old urban neighborhoods, which, through real estate speculation and lack of initiative on the part of local authorities, were deteriorating rapidly.

On January 1, 1994, 909,285 foreigners lived in Belgium (Centrum voor Gelijkheid van Kansen en voor Racismebestrijding, 1995b); this is 9.1% of the total Belgian population. Nearly 60% of these foreigners originate from member states in the European Union (EU), mostly from neighboring countries and Italy. Two thirds of the non-European Union foreign population comes from less developed countries (especially Turkey and Morocco), while one third comes from northern industrial countries. Within the total foreign population, the Italians are by far the largest group (24%), followed by Moroccans and Turks who form precisely one quarter of the foreign population.

The proportion of foreigners in the Belgian population has been stabilizing since 1980, because more foreigners acquired Belgian nationality. Until 1991, the annual number of foreigners who became Belgian citizens was about 8,000, with the exception of the year 1985 when, following the Act of June 20, 1984, the number was 63,000. A revision of the 1984 law (dating from June 13, 1991), established the right of second- and third-generation foreigners to acquire Belgian nationality. This caused another increase in the number of naturalizations. The foreign population described here does not include foreigners without a valid residence permit. In 1989, the Minister of Justice estimated this number to be 90,000, or about 10% of the foreign population in Belgium.

Within the foreign population from EU-member countries, there are few youngsters under age 15, which is comparable to the general Belgian population. The group of non-EU foreigners, however, can be characterized as a young group—with many children, with proportionally more youngsters (32%), and fewer elderly people than the native Belgian population.

According to the results of the 1991 census, 42.9% of the Belgian population was active in the labor market (i.e., either employed, self-employed, or unemployed). The proportion varies from 26% of the Moroccan population (this group includes a high number of youngsters) to 48% of foreigners from non-Meditteranean member states of the EU. The precarious situation of foreigners on the labor market is striking. Only 58% of the "active" Turks and 62% of the Moroccans had, at the time of the census, a job. At that time, only 13% of the active Belgian population was unemployed. Among the foreigners from EU-member states, there are significant variations in unemployment. The foreign population from neighboring countries had an unemployment rate (11%) close to the rate for the native Belgian population, whereas one in five foreigners from southern EU-member states was unemployed.

ETHNIC MINORITIES AND
IMMIGRANTS AND CRIMINALITY

Quantitative information on crime and criminal justice is extremely scarce in Belgium. This is rather surprising in view of the fact that Belgium held a primary position in this field more than 100 years ago. The Belgian Quetelet (1796 to 1874) is by rights globally recognized as the founding father of scientific criminography (Van Kerckvoorde, 1993). Data on the criminality of foreigners in general, and on the criminal involvement of ethnic minorities who have lived in Belgium for a long time in particular, are even scarcer.

Police Data

Three police forces operate in Belgium: the gendarmerie, the municipal police forces, and the judicial police. The different police forces are required to send a copy of criminal records involving foreign suspects to the Administration of Foreigner Affairs, which until 1993 came under the Minister of Justice, but now falls under the Minister of the Interior. The Administration of Foreigner Affairs has thus far not published any data from this file. Until now, no single scientific researcher has been allowed to consult this database.

Until November 1, 1983, no integrated data on the crimes recorded by the gendarmerie, the municipal police, and the judicial police (including data on the nationality of offenders) were available. Every police force recorded crime in its own way; the three police forces only rarely published their annual statistics; when published, there were no data on the nationality of offenders. In 1983, it became obligatory for the municipal and judicial police to sent some basic data to the gendarmerie. Thus, since November 1983, some integrated data on the crimes recorded by the three regular police forces are available.

Beginning in 1984, there have been a few publications on data concerning the nationality of police-recorded offenders (Bruggeman, 1992). In 1984, the population of suspects in the computerized "persons' file" totalled

320,057 people, 45.16% of whom were foreigners, not taking into account whether or not they had a known residence in Belgium (Bruggeman, 1992). Based on these police data, combined with the data recorded by the Administration of Foreigner Affairs, Bruggeman calculated the criminal involvement of the different nationalities living in Belgium. He found that 10.20% of Tunisians, 8.68% of Algerians, 5.72% of Moroccans, 3.78% of Turks, and 3.37% of Italians had been registered as suspects. Using a somewhat different method, Bruggeman was also able to estimate the level of official criminal involvement of foreigners with a residence in Belgium: 12.31% for Tunisians, 9.75% for Algerians, 6.69% for Moroccans, 4.31% for Turks, and 3.95% for Italians. The average criminal involvement level for foreigners with a residence in Belgium was 5.39%, for Belgians it was 2.04%.

During the last few years, representatives of the *gendarmerie* and the judicial police have presented selected data concerning the crimes recorded by the three regular police forces over the last year (Generale Staf van de Rijkswacht—Commissariaat-generaal van de Gerechtelijke Politie, 1991/1992/1993). At their annual press conferences (1990, 1991, 1992), data were given on the nationality of apprehended offenders; however, only for infractions of the narcotics law. The number of arrested offenders has risen from 3,917 in 1985 to 6,393 in 1987, remained pretty stable until 1990, and has increased dramatically to 17,442 in 1992. My own calculations (using the figures provided at the press conference) indicate that the percentage of foreigners among the known (drug) offenders was about 46% from 1986 to 1990, and approximately 40% in 1991 and 1992. Among the foreign-born apprehended (drug) offenders, the percentage of foreigners living in Belgium increases from 47% in 1990 to 66% in 1992 (53% in 1991). A striking fact is that in 1990 and 1991 a large majority of the foreign women arrested for violations of narcotics laws did not live in Belgium. According to 1992 data, however, the majority of foreign women arrested do have a residence in Belgium. Among the male offenders arrested for narcotics, the percentage of foreigners fluctuates around 47% between 1986 and 1990. This percentage declines to about 28% for 1991 and 1992. Among the foreign offenders arrested for drugs, the proportion of females fluctuates around 8% between 1986 and 1992.

Minorities and Crime in Antwerp

Police data collection in Belgium has made major advances since 1988 (Buellens, Devroe, & Ponsaers, 1995). The newly founded General Police Support Services publishes annual reports, based on the uniformly registered, centralized, and computerized police statistics. Integrated criminal statistics for 1994 (recorded by the municipal police, the gendarmerie, and the judicial police), containing data on the nationality of apprehended offenders, were recently published for the first time. The annual report of the municipal police of the city of Antwerp, the largest Dutch-speaking city in Belgium, with a high concentration of inhabitants with a foreign nationality, contains detailed information on the nationality of suspects arrested in Antwerp in 1994 (Stad Antwerpen Politie, 1995). For every offense, it is noted whether the offender with a foreign nationality (Moroccan, Turkish, etc.) lives officially in Antwerp, outside of Antwerp but in Belgium, or outside of Belgium.

According to these joint data on the city of Antwerp, in 1994, 43,131 crimes were recorded as having been committed in Antwerp; 21% of these crimes were cleared up by apprehending a total of 10,210 offenders. Of the arrested, 60% were Belgian, 40% had a foreign nationality (41% Moroccan, 7% Turkish, and 52% another foreign nationality). Of the total number of apprehended, 16.6% were Moroccan, 2.7% were Turkish, and 21% had another nationality. Of the total number of suspects arrested in Antwerp in 1994, 13.8% were Moroccans living in Antwerp, 2% were Moroccans living outside of Antwerp, and 0.8% were Moroccans who lived outside of Belgium. Furthermore, 2.3% of the total number of apprehended offenders were Turks living in Antwerp; the remaining Turkish offenders were living elsewhere in Belgium (.2%) or outside Belgium (.2%). Foreign suspects other than Moroccans or Turks lived either in Antwerp (8.7%), outside Antwerp but in Belgium (2.6%), or outside Belgium (9.6%). In Antwerp in 1994, approximately one out of three offenders caught for indecency offenses, violence against persons, and vandalism was of foreign nationality. The proportion of foreigners arrested rises to two out of five for drug offenses (see previous text) and arson, and approaches about 50% for swindle, abuse of trust, fencing, illegal weapon possession, and all sorts of organized theft.

Penitentiary Statistics

Space limitations prevent a discussion of the sad condition of Belgian penitentiary statistics. The Free University of Brussels published a study on the problem of overcrowded prisons (Beyens, Snacken, & Eliaerts, 1993). The distinction between Belgians and foreigners in prison statistics has only been made since 1980. The term *foreigner* refers to all those persons not having Belgian nationality. Among the foreign prison population, foreigners without means of support who were incarcerated because they were found on Belgian territory without means of support and without legal residence, were counted as well. Until 1993, these individuals could be locked up for a maximum period of 30 days at the discretion of the Foreigners Affairs Administration, which arranges the expulsion, or decides on a reconsideration within this period. (In 1993, the custody period was extended to 2 months.) These foreign detainees, then, have not committed a crime but ended up in prison because of an administrative measure.

Table 7.1 shows the distribution of Belgians and foreigners in the end-of-the-year population between 1980 and 1991 (Beyens et al., 1993, p. 60).

The number of Belgians in prison by the end of the year shows a somewhat erratic but still overall declining trend. On the other hand, the share of foreigners in the end-of-the-year population shows, both in relative percentage (%) and absolute numbers, a steady and pronounced increase. Their presence is so overwhelming that the increase in the total prison population may be completely explained by the ever-growing share of foreigners. By the end of the 1980s, Belgian prisons had a one-third occupancy by detainees of a foreign nationality. Everything indicates that this trend will continue during the 90s. The proportion of foreigners in the day population was 37% in February 1992. At that time, Moroccans comprised the largest group in the foreign prison population (37.4%), followed by the group of foreign prisoners of European origin (30.5%)—mostly French and Italians. Prisoners from Eastern European countries made up 10% of the foreign prison population.

The proportion of foreigners imprisoned because of lack of means of support rose from 0.6% in 1975 to 1.6% in 1980, remained stable around 0.8% until 1985, and increased thereafter to 4% in 1991 (Beyens et al., 1993, pp. 38-39).

Table 7.2 outlines the trends in the number of prison admissions between 1982 and 1991 as well as the share of Belgians and foreigners in these admissions.

After a maximum number of admissions in 1984, there was a sharp decline starting in 1986. Among Belgians, the decline of the number of admissions is even stronger than that observed within the end-of-the-year population (Table 7.1). Although in 1982 the share of foreigners (in total prison admissions) was only 25%, the proportion of foreigners has steadily risen to 45% in 1991. There is a marked increase since the early 1990s. This

TABLE 7.1 End-of-the-Year Prison Population, Belgians and Foreigners: 1980 to 1991

| | Belgians | | | Foreigners | | | Total | |
Year	Number	Percentage	Index	Number	Percentage	Index	Number	Index
1980	4,459	78.6	100	1,212	21.4	100	5,671	100
1981	4,718	77.1	105	1,400	22.9	115	6,118	107
1982	4,976	79.0	111	1,323	21.0	109	6,299	111
1983	4,942	76.8	110	1,496	23.2	123	6,438	113
1984	4,751	74.8	106	1,601	25.2	132	6,352	112
1985	4,570	74.0	102	1,602	26.0	132	6,172	108
1986	4,773	72.5	107	1,806	27.5	149	6,579	116
1987	4,441	69.1	99	1,985	30.9	163	6,426	113
1988	4,092	67.3	91	1,991	32.7	164	6,083	107
1989	4,569	68.2	102	2,133	31.8	175	6,702	118
1990	4,109	69.4	92	1,815	30.6	149	5,924	104
1991	3,985	63.1	89	2,326	36.9	191	6,311	111

increase coincides with the growing number of administrative incarcerations of illegal foreigners. This, then, forms the most important explanation for the spectacular rise in the number of prison admissions of foreigners.

It is clear that over the last several years, the number of admissions of illegal aliens has increased (Beyens et al., 1993). In 1991, one half of the prison admissions of foreigners occurred without a crime being committed (i.e., because they were without means of support); in 1982, only 22% of the foreigners admitted were without means of support. It should be noted here that the "average day population" and admission figures concerning foreigners without means of support display huge differences. Their minimal share in the day population is caused by their very short length of stay.

MINORITIES AS VICTIMS OF CRIME

The police and judicial criminal statistics contain no information on the victims of crime. Belgium does not conduct a national victimization survey; however, the country has participated in international victim surveys. Unfortunately, these data do not contain information on the nationality of the victims. Two small-scale victim surveys have been carried out among Moroccan

Table 7.2 Number of Prison Admissions of Belgians and Foreigners: 1982 to 1991

| | Belgians | | | Foreigners | | | Total | |
Year	Number	Percentage	Index	Number	Percentage	Index	Number	Index
1982	15,819	74.5	100	5,407	25.5	100	21,226	100
1983	16,670	73.3	105	6,061	26.7	112	22,731	107
1984	17,142	73.0	108	6,336	27.0	117	23,478	110
1986	14,205	69.3	89	6,288	30.7	116	20,494	96
1988	10,913	61.9	68	6,715	38.1	124	17,628	83
1989	12,056	64.9	76	6,530	35.1	120	18,586	87
1990	10,671	60.3	67	7,033	37.8	130	17,707	83
1991	10,164	54.8	64	8,376	45.2	154	18,545	87

youngsters in Antwerp, and among Turkish inhabitants of two working-class neighborhoods in Ghent.

Victimization Among Moroccan Youngsters in Antwerp

During the first half of 1989, Muhring (1989) conducted a survey on victimization among 120 Moroccan youngsters (59 girls and 61 boys), ranging in age between 15 and 21, and attending Catholic, public, or Flemish community schools. These youngsters lived primarily in Borgerhout, a suburban area of Antwerp with a high concentration of Moroccan migrants. The sample of respondents was not representative of the Moroccan youngsters of these neighborhoods. Of the youngsters, 82 were considered second-generation immigrant (i.e., they had lived in Belgium since their birth or before the age of 2); the others were considered first-generation immigrants. All respondents were unmarried, lived with their parents, and had no children themselves. Questions were asked about victimization over the last 15 months. Almost four out of five Moroccan youngsters had, during the last 15 months, been the victim of one or more of the events mentioned on the survey form. The boys reported more victimization than the girls. Victimization with a racist motive (mainly racist remarks) occurred frequently. Although the survey indicates that Moroccan youth are frequently victimized, without comparable figures about the victimization of native Belgian youth it is impossible to draw any conclusions about whether Moroccan youth have a higher risk of victimization.

Victimization of Turkish Inhabitants in Ghent

The Criminology Research Group of the University of Ghent has conducted surveys measuring feelings of insecurity, victimizations during the past year and before, and relationships with the police (Hebberecht, Hofman, Philippeth, & Colle, 1992) in four different neighborhoods, as well as among two groups of Turks in Ghent. The sample was representative for the Turkish population of two working-class neighborhoods in Ghent (St-Macharius $(n = 50)$ and Ham $(n = 70)$. Both multiethnic neighborhoods are located in the 19th-century belt around the center of Ghent. For St-Macharius, the data from the Turkish respondents were compared with those from the native Belgian respondents $(n = 153$; Hebberecht, 1993).

The native Belgian group differed from the two Turkish samples with respect to gender, age, civil status, living arrangement, education level, and employment, notwithstanding the fact they live in the same type of working-class neighborhood. To measure victimization, a list of 24 facts and events (property, violent and indecency crimes and threats) was submitted to the respondents. About one out of three Turkish respondents from the two working-class neighborhoods reported having been victimized at least once during 1989. Almost one out of two native-born respondents, however, also reported one or more victimizations. The surveys suggest some additional differences in victimization between native Belgians and Turkish respondents, but without a clear and consistent pattern.

RESEARCH AND THEORY ON THE
CRIMINAL INVOLVEMENT OF MINORITIES

The rather scant scientific attention Belgian criminologists have been paying to ethnic minorities and crime contrasts sharply with the numerous social-scientific studies on the position of ethnic minorities that have been conducted in Belgium (Ramakers & Vandevelde, 1992). Although much public opinion and many criminal justice officials have associated ethnic minorities, ever since their arrival in Belgium, with insecurity and criminality, only a few criminologists focused on this issue before the late 1980s. It was only when the electoral success of the extreme right-wing Flemish party, Vlaams Blok ("the Flemish Block"), made the "migrant question" a political problem for traditional Belgian political parties that a small number of criminological research projects were undertaken, financed by the Royal Commissionership for Migrants Policy, the Ministry of Scientific Policy, the Ministry of the Interior, and the French Community Authorities.

The Criminal Involvement of Ethnic Minorities

Until the end of the 1980s, criminologists interested in ethnic minorities were mainly concerned with the extent, the specificity, and the etiology of the criminal involvement of minorities. Most criminologists relied on judicial statistics. Data from a self-report study and police records have been used as research material by others. Until the 1970s, researchers assumed that these official crime data gave a reliable reflection of the extent and the nature of crime committed by ethnic minorities. Thereafter, critical reflection on these statistical data emerged, and the constructed and selective nature of these data was increasingly stressed. The question whether ethnic minorities committed more crime than Belgians often was central to these researchers.

An early study examined criminality among Italian youth aged between 16 and 25 living in an area with a concentration of Italian migrants, and working in the Walloon mining area. Liben (1963) studied all prosecutors' files from the judicial district of Liège for 1956 and 1957 related to crimes committed by Italian youngsters between 16 and 25. One out of five of the youngsters studied had been in contact with Belgian penal justice before 1956. According to Liben, Italian youngsters did not commit more crime than their Belgian contemporaries. Most interpersonal violence for the Italian youth involved another Italian.

In a document on delinquency by foreigners, written for a conference on criminality among European migrants and organized by the Council of Europe, Debuyst (1970) developed a first critique of the use of conviction rates for analyzing delinquency by foreigners. According to Debuyst, delinquency rates of native born and migrants are hardly comparable when based on conviction data. The migrant population counts more men and youngsters who, as research has shown, commit more crimes. Moreover, the police react much more rapidly against foreigners, courts pronounce harsher punishment, and there exist many administrative legal rules that, by definition, only can be violated by foreigners. Based on some European research findings, Debuyst argued that the crime rate of migrants was slightly lower than that of native-born Belgians. The crime pattern of immigrants shows more public order infractions and traffic offenses; aggravated property crimes (robbery) are also more often committed by migrants, although this type of offense remains rather exceptional.

Junger-Tas (1976) conducted research concerning hidden and unrecorded juvenile delinquency by using a self-report survey on a representative sample of youngsters aged between 15 and 18 from a small municipality in the Brussels metropolitan area. Of the town's population, 31% was considered foreign. Junger-Tas conducted 399 interviews—35% involved young foreigners (17.6% southern Europeans and 17.2% North Africans). Most southern European youngsters had been settled in Belgium for a longer period than most of the North African juveniles. Her analysis showed that foreign juveniles committed fewer offenses and manifested less serious and less frequent delinquent behavior. This result was even more marked for North Africans when compared to southern European youngsters: Youths from southern European origins committed more crimes than North African youngsters. Foreign juveniles committed fewer than the average property offenses, but they were involved in more aggressive offenses than Belgians.

In a special issue of the progressive Brussels periodical *La Revue Nouvelle,* Jerkovic (1980) discusses the quantity and nature of criminality committed by migrants. In a polemical and critical book concerning migrants and racism in Belgian politics, the link between migrants and increasing criminality is interpreted as a myth sustained and activated by the media and conservative political parties (Gijsels, Hobin, & Boukhriss, 1988). Overrepresentation of migrants in police crime statistics is put into perspective by referring to the larger number of men and juveniles in the migrant community, the greater willingness to report foreign offenders, the willingness of police to investigate crimes committed by foreign offenders, the greater visibility of migrants and the numerous and severe police controls of migrants, and the special regulations and legislation that exist for foreigners only.

Poulet (1990a, 1990b) examined files from the Juvenile Prosecutor's Office of the Walloon judicial district of Charleroi for 1986. Almost 19% of the population in this judicial district consisted of foreigners, especially Italians and, to a lesser degree, North Africans and Turks. This region had been hard hit by economic recession; unemployment enhanced the social vulnerability of large parts of the population, who remained firmly rooted in traditional working-class culture. The nationality of the father was used as the criterion to divide the minors. For Belgian and Italian juveniles, a stratified random sample was drawn. All files of North African and Turkish minors were analyzed. (Poulet acknowledged that official delinquency is the product of various selectional mechanisms.) She analyzed the files of 665 minors who were involved in 1,122 offenses in 1986, and examined also their official criminal career. Her analysis concluded that the pattern of delinquent involvement of migrant youth is not fundamentally different from that of native-born Belgian youth. Police, however, recorded more crimes committed by North African youngsters than by Italian or Turkish youngsters. Within the North African and Italian population arrested by the police, Poulet found twice as many girls than within the Turkish group of young suspects. Also, she found no ethnic differences with regard to likelihood of arrest for property offenses. Turkish and North African youngsters were less likely to be arrested for crimes against the person compared to Belgian youngsters. Italian youth, however, were more often caught for aggressive crimes than their Belgian counterparts.

Combining the official data employed by Poulet (1990a) with in-depth interviews with some of the youth, Bastenier (1990) focused on juvenile migrant groups. Of the recorded delinquent incidents, especially theft (70%) and drug-related incidents (83%), 65% were committed by youngsters acting in a group. Almost half (48%) of these groups consisted of only two offenders; in 29% of the cases, there were three offenders. Groups with more than seven offenders were exceptional. Of the delinquent boys, 84% were involved in group offending; for girls, the number was 67%. What is interesting about this is that over half (57%) of the incidents committed by a group were committed by a group with members of different nationalities. Belgian youngsters were more likely to be involved in single nationality, homogeneous groups (38%), followed by North African youngsters (23%), Italians (15%), and Turks (12%). Bastenier stresses that it is not the nationality of the youngsters, but rather their life environment that determines the composition of these delinquent groups; the multiethnic constellation of a neighborhood is reflected in the multiethnic composition of delinquent groups originating in those neighborhoods. Bastenier points at the temporary and loosely organized nature of most of these youth groups: 60% to 80% of the group-delinquent incidents were carried out by groups that had been operating only for a short time.

The Royal Commissionership for Migrants Policy (Koninklijk Commissariaat voor het Migrantenbeleid, 1990), in one of its reports, analyzed delinquency patterns of migrant populations. This report focused extensively on methodological problems concerning the interpretation of data on migrants in police records, judicial files, and penitentiary statistics.

The Etiology of Criminal Involvement
of Ethnic Minorities

Belgian criminologists are not particularly original in their explanations
of similarities and differences in criminal involvement of ethnic minorities.
They focus either on economic and social conditions, cultural differences,
or discrimination.

Economic and Social Conditions

Some criminologists point to the economic and social conditions of
ethnic minorities as the explanation for the crimes they commit; Belgians in
the same economic and social situation would have a level of criminal
involvement comparable to that of the immigrants. An example is Jerkovic
(1980), who argues that the economic and social position of migrants
constructs the base for their criminality. Because of educational deprivation,
living conditions in deteriorating urban areas, family conflicts, and their
working-class existence, migrants end up getting involved in crime. For the
Royal Commissionership for Migrants Policy (Koninklijk Commissariaat
voor het Migrantenbeleid, 1990), the factors that can lead young foreigners
to crime are related to the problems of socialization, which youngsters in
general are experiencing in a perpetually changing socioeconomic environment.

Cultural Differences

Liben (1963) explained the criminal involvement of Italian juveniles by
making reference to cultural differences. Cultural conflicts that exist among
most Italian youngsters create a sense of unease and result in criminal
behavior, behavior through which they try to free themselves from this
feeling. Adaptational problems experienced by second-generation migrants
are, according to Gijsels et al. (1988), at the base of their criminal behavior.
These difficulties in adaptation are caused by the conflict between their
culture transmitted to them by a harsh patriarchal upbringing, and the values
and traditions of Western society.

In her research concerning hidden and unrecorded juvenile delinquency,
Junger-Tas (1976) explained the differences between Belgian and foreign
juveniles, and the differences between southern European and North African

juveniles in Brussels, by taking into account the length of time the foreign juveniles had been in Belgium and their degree of assimilation into Belgian cultural patterns. She determined that a longer stay in Belgium resulted in a greater degree of assimilation as well as criminal behavior less distinctive from native-born Belgian criminality. Therefore, the delinquency of southern European juveniles approaches that of the Belgian juveniles because they are better integrated into Belgian society and less isolated than the North African juveniles.

According to the Royal Commissionership for Migrants Policy (Koninklijk Commissariaat voor het Migrantenbeleid, 1990), the more serious and profound cultural identity crisis young foreigners often experience may push the youth toward the delinquent path. Most of the delinquent offenses committed by (young) foreigners are to be considered manifestations of a desire to participate and to integrate in society, rather than as expressions of a cultural dissidence against the dominant cultural values in the host society. In his analysis of juvenile migrant gangs, Bastenier (1990) argued that many of the theft incidents were carried out in groups because of the social meaning (migrant) youngsters are attaching to this offense. Theft is, paradoxically, the expression of a desire of these youngsters to socialization and social integration. Drug-related crime is also viewed by Bastenier as reflecting a desire for social integration by (migrant) youngsters who are socially, economically, and culturally marginalized. On the other hand, offenses against persons, public disturbances, and acts of vandalism are expressions of aggressive reactions toward institutionalized forms of being social.

Discrimination

Junger-Tas (1976) claimed that the lower crime rates of southern European youngsters, but especially of North African youngsters, are explained not only by a lesser degree of integration, but also by the fear of extradition, kept alive by numerous and effective police controls. In another view, Debuyst (1970) stated that the negative attitude of many native-born Belgians toward migrants is one of the factors explaining the migrants' specific crime pattern. Likewise, the Royal Commissionership for Migrants Policy (Koninklijk Commissariaat voor het Migrantenbeleid, 1990) argues that discriminatory reactions of the population and of (police and penal) public and private institutions, can also enhance delinquency.

THE CRIMINAL JUSTICE SYSTEM
AND ETHNIC MINORITIES

The Police

We already referred to Junger-Tas's (1976) self-report study, in which she also explored the relation between police practices and the ethnic origin of the interviewed youngsters. Comparing the recorded and the nonrecorded offenses by nationality of offender, Junger-Tas found that North African youngsters were greatly overrepresented among those whose offenses were formally recorded by the police. She explained this by the multiple police patrols and the repeated police ID checks in migrant neighborhoods. Foreign youngsters also spend a great deal of their leisure time on the street, mainly because of cramped housing. She added to this that, with increased patrol, the police expect and observe more delinquent behavior. She further assumes that the aggressive delinquency of North African youngsters, because of its character, attracts more attention, and thus will be discovered sooner.

Using the results of a participant observation study of patrolling municipal police officers in the Brussels metropolitan area, financed by the Ministry of Interior, De Valkeneer (1987) found that men, North Africans, and people aged 18 to 45 years old were most likely to be stopped and interviewed (i.e., in an ID check) by the police. North Africans were twice as likely to be asked for identification than would be expected on the basis of their presence in the local population. The police also focused patrols in the neglected areas with a high concentration of North Africans.

Casman, Gailly, Gavray, and Pasleau (1992) explored the social images (i.e., representations) of migrants held by municipal police officers. They used participant observation as well as interviews with municipal police officers in Liège and the Brussels metropolitan area, as well as surveys conducted among Walloon police commissioners. This study showed the extent to which police officers associate young migrants with delinquency. Many police officers assumed that migrants engage in crime more than Belgians, and that they are taking advantage of the Belgian social security system. In their view, because of the laxity of the public prosecutor, the rather lenient decisions by judges, and the ambiguous statements of politicians, foreigners cause even more problems for society. Many policemen label the attitude of young migrants as self-assured and arrogant; immensely frustrated by this attitude, the police tend to approach young migrants with the attitude that they are untrustworthy. Participant observation showed that young migrants were the target of identity checks. The arbitrary character of many checks, combined with the disrespectful attitude of many police officers, escalated tense situations, which sometimes grew into open conflicts and riots between migrants and police. The researchers found among many police officers a certain amount of verbal racism—in a number of cases even resulting in racist violence. Although this racism was condemned by a number of colleagues, this seldom led to sanctions. Many police officers made a distinction between "good" and "bad" foreigners, between foreigners from the European Union and other foreigners. Within this second category they further differentiated among Asians, Turks, blacks, and Moroccans. Asians, in the eyes of many police officers, caused fewer problems. They were polite and hard working. Turks also did not cause many problems for the police because they regulate and solve their problems themselves, or so it was thought. Blacks were arrogant and specialize in falsifying documents. The lowest step in the hierarchy consisted of Moroccans who were labeled as liars and thieves. In view of these negative images of migrants, it is not surprising that many police officers are also advocates of tougher ways of dealing with migrants.

Between 1989 and 1992, a few serious incidents and riots took place between the police and youngsters from ethnic minorities (mainly of Moroccan origin) in the Brussels and Antwerp metropolitan areas. Since then, such incidents have occurred sporadically in different Belgian cities on a modest scale and with less media attention. For Hebberecht (1992), these riots and incidents form visible crystallization points of the troubled relationship that developed during the last 20 years between the police and ethnic minorities. Economic, social, and political marginalization processes within certain groups of youngsters from ethnic minorities have led to a subculture of social exclusion, desperation, and resistance that drives the least strong to drug addiction, and makes the skillful and able ones join organized crime and develop a criminal career. It brings others, who cannot manage to establish the right contacts with the criminal milieu, to street prostitution or acts of aggressive street criminality. It is this limited group of problematic youngsters whom police officers encounter in their daily police work; many policemen, however, are inclined to generalize their experiences to the whole young population of foreign origin.

Bastenier (1991) argues that the discriminatory intervention of the police plays a pernicious role in the ethnicalization of social relations in the large cities. Although the problems of education, housing, and employment, and the discrimination and racism that confront ethnic minority juveniles, do constitute the breeding ground of urban violence, these elements do not explain the violence and rioting of North African juveniles in Belgian and European metropolitan areas. Along with social class and gender, the ethnic group increasingly determines the social stratification. For some North African juveniles, belonging to an ethnic group becomes a factor in regrouping themselves with regard to the representatives of the social order. It becomes an element of the construction of their identity that cannot be separated from their particular social position of complete cultural integration but of economic and political exclusion. The violent protests of particular North African juveniles is a revolt of integrated juveniles who are being excluded. The police play a key role in these situations.

The Courts

The judicial reaction to crimes committed by foreigners has been the object of little research. In one of the reports of the Royal Commissionership for Migrants Policy (Koninklijk Commissariaat voor het Migrantenbeleid, 1990), the position of juvenile migrants in juvenile protection is discussed. Juvenile migrants are underrepresented in the voluntary social juvenile protection services, although nonvoluntary judicial juvenile protection shows an overrepresentation of migrant youths. Reasons mentioned include the lesser extent of attention to problem youngsters from ethnic minority families, migrant unfamiliarity with the system, and the selective intervention of the police and the juvenile court; also, the juvenile court refers juvenile migrants to public institutions more quickly.

It is notable that in Poulet's (1990b) study, which found that cases with youngsters of Italian and Turkish origin were more often dropped without consequence, cases of Belgian and North African youngsters were more likely to be referred to the juvenile court.

An interesting different approach to the issue of minorities and criminal justice is represented by the recent study of Brion, Verheyen, and Spiessens (1994), who estimated the social costs of a judicial conviction accompanying the execution of measures of extradition and the acquisition of a working permit. Based on interviews with migrants who had been confronted with the criminal justice system and with criminal justice officials, the concept of "inequality" was conceptualized and operationalized according to the theory of "differential social costs." These costs constitute all the negative social, economic, and political consequences that directly or indirectly result from the intervention by the criminal justice system. They concluded that interventions of the criminal justice system have different social costs for certain groups of foreigners; second-generation migrants experience most sharply the negative effects of primary and secondary criminalization.

In What Direction Should Belgian `Criminological Theory Go?

Belgian criminological research on crime, criminal justice, and ethnic minorities is largely descriptive, mostly empiricist, poor at generalizing, and mainly exploratory. Belgian criminologists who deal with this subject are only marginally involved in theory building; the theoretical foundation of their empirical studies is typically weak. In research, concepts and assumptions are uncritically adopted from the dominant political-ideological discourse; the existence of "ethnic minorities" is taken for granted. It is assumed that ethnicity is the most important social dividing line, that ethnic or cultural differences are "natural." The "minorization paradigm" worked out by the Dutch cultural anthropologist Jan Rath (1991) might provide a fruitful approach to studying criminal behaviors by members of ethnic minorities, their victimizations, and feelings of insecurity, and for research on police and judicial reaction toward ethnic minorities. According to the minorization paradigm, the position of migrants, in politics and in other social relations, is not the product of a process of "integration," but of a process of distribution of scarce resources. Although cultural factors may have some influence on the position of migrants, this is not the central determinant. Of much greater importance is the social significance attributed to real and imagined characteristics of these migrants by the state and other institutions.

DEBATE AND POLICY ISSUES

When, in the 1960s, Belgian authorities and industry were feverishly recruiting foreign Maghrebian and Turkish workers in an era of economic boom with a tight labor market, the Belgian population remained rather indifferent. The North African and Turkish immigrants were considered to be guest workers who happened to be living in Belgium for economic purposes. During that period, the Belgian government tried to make the country as attractive as possible to immigrants by allowing, although restrictedly, families of immigrants to join and to settle. This policy assumed that these families would stay for an extended period, or even permanently, which would require a policy of integration. Nevertheless, until the mid-1980s, Belgian authorities failed to develop and implement such policy in a coherent way. Furthermore, the police and judicial institutions acted in a discriminatory manner, sometimes even openly racist toward foreigners, and immigrants especially (Hebberecht, 1992).

After immigration was halted by the Belgian government in 1974, the authorities and large portions of the population were confronted with a "migrants problem," which, at that time, had not only a socioeconomic dimension but also a sociocultural component. Following the increase of racism among the Belgian population, the government issued the 1981 Act that penalized specific acts inspired by racism or xenophobia.

With the municipal elections of 1988, the Flemish Block (Vlaams Blok), an extreme right-wing political party, realized an electoral breakthrough. This electoral success was attributed primarily to the Block's anti-migrant program. The general atmosphere of increasing racism and the political success of extreme right-wing programs caused both the federal and regional governments to develop a "migrants' policy." In 1989, a Royal Commissioner for Migrants Policy was appointed for a period of 4 years. This Commissioner has only an advisory role, with only limited authority to take initiatives. The initiatives and proposals of the Royal Commissioner with regard to migrant integration were based on the concept of "insertion," a concept somewhere between "assimilation" and "segregation" (Van Loock & Deslé, 1994). Starting from the concept of insertion, the Royal Commissionership for Migrants Policy (Koninklijk Commissariaat voor het Migrantenbeleid, 1993) made several proposals and took numerous initiatives in housing, employment, education, and youth affairs. The proposed measures on police services and migrants, and on the judicial handling of migrant cases have been less developed (Hebberecht, 1991).

In the period between 1989 and 1991, the Royal Commissionership determined, to a large extent, the federal, regional, and local policy toward migrants. Riots between migrant youths and the police in Brussels and Antwerp, in 1991, and the extended electoral breakthrough of extreme right-wing political parties with the federal elections of November 1991, however, have caused the authorities to de-emphasize measures in support of migrant groups. Thus, migrant policy became part of an antipoverty policy, which pushed the whole of the migrant population under the "poverty" label, with stigmatizing effects.

In 1993, the Royal Commissionership was succeeded by the newly established Center for Equal Opportunities and Antiracism (Centrum voor Gelijkheid van Kansen en voor Racismebestrijding, 1995). Since 1993, the Center has been pursuing sociocultural work intended, among other things, to create a change of attitude and mentality within the police with regard to migrants. The gendarmerie and some of the municipal police services have been trying to improve relations with ethnic minorities. The employment of ethnic minorities by the police is, however, rather scant and poorly supervised. The gendarmerie, for example, employs only 38 foreign-born (out of a total of 16,000) employees. Only 16 of the 589 municipal police forces employ minorities, mostly males (Centrum voor Gelijkheid van Kansen en voor Racismebestrijding, 1996b).

Beginning in 1992, the Ministry of the Interior has been involved in several local projects to reduce the feelings of insecurity and malaise caused by activities of groups of migrant youth among the native Belgian population. Growing racism among the population and the conclusion that the 1981 Act (which penalized acts inspired by racism and xenophobia) had been applied only occasionally (Dejemeppes, 1996), resulted in a major modification of this law in 1994. Among other things, the penalty was raised significantly. The Center for Equal Opportunities and Antiracism established local complaint departments (Centrum voor Gelijkheid van Kansen en voor Racismebestrijding, 1996a).

Currently, an intense social and political debate is raging on a recent repressive law proposal concerning refugees, written by the Minister of the Interior under extreme right-wing political pressure. During the last few years, government policy toward ethnic minorities has been subordinated to a security policy toward foreigners and people of foreign origin. Now there is less and less talk of a policy of integration that would recognize the right of ethnic minorities to full social, economic, and political participation in Belgian society. Sadly, extreme right-wing political pressure is, to a large extent, determining today's political agenda concerning the Belgian policy toward ethnic minorities.

REFERENCES

Bastenier, A. (1990). Les bandes de jeunes d'origine étrangère. Importance et signification de la délinquence en groupe [Juvenile groups of foreign origin. The importance and meaning of group delinquency]. In A. Bastenier & F. Dasetto (Eds.), *Immigrations et nouveaux pluralismes. Une confrontation des sociétés* [Immigration and new pluralism. A confrontation of societies] (pp. 237-271). Brussels: De Boeck-Wesmael.

Bastenier, A. (1991). Violence urbaine des minorités ethniques [Urban violence and ethnic minorities]. *La Revue Nouvelle, 7/8,* 3-12.

Beyens, K., Snacken, S., & Eliaerts, C. (1993). *Barstende muren. Overbevolkte gevangenissen: Omvang, oorzaken, en mogelijke oplossingen* [Cracking walls. Overcrowded prisons: extent, causes, and possible solutions]. Antwerpen: Kluwer.

Brion, F., Verheyen, L., & Spiessens, G. (1994). *L'inégalité pénale. Immigration, criminalité, et système d'administration de la justice pénale* [Penal inequality. Immigration, crime, and penal administration system]. Brussels: Belgian Information and Documentation Service (INBEL).

Bruggeman, W. (1992). *Naar een vernieuwde statistiek voor de reguliere politiediensten in België* [Toward a renewed statistic for the regular police services in Belgium]. Brussels: Politeia.

Bryssinck, R., Boudart, M., & Boudart, M. (Eds.). (1990). *Modern Belgium.* Brussels: Modern Belgium Association.

Buellens, M., Devroe, E., & Ponsaers, P. (1995). *Statistiek van de geregistreerde criminaliteit: De stap naar de praktijk* [Statistic of recorded crimes: Moving into practice]. Diegem: Kluwer.

Casman, M.-T., Gailly, P., Gavray, C., & Pasleau, J. P. (1992). *Police et immigrés: Images mutuelles, problèmes, et solutions* [Police and immigrants: Mutual representations, problems, and solutions]. Brugge: Vanden Broele.

Centrum voor Gelijkheid van Kansen en voor Racismebestrijding [Center for Equal Opportunity and Antiracism Policy]. (1996a). *Krijgen allochtonen een kans bij de Belgische politiediensten?* [Do foreigners get a fair chance within Belgian police forces?]. Brussels: Nationale Informatie Dienst.

Centrum voor Gelijkheid van Kansen en voor Racismebestrijding [Center for Equal Opportunity and Antiracism Policy]. (1996b). *Op-stap naar gelijkwaardigheid. Jaarverslag 1995* [Steps to equality. Year report 1995]. Brussels: Nationale Informatie Dienst.

Debuyst, C. (1970). Notes sur la délinquance des étrangers [Notes on foreigners' delinquency]. *Annales de Droit, 4,* 557-568.

Dejemeppes, B. (1996). De bestraffing van racistische daden. Een stand van zaken anno 1996 [Punishing racist actions. The situation in 1996]. *Panopticon, 17,* 313-346.

De Valkeneer, C. (1987). *Missions des policiers patrouilleurs et des agents de quartiers. Volume I et II* [Tasks of police patrols and neighborhood police officers. Volumes I and II]. Louvain-la-Neuve, Belgium: Université Catholique de Louvain.

Generale Staf van de Rijkswacht—Commissariaat-generaal van de Gerechtelijke Politie [General staff of the gendarmerie—Commissionership-general of the judicial police]. (1991/1992/1993). *Statistieken 1990* [Statistical data 1990, 1992, 1993]. Brussels, Belgium: Author.

Gijsels, H., Hobin, V., & Boukhriss, H. (1988). *De barbaren. Migranten en racisme in de Belgische politiek.* [The barbarians. Migrants and racism in Belgian politics]. Berchem, Belgium: Éducation Prolétarienne/Proletarische Opvoeding (EPO).

Grimmeau, J.-P. (1992). Vagues d'immigration et localisation des étrangers en Belgique [Immigration and residence of foreigners in Belgium]. In A. Morelli (Ed.), *Histoire des étrangers et de l'immigration en Belgique de la préhistoire à nos jours* [History of foreigners and immigration in Belgium from prehistoric until contemporary times] (pp. 105-118). Brussels: Editions Vie Ouvrière.

Hebberecht, P. (1991). Migranten en criminaliteit. Kanttekeningen bij de rapporten van het Koninklijk Commissariaat voor het Migrantenbeleid [Migrants and crime. Remarks with the Royal Commissionership's final report]. *Panopticon, 12,* 213-220.

Hebberecht, P. (1992). *De rijkswacht en de migranten* [Gendarmerie and migrants]. Brussels: Koninklijke Rijkswachtschool.

Hebberecht, P. (with Caudron, B., Colle, P., Deduytsche, K., Hofman, H., Philippeth, K., Scheerlinck, A., & Verbeke, T.). (1993). *Eindrapport betreffende het onderzoek naar een globaal veiligheidsbeleid in stedelijke gemeenten met een grote concentratie aan migranten. Onderzoek verricht in opdracht van het Koninklijk Commissariaat voor het Migrantenbeleid* [Final report concerning the study on an integral security policy in urban cities with a high concentration of migrants. Research carried out by order of the Royal Commissionership for Migrants Policy]. Ghent: Universiteit Gent, Onderzoeksgroep Criminologie.

Hebberecht, P., Hofman, H., Philippeth. K., & Colle, P. (with Caudron, B., De Decker, P., & Deduytsche, K.). (1992). *Buurt en criminaliteit. Een buurtgericht onderzoek naar criminaliteit, onveiligheid, en preventie* [Neighborhood and crime. A neighborhood study on crime, insecurity, and prevention]. Brugge: Vanden Broele.

Jerkovic, J. (1980). Criminalité: L'ère du soupçon [Crime: The suspicion era). *La Revue Nouvelle, 9,* 164-171.

Junger-Tas, J. (1976). *Verborgen jeugddelinkwentie en gerechtelijke selektie. Een onderzoek in een stadsmilieu* [Hidden juvenile delinquency and judicial selectivity. An urban study]. Brussels: Studiecentrum voor Jeugdcriminaliteit.

Koninklijk Commissariaat voor het Migrantenbeleid [Royal Commissionership for Migrant Policy]. (1990). *Voor een harmonische samenleving. Deel III: Feiten en toelichting van de voorstellen* [For a harmonic society. Part III: Facts and explanations for the proposals]. Brussels: INBEL.

Koninklijk Commissariaat voor het Migrantenbeleid [Royal Commissionership for Migrant Policy]. (1993). *Tekenen voor Gelijkwaardigheid. Eindrapport van het Koninklijk Commissariaat voor het Migrantenbeleid* [Supporting equality. The Royal Commissioners's final report]. Brussels: INBEL.

Liben, G. (1963). Un reflet de la criminalité italienne dans la région de Liège [A reflection of Italian crime in the Liège region]. *Revue de Droit Pénal et de Criminologie, 44,* 205-246.

Martens, A., Bastenier, A., & Dassetto, F. (1990). Immigration and foreign minorities. In R. Bruyssinck, M. Boudart & M. Boudart (Eds.), *Modern Belgium association* (pp. 344-352.) Brussels: Modern Belgium Association.

Muhring, E. (1989). *Viktimisering van adolescente Marokkanen in Antwerpen* [Victimization of adolescent Moroccans in Antwerp]. Unpublished doctoral dissertation, University of Ghent.

Poulet, I. (1990a). *La délinquence enregistrée des jeunes d'origine immigrée* [Recorded delinquency of juveniles of foreign origin]. Brussels: Bruylant.

Poulet, I. (1990b). La délinquence officielle des jeunes d'origine immigrée dans l'arrondissement judiciaire de Charleroi [Officially recorded delinquency of migrant juveniles in the judicial district of Charleroi]. In A. Bastenier & F. Dasette (Eds.), *Immigrations et nouveaux pluralismes. Une confrontation des sociétés* [Immigration and new pluralism. A confrontation of societies] (pp. 209-235). Brussels: De Boeck-Wesmael.

Ramakers, J., & Vandevelde, V. (1992). De caleidoscoop van het migrantenonderzoek: Een stand van zaken [The caleidoscope of research on ethnic minorities: A state of affairs]. *Steunpunt migranten cahiers, 2.* Leuven, Belgium: Hoger Instituut van de Arbeid.

Rath, J. (1991). *Minorisering: De sociale constructie van etnische minderheden* [Minorization: The social construction of ethnic minorities.]. Amsterdam: Socialistische Uitgeverij Amsterdam (SUA).

Stad Antwerpen Politie [City of Antwerp Police]. (1995). *Jaarrapport 1994* [Year report 1994]. Antwerp: Antwerp Police Department.

Van Kerckvoorde, J. (1993). *Strafrechtsbedeling in België* (Criminal justice in Belgium). Deurne, Belgium: Kluwer.

Van Loock, L., & Deslé, E. (1994). Wetenschap en politiek: Het Vlaams-Belgisch migranten-
    beleid sinds het Witboek [Science and politics: Flemish migrants policy after the White
    Paper]. *Panopticon, 15,* 485-494.

8

MINORITIES, CRIME, AND CRIMINAL JUSTICE IN SPAIN

Rosemary Barberet
Elisa García-España

INTRODUCTION

Spain (population 39,433,942) is one of the 15 countries of the European Union and is located on the Iberian Peninsula in southern Europe. During the 20th century, Spain has gone from a republic to an authoritarian regime to its present status of a democracy, with a constitution dating from 1978. Spain is divided into 17 autonomous regions and 50 provinces; the largest cities are Madrid and Barcelona. The Spanish criminal justice system is marked by a mixture of tradition and innovation. The Spanish police system struggles to maintain coordination over two national traditional police forces, the National Police and the Civil Guard, and newly developed regional and local police corps. Criminal procedure reflects a mixed inquisitorial and accusatorial system. The Spanish prison system incorporates state-of-the-art institutions with antiquated provincial ones, all run under the challenges posed by one of the most progressive prison laws in Europe. The juvenile justice system has been reformed only recently to allow for due process elements. As is the case with other Spanish institutions, the Spanish criminal justice system is still democratizing and represents a political compromise between opposing groups and, increasingly, European mandates.

Numerous civilizations—the Iberians, Phoenicians, Greeks, Romans, Goths, Arabs, Jews, and Christians—have passed through Spain throughout its history and left their cultural mark. Although Spain has had a multicultural past, at present it is a relatively homogeneous country with regard to race and ethnicity, although regionalism has given Spain a new heterogeneity. In recent years, however, the phrase *minoría étnica* (ethnic minority)[1] has been used as a catch-all concept to encompass two recent phenomena in Spain: the historically constant case of Spanish gypsies, and the relatively new arrival of a group termed *los inmigrantes,* which commonly refers to immigrants from the Maghreb and South America. Each group is estimated at 700,000, and thus each constitutes about 2% of the Spanish population. Not surprisingly, both of these groups have been plagued with criminal stereotyping, and both profess to being disproportionately victims of crime, discrimination, and unfair treatment by the authorities.

SPANISH GYPSIES

A Brief History of Gypsies in Spain

Gypsies probably entered Spain in 1415. They are believed to be descendants of Egyptians, with their origins in northern India. Some evidence points to this: their language, Romany,[2] was found by the German linguist Grellman in 1782 to be the language spoken on the right bank of the Zind river in northern India (San Román, 1976, p. 17).

Four periods of relations between the gypsy minority and payo[3] majority can be identified in Spanish history. During the first "idyllic" period, gypsies entered Spain as religious pilgrims and were largely welcome; during the second period (1499 to 1633), they were seen as conflictive nomads and decrees were issued against them by the crown aiming to disperse, expulse, or sedentarize them (Sánchez Ortega, 1986, p. 19).

It was at this time that gypsies started to settle in neighborhoods at the outskirts of cities and towns; these neighborhoods came to be called *gitanerías* (San Román, 1976, pp. 31-32) and were the first instances of residential segregation. It was also during this period that criminal labels were applied to gypsies as a group. At one point, gypsies became so associated with deceitful horse selling that they were prohibited from selling or owning horses, or from owning firearms. Finally, they were even forbidden to engage in any occupation other than agriculture. Errant gypsies became so associated with the criminal underworld that any nonsedentary gypsy was considered a bandit and an outlaw (San Román, 1976, pp. 32-38).

The third period (1633 to 1783), was one of legal integration and refers to efforts by the enlightened King Carlos III to treat gypsies the same as all other subjects, while still "trying desperately to eliminate their nomadism and covert them into productive subjects" (Sánchez Ortega, 1986, p. 19).

The fourth period covers 1783 to the present, when gypsies settled definitively in Spain and acquired sociocultural traits that would come to identify them as Spanish gypsies. From 1860 onwards, no specific legislation existed that was directed at gypsies. A series of legal measures, however, frequently were used against gypsies, such as the *Ley de Vagos y Maleantes* (Vagrancy Law) and the later *Ley de Peligrosidad Social* (Social Dangerousness Law). Both laws allowed measures to be enacted against offenders without due process, for the mere reason that the offender had no means of making a living and was thus a potential criminal (San Román, 1976, pp. 38-42).

During the dictatorship of General Franco, the Guardia Civil (Civil Guard, Spain's militarized police force) in 1943 enacted an order that specifically included the persecution of gypsies, mandating officers to watch them carefully; to review the veracity of their identification and stated domiciles; to observe their dress; to investigate their means of subsistence to gain an idea of their movements and occupations; to note their comings and goings to prevent horse or other thievery; and to arrest gypsy horse traders who did not carry the appropriate license (Martínez-Pereda Rodríguez, 1993, pp. 535-536). It was not until after Franco's death, during the transition to democracy, that the 1978 Constitution prohibited racial and ethnic discrimination. In that same year, gypsy leader and now European Parliament Member Juan de Dios Ramírez Heredia led an effective campaign to strike this mandate from the 1943 order.

Current social policy in Spain toward gypsies is clearly integrationist. Within the Ministry of Social Affairs, there is currently a special Gypsy Development Plan that funds and supports outreach programs that aim to reduce gypsy marginalization by trying to ensure that gypsies have access to all the benefits that other Spaniards enjoy. Gypsy associations are also encouraged and enjoy increasing support from local, regional, national, and European Union administrations. Housing programs have resettled some gypsies from substandard living conditions in shacks on the outskirts of cities to high-rise flats, which has had a substantial impact on gypsy culture for this new generation. It is safe to say that most gypsies and gypsy advocates still feel there is a long way to go until gypsies achieve social equality with other Spaniards, citing grave problems of illiteracy, health, deficient living conditions, alienation from their own cultural tradition, and employment discrimination, among others.

Gypsy Culture

There are important cultural differences between gypsy and payo culture that are criminologically relevant. These differences are in constant flux, as the gypsy community evolves and responds to the pressures of majority society. Traditional anthropological literature stressed the importance of the extended family; virility, with the correlates of virginity as a marriage prerequisite for women, obedience of women and children to men, and fertility; respect for the authority of the elderly; honoring one's word; generosity; and community sentiment. Recent observations, however, point to the following: interest on the part of gypsies in participating in cultural activities (music, language reinforcement) that transcend family lines (not to be confused with participation in gypsy associations, which are a creation of the majority society and in which gypsies participate minimally); the increasing authority given to younger members of the gypsy community, especially in dealing with the payo world in which their higher levels of education are needed; more dialogue among the generations in decision making within the gypsy community; the more flexible roles accorded to women and children; a growing sendentarism; and the growing attraction of religious evangelism in the gypsy community (Fresno García, 1993, pp. 29-30).

These cultural differences are criminologically relevant in that they have ramifications for the espousal of behaviors that payo society considers illegal. For example, cultural differences regarding gender roles may mean that the gypsy community has a different attitude toward the victimization of women. On one hand, one could expect much greater outrage accorded to the rape of a gypsy virgin. On the other hand are Calvo Buezas's (1990) findings on the differing values in gypsy and payo communities regarding domestic violence. Of gypsy youths surveyed, 61% agreed with the statement, "It's not bad for a man to beat his wife if she doesn't attend to the children or to her husband's parents," whereas only 8% of the payo children agreed with the statement (p. 170). The importance of lineage and of community sentiment is also key to understanding the relations between the gypsy community and payo society, as we shall see in the following section on gypsy law.

Gypsy Law

A key difference between gypsies and other minorities is that gypsies have their own law, termed *La Ley Gitana,* or Gypsy Law, an oral tradition that specifies which kinds of acts are considered harmful, how they will be judged, how conflict will be resolved, and how sanctions will be imposed. Gypsy law considers most punishable acts whose results are harmful (although the intention may not have been); acts that affect not only the individual but also his or her lineage; and acts that occur either within the gypsy community or, if committed elsewhere, would bring great harm to the community (Torres Fernández, 1991, pp. 37-43). Gypsy law is usually interpreted and enforced by the elders in a gypsy community, and punishment can range from retribution to banishment to death. Punishment often falls on the offender's lineage, and thus it is not surprising that when processed for a crime in the payo legal system for a crime, the offender's lineage may decide who will take the blame and do the prison time, although this is not always the case.

Gypsy law exists most strongly in the most insular and structured gypsy communities. In many of the more marginalized communities, gypsy law has weakened to a series of customs. Although there is little, if any, legal recognition of gypsy law in Spain, there is an implicit challenge for the payo criminal justice system in deciding when it is appropriate to intervene, and when discretion should be used to respect gypsy laws and customs.

Gypsies and Criminal Involvement

Current empirical research on Spanish gypsies and criminal involvement is virtually nonexistent. Furthermore, the topic is taboo. Throughout Spanish history, gypsies have been persecuted by national and local authorities and rendered synonymous with marginal lifestyles and criminal behavior. Not only did classic Spanish literary works perpetuate this relationship, but Spanish positivist criminologist Rafael Salillas confirmed this linkage under the rubric of science, dedicating a third of his book *Hampa* to the topic (Salillas, 1898, pp. 127-322). For Salillas, the nomadic lifestyle of gypsies is what gives them special physiological and psychological traits that then facilitate their participation in criminal behavior. Yet since Salillas few social scientists have addressed the criminality of gypsies in empirical or theoretical terms. It seems that this topic of inquiry in current-day Spain, so sensitized to the new European xenophobia, is politically incorrect.

Research on the criminal involvement of Spanish gypsies is rendered difficult by the same factors that condition any quantitative study of gypsies in Spain. First, there are no census data on gypsies because it is considered unconstitutional to ask about one's race or ethnicity (but not one's nationality) in the Spanish population census. Second, objective and subjective measures of gypsy status are fraught with problems. Gypsies are not always "recognizable" to third parties; although they have discrete physical features (dark hair, olive-toned skin), quite often these features have melded and are hard to detect; furthermore, many payos, especially from Andalusia, share the same features. Some studies assume that all gypsies live in poverty in easily identified shantytowns, and simply count them in those habitats. Other gypsies, however, are not poor and live integrated with payos. These are the gypsies that are rarely counted and rarely studied. A subjective measure (such as asking a person to self-define his or her ethnicity) would also be problematic. There are those who were born in gypsy families who no longer consider themselves gypsies; there are half-gypsies who call themselves by other names; and most of all, there is a certain resistance on the part of gypsies to be identified and counted, which is a vestige of past—and present—persecution.

Despite the resistance to being counted and the practical impossibility of doing so, there is a need, both on the part of the government and on the part of gypsy organizations, to cite numbers. After all, numbers justify budgetary allocations for social programs. So periodically studies do get commissioned, and numbers do exist, but not without frequent criticism from the gypsy community. Presently, sources at the Ministry of Social Affairs cite the number of gypsies at around 700,000 in Spain, although other sources cite between 400,000 and 500,000 (see Fresno García, 1993, p. 6) and some gypsy organizations claim to have counted more than one million.

Police, court, and prison statistics do not report racial or ethnic variables. Official files, however, may contain these data. For example, outdated Guardia Civil arrest forms (still in use in some rural areas), contained the category of *aceitunado* (olive-toned) under "complexion," and this was how gypsies were recorded. Nevertheless, criminal justice professionals and gypsy leaders interviewed for this chapter[4] were all in agreement that gypsies are disproportionately represented in police arrests, court hearings, and prison populations. Furthermore, these interviewees observed that gypsies tended to be arrested, processed, and imprisoned for a subset of crimes and with very particular circumstances: for small- to medium-scale drug trafficking, for property crimes that are the result of a heroin addiction or economic necessity, and for violent crimes that occur as a result of family feuds.

A few criminological studies that have delved into the official files of processed offenders have found the same result. Serrano Gómez and Fernández Dopico's (1978) study of 2,049 prison inmates found that gypsies were overrepresented, with their involvement in the sample being more than double of what it should be (p. 125).

Cea D'Ancona's (1992) study of Madrid juvenile court cases from 1975, 1977, 1979, 1981, and 1983 also found a disproportionate number of gypsies. During those years, gypsy cases made up 8% of the sample. The reasons for juvenile court referral were also different for gypsy and payo children. Gypsy children were rarely referred to the court by their families for intractable behavior, but rather appeared before the court due to repeated acts of delinquent behavior (Cea D'Ancona, 1992, pp. 12-19).

Although there may not be much data on the criminal involvement of gypsies, there is a small but growing area of research on the public perceptions of gypsies by nongypsies. These data show that many Spaniards still associate gypsy status with criminal status. A 1987 survey of 1,110 elementary, secondary, and vocational school teachers showed that 46% believed that gypsies were "worse" than payos in the area of criminality. This represents a change for the better from 1977, however, when the same question was asked on a different survey and 73% of the teachers voiced the same opinion. A survey taken in 1987 of 1,410 elementary, secondary, and vocational school students showed that 46% believed that gypsies "stole more" than payos (Calvo Buezas, 1990, pp. 130-132).

The Gypsy Community's Reaction to Crime

The gypsy community is increasingly sensitive to the criminal label. Furthermore, the admitted presence of certain types of criminal behavior among gypsies is a source of great shame and scorn. Often, those gypsy offenders that end up incarcerated have been shunned long ago by many of the members of the gypsy community. Some, then, are outcasts from the gypsy community, although they most likely still receive support from their families. There appears to be a very real rift in gypsy society, then, between gypsies who lead licit and illicit lifestyles, perhaps more pronounced between those who are involved in the drug trade and those who are not, and particularly strong among upwardly mobile gypsies. This rift is accentuated by sporadic attempts by the authorities to blame Spain's drug problem on the gypsy community. In 1991, Rafael Vera, Secretary of Internal Security of the Ministry of the Interior, declared before the press that 70% of the small-scale drug trafficking networks were controlled by gypsies, and that the gypsy elders *(patriarcas)* were unable to control this issue. The very same day of his declaration, 2,000 people marched in Madrid to protest this accusation, under signs reading "Gypsies Against Drug Trafficking." One gypsy leader noted, "It is not fair that just because a few of our own are involved in drugs, that the rest of us become labelled traffickers (*Vera Asegura Que los Gitanos,* 1991, p. 17).

Gypsies, Victimization, and Police Protection

Victimology and policing are topics new to Spanish criminology, and so explain the almost total lack of research regarding gypsies in these areas. Our interview data here are enlightening (see Note 4). There appears to be a real rift between gypsies who are and are not engaged in certain types of illicit behavior, and the presence of this behavior (especially drug trafficking, seen as a bad influence on children) highly frustrates sections of the gypsy community. The frustration comes from the fact that in some gypsy neigh-borhoods, the elders have lost control over misbehavior within the commu-nity; police protection is not necessarily the answer either, as we shall see shortly.

Gypsies are also victims of crime on the part of payos. Over the last several years in Spain, press coverage has been given to instances of racial attacks and discrimination. Gypsies in Mancha Real (in the province of Jaén, Andalusia) were the center of attention recently when their payo neighbors, after a criminal incident between a gypsy and a payo, refused to let gypsy children attend school and later burned down their houses, with the tacit consent of the mayor of the town and the passivity of the police. Other instances of gypsy-payo conflict are becoming increasingly common.

It is on the issue of police protection that interviews with police officials and gypsies demonstrate real differences. The police see little involvement on the part of gypsies in terms of demanding police protection, reporting crime, and providing information that could lead to an arrest. They see gypsies as generally distrusting of the police and apparently able to solve their own problems, especially family feuds. Gypsy leaders, on the other hand, express a great need for police protection, for themselves and their children, for certain types of crime (notably drug trafficking). They admit their "ancestral fear and distrust" of the police, however, and caution that police in general are ignorant of gypsy culture, unfamiliar with the gypsy community, and thus act too impulsively in their community. One gypsy leader, referring to gypsy law, notes that he would prefer the police to intervene preventively in interlineage conflicts before blood is spilled: "I know that if the conflict results in a victim, the victim's lineage will most likely be banned, and I might have to pack up my family's things and leave the area."

Gypsies and Criminal Justice Careers

There are no data on the number of gypsies in law enforcement, court, or prison positions. Interviews conducted in Seville yielded little information. Apparently, there are isolated numbers of gypsies employed in police forces, and there are a growing number of gypsy lawyers. The numbers, however, are very small. There appears to be no special recruitment of minorities for criminal justice positions. Gypsy leaders in Seville admitted attaining a criminal justice career was not a common aspiration for gypsy youth, because of the bad experience many gypsy families have had with the criminal justice system. In any case, gypsies' lack of education, a prerequisite for criminal justice positions, is a strong barrier. A study of Andalusian gypsies by University of Granada anthropologist Juan Gamella, calculated that only 1% of gypsy children currently in elementary school will proceed to secondary school, largely due to absenteeism; and, only 70 Andalusian gypsies are currently pursuing college degrees, while proportionately there should be 6,000 enrolled ("Los Andaluces Profesan," 1995, p. 15).

Theoretical Approaches

Because there is no developed body of literature in Spain on gypsies and criminal involvement or victimization, there is consequently no developed theoretical approach. "Street theory," at least that embraced by police leaders and gypsy leaders interviewed for this chapter, however, points to five causal mechanisms. The first explains gypsy criminality through the marginalized lifestyle of poor gypsies. In this case, deficient housing conditions and health care, insufficient educational opportunities, and unemployment or underemployment lead to the adaptation of a criminal lifestyle to satisfy vital needs; often drug addiction is an intervening variable between a deficient environment and criminal behavior. The second theory, more often espoused by gypsy leaders, points to the increasing restriction of traditional gypsy occupations as the main cause of criminal involvement. Increasing regulation and restriction of open-air market peddling, one of the main traditional occupations for gypsies, and of other traditionally gypsy occupations, such as cardboard and metal collecting and recycling, means that gypsies must find other ways of making a living, which may include property crime and drug trafficking. The third theory points to police harassment of gypsies in general (gypsies complain that they are frequently stopped and asked to show identification), and a judicial system that takes advantage of gypsies and suggests that police spend more time arresting "accessible" small-scale gypsy drug traffickers than more important medium- and high-level traffickers. Thus a reason for the disproportionate number of gypsies involved in the criminal justice system may be due to a disproportionate law enforcement effort against gypsy offenders. A fourth theory points to the effects of modernization on gypsy society, which has traditionally eliminated adolescence: Gypsy children are married off quite early, and begin working or childbearing immediately after marriage. Modernization, and the lack of employment for younger gypsies, has created a gypsy adolescence and its crime-prone properties. A fifth theory emphasizes the aspects of gypsy culture that conflict with majority culture and condone certain types of behavior that payo society criminalizes. In our view, explanation of criminal behavior among gypsies probably requires a combination of all of these theories.

Although there is a clear lack of empirical data and theory testing on gypsies and the criminal justice system in Spain, it appears that due to a historical persecution of gypsies in Spain and the ensuing association between gypsy status and criminal behavior, a minority group has emerged that, in the midst of cultural adjustment to an increasingly modern society, is sensitive to this label and distrusting of the criminal justice system. Clearly much more work is needed by Spanish criminologists to clarify the causes of crime and victimization among gypsies and payos in Spain.

IMMIGRANTS

Spanish Immigration Trends and Policy

From the 1950s onward, a few countries of the European Union became focal points for immigration due to the postwar economic recovery and the need for manpower; laborers were recruited first from former colonies, then from southern European states (including Spain), and then from Third World countries. Since the 1950s, apart from Great Britain, France, and Germany, other countries such as Belgium, The Netherlands, and Luxembourg became host countries for immigration. In the 1970s, there was an economic boom in certain parts of southern Europe, including Spain, and within Spain, quite notably the region of Catalonia. This boom provoked a change in migratory flow, and converted Spain, among other countries, from being a country *from* which workers migrated into a focal point for non-European immigrants. Although sub-Saharan African emigres initially reached Europe through the borders of southern Italy, when that country stiffened its entry requirements, the flow of emigres entered Europe through Spain from Morocco (Adroher et al., 1995, p. 208).

From the 1980s onward, the number of illegal or irregular foreigners who lived in Spain began to increase, without any regulation of this phenomenon. This caused the government at that time to present a bill that would regulate the rights and liberties of foreigners residing in Spain, developing at the same time guarantees from the Spanish 1978 Constitution.[5]

The growth of the immigrant population continued throughout the 1980s due to the development of an underground economy and the increasing segmentation of the labor market. Spain established itself as one of the mediterranean host countries for immigration (see Table 8.1). Nevertheless, the legislation regarding foreigners was not passed into law until July 1, 1985.[6]

During the legislative debates that ensued prior to the passage of the bill, it became obvious that the main rationale behind the need for the law was the great problem of international crime in Spain. Other justifications, such as the need to legalize the situation of many illegal residents in Spain, contributed to the urgency that accompanied the debate. As such, the debates clearly assimilated criminals and foreigners: "Even today, 10 years after the passage of the Foreigners' Law, the administration continues to use this argument with data that do not respond to reality" (Adroher et al., 1995, p. 487). One study (Pereda, De Prada, & Actis, 1991, p. 19) qualified this policy period as a failure, due to the scarce publicity of the amnesty law, but especially due to the difficulties in meeting the conditions imposed by the law itself. The law is considered, then, to be restrictive, in that it attempts to hinder the legal entry to and residence of immigrants in Spain.

The inefficacy of Organic Law 7/85 was clear in 1991 when the presence of large numbers of illegal residents in Spain forced the government to reanalyze the situation. In a resolution dated June 7, 1991, a series of criteria

TABLE 8.1 Legal Resident Foreigners in Spain

1960	64,660
1965	99,582
1970	148,400
1975	165,039
1980	183,422
1985	241,971
1990	407,647

SOURCE: Data from the Spanish population census, as cited in the Instituto Nacional de Estadística (1960, 1965, 1970, 1975, 1980, 1985, 1990).

were adopted for a new period of legalization of foreigners who were working in Spain illegally (Areste, 1995, p. 182). This resolution was in accordance not only with the Foreigners Law, but also with the new migratory policy that was a product of Spain's entry into the European Union in 1985 and the philosophy of the 1993 Single European Act, which has been brought forth in the 1990 Schengen agreements (regarding open borders within the European Union [EU]; this agreement resulted in stricter immigration policy in Spain, especially regarding the Maghreb), those of the Trevi Group (a forum of EU Ministers of the Interior that deals with common security issues such as terrorism, international drug trafficking, and immigration), and so on.

One of the consequences of the process of legalization was the change that took place on the Spanish immigration map (Fernández, 1992, p. 18). Up until a few years ago, the majority of the legal foreigners who resided in Spain were European. After legalization, and according to official sources, it appears that legalized foreigners from other origins have increased. Due to the constant migratory pressure from the Third World, the immigration policy adopted in recent years has been by quotas. An agreement of the Council of Ministers on May 26, 1993, established a limit on the number of foreign workers who would be authorized during that year; this measure would serve to control migratory fluctuations and has been in effect since that time (Areste, 1995, p. 190). In 1996, a new series of regulations of the Foreigners Law of 1985 was published that call for another period of legalization. These regulations do not change the restrictive immigration policy, but merely provide an open door for those immigrants whose residency or work permits have not been renewed and who are currently out of status.

Illegal Immigrants in Spain

The existence of illegal immigrants is a consequence of the migratory fluctuations toward certain countries and the restrictive immigration policies established by the receptor states. In the case of Spain, this involves not only the framework of the European Union but also the existing relations with the native countries of the illegal immigrants, most of whom are from the Third World (Colectivo IOE, 1992). The restrictive policy adopted by Spain has had the effect of increasing the number of illegal immigrants. De Lucas (1991) affirms, regarding these "clandestine workers," that "we are dealing with a problem provoked by the government, by the administration, and by the economic model prevailing in western countries, in that they constitute a cheap workforce that helps the system grow" (p. 22).

Quantitatively we will concentrate on data obtained by the organization Colectivo IOE (a private nonprofit organization that helps immigrants) in 1986, which holds that in that year a total of 294,000 illegal immigrants resided in Spain, originally from former Spanish colonies and underdeveloped countries. Three years after the Colectivo IOE study, a study commissioned by the Spanish Institute for Emigration corroborated this number, concluding that 260,000 was the minimum number of illegal immigrants in Spain. The fieldwork for this study was based on a new, yet questionable, source; the number of illegal immigrants who had approached the Spanish social service network. During that same year of 1989, a comparative European study brought forth the results shown in Table 8.2.

Table 8.3 shows that only in Italy does the number of illegal immigrants surpass the number of legal immigrants; however, these figures are hardly comparable given the different internal policies of each country. The government of Spain did not agree with the figures referring to Spain, given that official estimates provided to the Spanish parliament in 1990 set the number of illegal immigrants before the 1991 legalization at 170,000—124,000 fewer than cited in Table 8.2. When the legalization process opened up in 1991, 132,934 illegal foreigners applied, suggesting that the official figures were close to reality in Spain. Nevertheless, as part of fieldwork research conducted at the Málaga detention center for foreigners, it was found that only one out of three illegal immigrants who were in Spain at that time applied for legalization. The rest alleged that they did not know about or mistrusted the process. Therefore, it appears that the number of illegal immigrants in Spain in 1991 was somewhat greater than the number of applications presented during the legalization period. In any case, the foreign

TABLE 8.2 Legal and Illegal Immigration in the South of the European Community

Country	Legal Immigration	Illegal Immigration
Italy	572,103	850,000
Spain	484,334	294,000
Greece	183,577	70,000
Portugal	94,553	60,000

immigrant population in Spain (legal and illegal), even in 1995, is relatively small compared to other European countries and as such is only beginning to achieve social visibility.

The oldest immigrant group in Spain originates from European Union countries, mainly Portugal. Among the non-European Union countries, Moroccans are the oldest immigrant group, especially those who had established their residence in Ceuta and Melilla. Nevertheless, in the 1970s Spain witnessed great increases in the number of immigrants from South America, the Philippines, and central Africa. The majority of these non-European Union immigrants tended to come from former Spanish colonies.

Because of the recent influx from citizens from non-European Union countries, the following section focuses on these immigrants, detailing data from a study published by the Colectivo IOE in 1992. According to this study, there was an increase in the number of immigrants from North Africa in 1991, right after a visa became an entry requirement for these citizens. Earlier immigrants from these countries had been largely illiterate, whereas the more recent ones usually possess secondary education; yet, they are usually willing to work wherever they can to better their living situation. They are usually more politicized and pressured by unemployment. Black Africans are those who find it the most difficult to enter Spain, arriving by boat or as stowaways with fishermen. Black African immigrants usually seek refugee status.

Latin American immigration intensified in 1990 and 1991. The countries of origin are usually Perú and Argentina. They usually enter as tourists, for which they need no visa. They often use organized networks that find female immigrants employment in domestic work.

Regarding Asian immigrants, the flow of Filipinos has lessened although there are intermittent waves of immigration from the Philippines through Portugal and Barcelona. Often these immigrants use organized networks that falsify visas and find the women employment as live-in domestic help. As for the Chinese, despite their number, they have little social visibility. They tend to find work almost exclusively in the service sector and their integration into Spanish society is particularly difficult.

In Spain, there are many illegal immigrants among those arriving from the Third World; because of the current restrictive immigration policy, all these immigrant groups are likely to remain illegal and thus are unprotected from a legal standpoint. Another study conducted by the Colectivo IOE in 1987 confirms this point and adds:

> Their situation of social marginality is confirmed by objective indicators of their living conditions (work, social security, income and savings, housing) and also by subjective indicators (perception of social rejection, legal insecurity, fear of the police, xenophobic nationalism as reflected in public opinion, and so on). (Colectivo IOE, 1987, p. 25)

This sociological report describes undocumented or illegal foreigners as uprooted individuals, half of whom do not live with their family. Few own property, and most live in poor dwellings on the outskirts of cities. Many of them are affected by different kinds of crowding, which happens most often with the Moroccans. The income of these illegal foreigners tends to be quite low, causing them to suffer extreme poverty, and when their own survival is at stake and they have exhausted all other resources, they often resort to begging, homelessness, prostitution, drug trafficking, or criminal behavior in general. Nevertheless, and as we shall see in detail, the Colectivo IOE report differentiates between the professionalized crime committed by European Union immigrants and the less serious crime committed by those from the Third World, excluding of course, those tied to drug trafficking mafias.

Furthermore, when one analyzes police statistics (see the following), the media have exaggerated the dangerousness of immigrants. This has resulted in distorting the social visibility of immigrants and highlighting the association between conflict and immigrants. The immigrant is conceived as a social danger in all aspects; part of society begins to state that "those people are taking jobs away from the nationals and that is why unemployment is so high in Spain." At the same time, they are held responsible for the lack of public safety on the streets, without reference to any objective data indicating that this is the case.

Similarly, a study conducted to capture Spanish public opinion on the topic established that, although the theoretical attitude toward visitors is positive, understanding diminishes with the fear of a possible impact on the economy and on employment. (Centro de Investigación Para la Realidad Social, 1995, p. 16)

The study also notes that 52% of those surveyed thought that immigrants make the crime rate increase. Nevertheless, according to another more recent study (Centro de Investigaciones Sociológicas, 1995), in Spain there is less xenophobia than in other neighboring European countries, perhaps explained partly by the fact that Spain has one of the lowest immigration rates in the European Union.

Foreigners and Criminal Behavior

A great disadvantage of official statistics in Spain is that they give breakdowns according to foreign or national origin, but do not differentiate among legal and illegal immigrants, tourists, or others simply passing through Spain. This is an important caveat in drawing conclusions from these statistics.

Police Statistics

Arrests of foreigners, relative to the number of foreigners residing in Spain, have been practically the same from 1993 to 1995 (see Table 8.3).

It must be noted that the number of foreign residents in Spain cited previously is from official immigration sources and does not include the undocumented foreign immigrant population residing in Spain; therefore, it is an underestimate. To this number, one would need to add not only undocumented immigrants but also the floating populations of asylum and refugee seekers, seasonal workers, people in transit, and tourists. Although efforts to obtain correct figures of undocumented immigrants in Spain have not been successful, estimates are that they probably total a number similar to that of documented immigrants (Colectivo IOE, 1992, p. 11).

Given these caveats, if one were to assume that the total number of immigrants, legal or illegal, in Spain were around 800,000, that would mean they constituted 2% of the Spanish population. Only 9.6% of the 800,000 are arrested by the police, but because these arrests include administrative infractions, if one limited the analysis to criminal infractions, we are probably talking about 9%. Therefore, 9% of the foreign population of Spain is arrested yearly, which constitutes approximately 8.5% of the total number of arrests in Spain.[7] This is obviously disproportionate, considering that the

TABLE 8.3 Arrests of Foreigners as a Percentage of Legal Foreign Residents in Spain, 1993 to 1995

Year	Arrests	Legal Residents	Percentage
1993	78,713	430,422	18.28
1994	77,071	461,354	16.70
1995	74,134	499,773	14.80

SOURCE: Data from Centro de Proceso de Datos del Ministerio del Interior (1993, 1994, 1995).

estimate of 800,000 foreigners is only 2% of the Spanish population. There is no research in Spain that attempts to explain this disproportion, but we offer several alternatives: First interviews with accused immigrants (García-España, 1995) suggest that those arrested felt that there was a racial factor that prompted their arrest; in other words, they believed that police exerted greater scrutiny at checkpoints and at roundups toward the immigrant population—especially people of color. Second, official statistics include not only immigrants but also tourists, transients, and other foreign nonimmigrants. Third, the overrepresentation of immigrants could be explained by the demographic composition of this group (mainly young and male), characteristics that are also associated with greater involvement in criminal acts.

Judicial Statistics

From 1981 to 1989 the foreign proportion among the total population convicted in Spain rose from 2.91% to 4.16% (see Table 8.4). These percentages must be interpreted with caution because the population of foreigners in Spain also increased during that period. The latest data available are from 1989 (Instituto Nacional de Estadística, 1989) and describe the convictions of foreigners by the provincial and investigative courts. In that year, 4% of the convicted were foreigners. The convictions were concentrated mainly in property crimes (42%), then risk crimes (a category in Spanish penal code that includes drug trafficking; 32%), followed by fraud (7%). Property and drug-related crimes are, however, also the most common convictions for the Spanish population overall. As for specific nationalities of convicted foreigners, in absolute terms Moroccans displayed the highest prevalence (i.e., proportion of people convicted); Germans, however, the highest incidence (i.e., frequency of convictions). Risk crimes were committed most often by Moroccans and French citizens, and fraud was committed most often by Moroccans.

TABLE 8.4 Convicted Foreigners and Spanish Nationals, 1981 to 1989

Year	Spanish Nationals	Foreigners	Foreigners Percentage of Total
1981	60,687	1,768	2.91
1982	61,542	1,620	2.63
1983	59,044	1,533	2.59
1984	72,619	1,810	2.36
1985	76,566	1,838	2.40
1986	78,893	2,711	3.43
1987	78,069	3,009	3.85
1988	69,255	2,812	4.95
1989	56,794	2,363	4.16

Prison Statistics

According to the *Annual Report of the Penitentiary Institutions* in 1991 (Dirección General de Instituciones Penitenciarias, 1992), 16% of the prison population in Spain are foreigners. There has been a progressive increase in the number of foreigners incarcerated in Spanish prisons between 1983 (7.6%) and 1994 (15.9%; Secretaría de Estado de Asuntos Penitenciarios, 1995; Tournier, 1983). In 1994, the Spanish Attorney General announced ("Declaraciones del Fiscal General," 1994) that there were 6,563 foreigners imprisoned in Spain, of which 3,000 had been convicted for "less serious offenses," that is, those offenses that carry a sentence of 4 to 6 years.

In December of 1994, 60% of the foreign prison population was awaiting trial, compared to 35% of nationals. These data suggest that pretrial detention is more often applied to foreign offenders, perhaps because of their lack of ties to Spain and the possibility that they might not appear at trial.

Comparison of the data from the three criminal justice sources (police, judicial, and prison statistics) reveals a higher percentage of foreigners incarcerated (16%) vis-à-vis arrested (8.5%) vis-à-vis convicted (5.5%). This can be explained by the apparently habitual use of pretrial detention for foreign detainees.

The Immigrant as Victim

Racially motivated assaults on foreign immigrants are becoming a problem in some areas of Spain. The "Defender of the People," a public ombudsman, in his 1993 annual report, noted the existence of xenophobic attitudes toward and the social rejection of certain ethnic groups; he also noted that these sorts of displays already existed in Spain against gypsies (*Defensor del Pueblo*, 1993, p. 15-23). Likewise, a report issued by the organization Jóvenes Progresistas (Progressive Youth) notes that whereas in 1991 there were three instances of xenophobic assaults against immigrants, in 1994 there were 241 (*Jóvenes Progresistas*, 1994). The circumstances surrounding the assault often include a person of color as a victim and a Skinhead as the aggressor. The newly reformed penal code, passed in November of 1995, includes racial, ethnic, or religious motivation as an aggravating factor in sentencing. (Unfortunately, Spanish victimization surveys do not give us data on the immigrant or nonimmigrant status of the victim.)

Immigrants are not only victims of assaults in Spain, but also victims of illegal employment contracts and working conditions. According to Spanish legislation, the employer in this circumstance may be punished. Employers, however, are rarely punished; whereas illegal immigrant workers, when discovered, are deported from Spain and cannot reenter the country for the next 3 to 5 years.

Treatment of Immigrants by the Criminal Justice System

Deportation

Immigrants may be deported by Spain even if only accused and not yet convicted of a crime; the Foreigners Law refers to "illegal activities" (a very broad and vague term) as a reason for deportation. In any case, deportation as a substitute for a prison sentence for foreigners is a hotly debated issue among Spanish legal scholars. Some argue that it is the only solution in keeping with the Spanish legal system—because the mandated purpose of a prison sentence is the social reintegration of prisoners, and because a foreign prisoner cannot be reintegrated because a criminal record will prohibit him or her from residing and working in Spain, the only alternative is deportation. There are other arguments that see deportation as either negative or positive discrimination: positive, because it may involve less "punishment" than the prison sentence that Spanish offenders receive; negative, because where a Spanish offender, for example, would have received a $1,000 fine, deportation seems an unfair substitute (Rodríguez Candela, 1995, p. 39).

Immigrants awaiting deportation may be kept in detention centers for a maximum of 40 days, but the Foreigners Law specifically denotes that these centers are never to be penitentiary in nature. These detention centers lack needed resources, however, such as social workers and internal regulations, which renders the conditions of the detention centers less than optimal.

Prisoner Rights and Privileges

Although Spanish and foreign prisoners are entitled to the same rights and privileges, in practice foreigners rarely receive these privileges. Because foreigners seldom have family or social support on the outside, they hardly receive visits, are granted furloughs, or are granted the privilege of only returning to prison at night. The latter two privileges are tied to the finding of work on release, which for foreign prisoners is legally impossible (see Giménez-Salinas i Colomer, 1994a, 1994b; Montijano, 1994). Although many would have solicited deportation to their countries of origin, it is a bureaucratic nightmare for the prison system and few have actually been deported (see Adroher et al., 1995, p. 208).

CONCLUSIONS

Persons of foreign origin in Spain appear to be disproportionately represented in police, judicial, and prison statistics. They also appear to be increasingly victimized by xenophobically motivated crime. They also are at a disadvantage in terms of treatment by the criminal justice system. The small amount of data available, however, do not often clarify whether the persons of foreign origin are (a) tourists or others simply passing through Spain, (b) illegal immigrants, (c) legally documented immigrants, or perhaps more important for theoretical purposes, (d) second-generation immigrants. Furthermore, nationality breakdowns are rarely available. These distinctions are key to the development of hypotheses. In any case, it appears that there is something about a person's foreign origin that either pushes one to engage in criminal behavior or be disproportionately victimized—or causes a behavior to become more noticed by agents of formal social control. Certainly the poor socioeconomic conditions of certain immigrant groups; the severance of social bonds, which is the nature of the migratory experience; and the degree of hostility encountered in the host country may all be criminogenic factors.

Although there is a dearth of research in the area of minorities and crime, Spain presents an interesting case of analysis of the relationship between the criminal justice system and ethnic minorities, given the historical contrast between its multicultural past and homogeneous present. The situation of gypsies and foreign immigrants in Spain suggests that the marginalization and criminalization of these minorities is a growing problem, or perhaps, in the case of Spanish gypsies, an age-old problem that is only beginning to come to light.

NOTES

1. Unless otherwise indicated, all translations in this chapter are the authors'.
2. In Spain, Romany is termed *Romanó* or *caló*.
3. *Payo* is the term in Spain for anyone who is not a gypsy.
4. Interviews were conducted with the following: representatives from the community relations department of the National Police in Seville; from the Seville archdiocese's gypsy outreach program; from the Romany Union in Seville; the Asociación Secretariado General Gitano in Madrid; and the Seville-based neighborhood association, Villela or Chivé. The first author also attended a meeting of a research working group on crime and the gypsy community organized by the Asociación Secretariado General Gitano in Madrid, and a workshop on the Criminalization of Gypsies sponsored by the International Institute for the Sociology of Law in Oñati, Spain.
5. Article 13.1 of the Spanish Constitution establishes that "foreigners will enjoy in Spain all the public freedoms guaranteed by the present Title in terms established by treaties and by law."
6. The content of Organic Law 7/85 on the Rights and Liberties of Foreigners in Spain shows a clear contrast between the generosity of its preamble and the restrictive character of its articles, given that the law limits itself to regulating the conditions of entry into Spain, residency and work permits, and the sanctions to be applied; only seven articles refer, and only vaguely so, to the rights of foreigners.
7. The total number of arrests in Spain in 1994 was 901,686, according to data from the Ministry of the Interior (Serrano Maillo, 1995).

REFERENCES

Adroher, S., Benlloch, P., Charro, P., Gortazar, C. J., Lazaro, I., Navarro, C., Ruiloba, J., Ruiz de Huidobro, J. M., & Vasquez, D. (1995). *La Inmigración: Derecho Español e Internacional*. Barcelona: Bosch.

Areste, P. (1995). La evolución del tratamiento administrativo: C. regularizaciones. In A. Borras (Ed.), *Diez Años de la Ley de Extranjería: Balance y Perspectivas* (pp. 182-190). Madrid: Fundación Paulino Torras Domenech.

Calvo Buezas, T. (1990). *El Racismo Que Viene*. Madrid: Tecnos.

Cea D'Ancona, M. A. (1992). *La Justicia de Menores en España*. Madrid: CIS/Siglo XX.

Centro de Investigación Para la Realidad Social—CIRES. (1995, April/June). La Realidad Social en España 1993-1994. *Observatorie Permanente de la Inmigración*, pp. 15-16.

Centro de Investigaciones Sociológicas—CIS. (1995). *Actitudes ante la Inmigración.* Madrid: Author.

Centro de Proceso de Datos del Ministerio del Interior. (1993). *Extranjeros Detenidos.* Madrid: Ministerio del Interior.

Centro de Proceso de Datos del Ministerio del Interior. (1994). *Extranjeros Detenidos.* Madrid: Ministerio del Interior.

Centro de Proceso de Datos del Ministerio del Interior. (1995). *Extranjeros Detenidos.* Madrid: Ministerio del Interior.

Colectivo IOE, Los Inmigrantes en España. (1987). *Documentación Social, 66*(January-March), 1-376.

Colectivo IOE, Los Inmigrantes en España. (1992). *Inmigrantes Indocumentados en España* [Mimeo]. Madrid: Author.

Declaraciones del Fiscal General del Estado. (1994, March 3). *El País,* p. 15.

De Lucas, J. (1991). Xenofobia y Racismo en España. *Claves de Razón Práctica, 13,* 14-26.

Defensor del Pueblo. (1993). *Informe Anual de 1993 y Debates en las Cortes Generales.* Madrid: Publicaciones del Congreso de los Diputados, Secretaría General (Dirección de Estudios).

Dirección General de Instituciones Penitenciarias. (1992). *Informe General 1991.* Madrid: Ministerio de Justicia, Edición Centro de Publicaciones del Ministerio de Justicia.

Fernández, A. (1992). Regularizaciones: El Fin del Proceso. *Cartas de España, 456,* 16-18.

Fresno García, J. M. (1993, May). *Análisis Socioantropológico Sobre la Situación Actual de la Comunidad Gitana en España.* Paper presented at the I Encuentro Estatal Sobre Programas de Desarrollo Gitano, Zaragoza, Spain.

García-España, E. (1995). *Analysis of the situation of 246 foreigners at the Alhaurin de la Torre Detention Center in Málaga, Spain.* Unpublished doctoral dissertation, University of Málaga, Málaga, Spain.

Giménez-Salinas i Colomer, E. (1994a, March). *Los Extranjeros en Prisión.* Paper presented at Simposio Internacional sobre la Condición del Extranjero, ESADE-Consejo de Europea, Barcelona.

Giménez-Salinas i Colomer, E. (1994b). Extranjeros en Prisión. *Cuadernos del Instituto Vasco de Criminología, 7,* 133-146.

Instituto Nacional de Estadística. (1960). *Anuario del Instituto Nacional de Estadística.* Madrid: Author.

Instituto Nacional de Estadística. (1965). *Anuario del Instituto Nacional de Estadística.* Madrid: Author.

Instituto Nacional de Estadística. (1970). *Anuario del Instituto Nacional de Estadística.* Madrid: Author.

Instituto Nacional de Estadística. (1975). *Anuario del Instituto Nacional de Estadística.* Madrid: Author.

Instituto Nacional de Estadística. (1980). *Anuario del Instituto Nacional de Estadística.* Madrid: Author.

Instituto Nacional de Estadística. (1985). *Anuario del Instituto Nacional de Estadística.* Madrid: Author.

Instituto Nacional de Estadística. (1990). *Anuario del Instituto Nacional de Estadística.* Madrid: Author.

Instituto Nacional de Estadística. (1989). *Estadísticas Judiciales.* Madrid: Author.

Jóvenes Progresistas. (1994). Datos Sobre Agresiones a Inmigrantes [Mimeo]. Madrid: Author.

Los Andaluces Profesan un "Intenso Rechazo" al Colectivo Gitano. (1995, June 30). *Diario 16,* p. 15.

Martínez-Pereda Rodríguez, J. M. (1993). Marginación, Magia y Delincuencia del Pueblo Gitano. *Revista de Derecho Penal y Criminología, 3,* 513-552.

Montijano, F. (1994, May). *Regimen Sancionador, Garantías y Régimen Jurídico de los Extranjeros*. Paper presented at I Congreso Internacional Sobre Derecho de Extranjería, Zaragoza, Spain.

Pereda, C., De Prada, M. A., & Actis, W. (1991). *Situación y Problemática de los Inmigrantes en España: Informe Contextual 1991*. Madrid: Cáritas Española.

Rodríguez Candela, J. L. (1995). Las Expulsiones Con Intervención Judicial en la Ley de Extranjería. *Cuadernos Jurídicos, 28,* 26-47.

Salillas, R. (1898). *El Delincuente Español: Hampa* (Antropología Picaresca). Madrid: Librería de Victoriano Suárez.

Sánchez Ortega, M. H. (1986). Evolución y Contexto Histórico de los Gitanos Españoles. In T. San Román (Ed.), *Entre la Marginación y el Racismo: Reflexiones Sobre la Vida de los Gitanos* (pp. 13-60). Madrid: Alianza.

San Román, T. (1976). *Vecinos Gitanos*. Madrid: Akal.

Secretaría de Estado de Asuntos Penitenciarios. (1995). *El Sistema Penitenciario en España*. Madrid: Secretaría de Estado de Asuntos Penitenciarios, Ministerio de Justicia e Interior.

Serrano Gómez, A., & Fernández Dopico, J. L. (1978). *El Delincuente Español: Factores Concurrentes (Influyentes)*. Madrid: Publicaciones del Instituto de Criminología de la Universidad Complutense de Madrid.

Serrano Maillo, A. (1995). Estadistica. *Revista de Derecho Penal y Criminologia, 5,* 1095-1151.

Torres Fernández, A. (1991). *Vivencias Gitanas*. Barcelona: Instituto Romaní.

Tournier, P. (1983). Estadística Sobre la Poblaciones Carcelarias en los Estados Miembros. *Bulletin d'Information Pénitentiaire*. Strasbourg, France: Council of Europe.

Vera Asegura Que los Gitanos Controlan el 70% del Menudeo de Heroína en España. (1991, October 26) *El País*, p. 17.

9

MINORITIES, CRIME, AND CRIMINAL JUSTICE IN THE NETHERLANDS

Willem de Haan

INTRODUCTION[1]

The Netherlands is a small European country with a population of 15.5 million; it is densely populated. Its traditionally industrial and agricultural economy is gradually developing into a transport and service economy. The Netherlands is a typical example of a continental welfare state that provides welfare and medicaid for the poor, state pensions for the elderly, unemployment and medical disability benefits, guaranteed minimum wages, extensive social housing, and subsidies and rent control.

Given that the Dutch welfare state suffers from a relatively low labor participation and a relatively high welfare dependency, the government faces increasingly serious financial problems, and in the current phase, 1981 to 1995, the level of material and immaterial welfare is in the process of being cut down to size. As far as these cuts relate to welfare benefits, they are

AUTHOR'S NOTE: I wish to thank Frank Bovenkerk for allowing me to draw on Dutch publications written in collaboration with him, and Siep Miedema for reading an earlier draft of this chapter.

strongly opposed by the citizens who count on them and consider them as their right. Nevertheless, a reconstruction of the welfare state is in progress,[2] and the debates concerning risk and responsibility, social justice and care, create the context in which discussions of criminal policy issues take place.

LEGAL CULTURE

An important and unique cultural feature of Dutch society is that it has traditionally been structured along religious, political, and ideological rather than class-based divisions. The major denominational groupings created their own social institutions in all major public spheres. This process, which has been called *pillarization,* is considered responsible for transforming a pragmatic, tolerant, general attitude into an absolute social "must" (Lijphart, 1975). In this sense, there has always been a structural basis for a certain amount of tolerance toward deviancy within Dutch society.

Historical research has shown that in the past immigrants and refugees have been received with considerable hospitality (Lucassen & Penninx, 1994). More recently, however, there are indications that this tradition of tolerance is withering in a more intolerant social climate (Sociaal en Cultureel Planbureau, 1994).

A pragmatic attitude is manifest in both the process of legislation and prosecution. At the legislative end, coalition parties often need to compromise on issues on which they do not fully agree, or that they even disagree on in fundamental ways. Related to the politics of accommodation is the phenomenon that the criminal justice system, like other institutions, has traditionally been based on a generalized trust in the integrity of the authorities. It is assumed that decision makers act in the general interest of the public and are not corrupt. It explains why a certain skepticism against criminal law as a problem solver and a reluctance to send people to prison have resulted in one of the smallest prison populations in the world.[3]

More recently, however, The Netherlands have experienced a dramatic change in penal climate. From the mid-1970s to the mid-1980s, the official crime rate increased almost tenfold, and between 1980 and 1995 the prison population roughly tripled in size. The soaring crime rate tends to be explained by a general process of secularization and the crumbling of the "pillars" in the 1960s, an increasing material affluence, the protest movements, and the transformation of tolerance into permissiveness in the 1970s.

The resulting erosion of informal social control needed to be compensated by an increase in formal social control. The rapid growth of the prison population and the expansion of the prison system has not only been the result of a general stiffening of sentences for the bulk of criminal offenses. More important is an increasing number of long-term sentences for a relatively small number of offenses such as business robbery, sexual violence, and drug trafficking. Almost half of the increase of the prison population is accounted for by long-term sentences for drug trafficking. For this offense, foreigners and ethnic minorities are disproportionately imprisoned.

ETHNIC MINORITIES

Ethnic diversity has been a characteristic of Dutch society from the 17th century on when tens of thousands of people from Eastern Europe and Germany came for economic reasons to the "boom town" of Amsterdam whose population tripled from 50,000 in 1600 to 150,000 in 1650. In following centuries, immigrants and refugees (protestant Hugenots) came from France, Italy, Portugal and, in the 1930s, again from Germany. After World War II, immigrants came to The Netherlands mainly for three different reasons.

First, people immigrated to The Netherlands because of the decolonization of their native countries. After the declaration of independence of Indonesia in the 1950s, more than 300,000 people repatriated from Indonesia and the Moluccan Islands. In the 1970s, more than 200,000 people from Surinam (Dutch Guinea) and 66,000 from the Caribbean Islands (Antilles) immigrated to The Netherlands.

A second form of immigration took place from the mid-1950s to the mid-1970s when migrant workers were hired in the Mediterranean area (Italy, Spain, Greece, Yugoslavia, Turkey, and Morocco). From the mid-1970s until the mid-1990s, this process of labor migration halted. A process of family reunion (chain-migration), however, continued until about 400,000 people from the Mediterranean area had immigrated to The Netherlands.

A third category of immigrants consists of refugees and asylum seekers—in the 1950s from Hungary and Czechoslovakia, in the 1970s from South America and Africa, and in the 1990s from countries such as Iran, Syria, Somalia, and the former Yugoslavia. Between 1945 and 1990, about 33,000 refugees were officially given asylum. By 1990, about one half of them had acquired citizenship or had left the country to return to their home or to go elsewhere. The other half lived in The Netherlands as part of an increasing number of ethnic minorities.

The Netherlands considers itself a multiethnic society, even though in a general population of 15.5 million not even 10% are foreign born or of foreign descent. Using a more restricted definition, which excludes immigrants from industrialized areas such as Western Europe, the United States, or Japan, about 6% of the general population is considered an ethnic minority— these are the target groups of official social policies. In the population group who are under 19 years of age, however, 13% is of ethnic origin.

Currently, the main ethnic minorities are of Surinamese (1.7%), Turkish (1.6%), Moroccan (1.3%), and Caribbean (0.6%) descent. Another 0.9% include immigrants from other nonindustrialized nations, caravan dwellers, and gypsies. Not included are about 26,000 illegal immigrants who are, in fact, condoned; a similar number of asylum seekers awaiting a judicial decision with regard to their request to stay; and a smaller but fluctuating number of officially invited, subsequently recognized, or both political refugees. Obviously, not included is an unknown number of undocumented illegal immigrants. The number of illegal immigrants, who mainly live in the four major cities, has been officially estimated by the immigration service as between 50,000 and 100,000.

There are significant differences among the legal immigrants in terms of both their social and cultural background and their accommodation and integration into society. About 94% of the Surinamese and 100% of the Antillians (Caribbean) are Dutch citizens, and most of them have far fewer difficulties with the language than immigrants of Turkish and Moroccan descent (only about 10% of whom have acquired Dutch citizenship). Surinamese and Antillians also have much more contact with native Dutch citizens and fewer reservations with regard to accepting white Dutch people as personal friends or as playmates of their children. About one third of the ethnic minorities are second-generation immigrants who were born and raised in The Netherlands. Within 10 to 15 years there will be a substantial number of third-generation immigrants.

Since 1985, discrimination against ethnic minorities has become more widespread as a result of the increasing number of refugees and asylum seekers, as well as the decreasing confidence in the economy. Research has shown widespread ethnocentric prejudice, especially among segments of lower-class youth, and increasing, often hidden discrimination in the labor market.

Labor

The position of ethnic minorities in the labor market is characterized by a high unemployment rate for longer periods of time, and an overrepresentation in lower-paying positions. Although all ethnic minorities are, in general, in a position of relative deprivation, there are distinct differences between men and women, juveniles and adults, and among different ethnic groups. In 1991, 7% of the native Dutch were unemployed compared to 31% of the Turks, 36% of the Moroccans, 26% of the Surinamese, and 31% of the Antillians (Veenman & Roelandt, 1994, p. 23). Generally, unemployment of second-generation immigrants tends to be slightly lower than that of first-generation immigrants. When, however, the economic developments of the 1980s generally resulted in a high level of unemployment (12%), unemployment, particularly among foreign-born juveniles (between 15 and 24 years of age), was extraordinarily high and well over 50%.[4] Of those who had a regular job, many (60% to 70%) did unskilled, low-paid work, and perhaps for that reason seemed to have difficulty holding on to work once they had found it (Veenman & Roelandt, 1994, p. 88).

When compared to other Western countries, the current social position of Turkish, Moroccan, Surinamese, and Antillian immigrants in The Netherlands can be roughly described as relatively unfavorable in the labor market but relatively favorable in education and in the housing market. The reason for this is that the state has rather powerful instruments for regulating entry into the educational system and the rent-subsidized housing market, whereas it is rather powerless as far as the labor market is concerned.

Housing

Ethnic minorities predominantly live in the cities rather than the rural areas. In fact, 44% of the ethnic minorities live in the four largest cities—Amsterdam, Rotterdam, The Hague, and Utrecht—making a substantial part of these urban populations of foreign descent. In Amsterdam, for example, currently 42% of the inhabitants and 58% of those under the age of 20 are ethnic minorities. In some of the lower-income neighborhoods of these cities, a majority is of foreign descent. Ethnic segregation—that is, segregation between ethnic groups—however, hardly exists. For example, in a typical "ethnic neighborhood" in Amsterdam, 18% are Moroccan, 14% Surinamese, 12% Turkish, and 9% are from "other nonindustrialized nations." Urban segregation in The Netherlands is developing not so much along ethnic ("racial") lines as according to the distribution of income ("class"). To a large extent, however, ethnic minorities and low-income classes overlap. Thanks to governmental housing policy, the areas where concentrations of ethnic minorities live are much better places to live than the urban ghettos in the United States.

Education

On the average, ethnic minorities are also less successful in the Dutch educational system than their Dutch-born peers. They are less likely to move on to higher education and more likely to be found in lower forms of compulsory vocational training, where they also accomplish less and tend to drop out more than the native Dutch. Of people aged between 15 to 65 years, two thirds of the Moroccans in The Netherlands have had no education whatsoever—the same holds true for 20% of the Turks, 12% of the Surinamese, 9% of the Antillians, and 2% of the native Dutch. Of the native Dutch, 20% have a degree in higher education, whereas only 7% of the Surinamese and Antillians, 2% of the Turks, and 1% of the Moroccans have such a degree. Among the second generation of these ethnic groups, the situation has somewhat improved, in particular among the Surinamese and Antillian youth. Only the Antillians have, generally speaking, a comparable high level of education (*Integrale Veiligheidsrapportage,* 1993, p. 88). Youth from the other ethnic minorities, and especially Moroccan youth, are still overrepresented among school dropouts. This is particularly the case when they were born outside The Netherlands and came as a result of family reunion.

SOCIAL VISIBILITY AND MEDIA FOCUS

Between 1970 and 1995, the Moroccan and Turkish minorities increased more than tenfold and the number of juveniles of Moroccan or Turkish descent grew even more rapidly. Because the number of native Dutch juveniles dropped dramatically over the same period, minority youth become more visible, especially in the public domains of larger cities.

Generally, media attention to ethnic minorities is largely stereotypical and tends to be focused strictly on negative topics rather than contextualizing issues and balancing them with positive aspects in a more constructive approach. Ethnic minorities, immigrants, and refugees are depicted as problem populations. Their arrival is described as an invasion of aliens, and their presence is discussed in terms of an unwanted social, cultural, and economic burden. They are held responsible for increasing violence and crime rates (drugs, mugging, street gangs). Their different cultural backgrounds create problems of integration and social conflicts. They enjoy welfare and social security benefits and allegedly pose a threat to those who consider them as competitors for cheap housing and scarce jobs (Van Dijk, 1994).

Prior to the large postwar immigration up until the late 1950s, "minorities" consisted primarily of people from "a-social" milieus, who had dealings with the police—caravan dwellers and gypsies played a prominent role. The Moluccans came to the attention of the public in the 1970s with a series of spectacular terrorist activities aimed at achieving an independent Moluccan Republic. Although only a few Moluccans were actually involved, the events were regarded as part of a major second-generation problem. With the rise of trade and the use of hard drugs, in particular heroin, in the second half of the 1970s, the Surinamese became the number one problem group. As a result, the national newspapers devoted considerable attention to their criminality. In the 1980s, the second generation of former "guest workers" and the Moroccans in particular, were the object of moral panics and deviance amplification.

After the Second World War, when it became publicly known that the Nazis had been "allowed" to deport as many as 80% of the Dutch Jews to concentration and extermination camps, which is far more than in any other country occupied by the German army, the common self-image of the Dutch as being tolerant and humane toward immigrants, refugees, and asylum seekers was shattered. As a result, a high sensitivity to the issue of antisemitism and political correctness developed. The notion of "race," which in Dutch has a much more specific meaning than in English, became contaminated with feelings of guilt and shame and, therefore, was eliminated from current discourse in The Netherlands. As a result of this taboo on racial issues, negative information concerning ethnic minorities tends to be avoided; ethnic differences, in crime for example, are dealt with as differences in "culture" rather than of race. Whereas many native Dutch please themselves with the fact that in comparison with other European countries the number of overt racist attacks in The Netherlands is relatively small, researchers in the field of ethnic studies have vigorously criticized the tendency to deny "everyday racism" (Essed, 1991). The national self-image of the Dutch as being nonracist is debunked as a collective myth.

In the 1980s, a growing awareness of latent and manifest racial discrimination resulted in efforts to make racism a social and political issue. In 1985, a National Office for the Prevention of Racism was established, followed by antidiscrimination legislation and equal opportunity and affirmative action programs. Since the beginning of the 1990s, however, the political culture in The Netherlands changed and the position of immigrants, refugees, and asylum seekers became an explicit political issue. In public debate, a vocabulary of restricting civil rights to those who are legal citizens overshadowed a vocabulary of ethics that stressed the solidarity with those who have good intentions and have come in good faith. Native Dutch citizens and, more generally, Western Europeans are seen as forced, as well as entitled, to defend their hard-won and well-deserved welfare against profiteers and conquerors from the Third World (Lutz, in press).

CRIMINAL INVOLVEMENT

In the context of the general policy and a growing awareness of civil rights and privacy protection for minorities, the ethnic background of people arrested by the police was no longer recorded after 1974. Fortunately, there are a number of other sources from which the involvement of ethnic minorities in crime can be estimated: the ethnic composition of the prison population, studies of police files and self-report in the areas of juvenile crime and undocumented illegal foreigners, and studies in organized crime.

Prison Population

Parallel to a change in the ethnic composition of the general population, the prison population has also changed. Statistics of trends are not available. We can only provide data concerning the current ethnic composition of the prison population. In 1994, 50% of the prison population consisted of white Dutch prisoners. Of the remaining 50%, roughly one half are residents with a foreign ethnic background (foreign born or of foreign descent) who either possess Dutch citizenship or have a legal permit to stay.[5] Of the 1994 prison population, 11% are Surinamese, 8% Moroccan, 5% Turkish, 7% Antillian, and 5% from various other European countries. The majority of these individuals are legal residents. This is unlike most of the 13% from non-

European countries (of whom people from Africa, Latin America, and the Middle East are the majority) who have never lived in Dutch society and do not have a legal permit to stay.

Of the prisoners, 95% are male, but the percentage of female prisoners, especially those over 30 years of age, is increasing. Among female prisoners, Turkish and Moroccans are by and large absent but the percentage of Latin Americans and Germans is much higher than among male prisoners. This is in part explained by differences in the kind of offenses for which women are imprisoned. The most striking difference is that 45% of all women are convicted for violation of the Opium Law—largely, drug trafficking (Van Swaaningen & De Jonge, 1995).

Juvenile Crime and Delinquency

In a survey (Junger, 1990b) of 800 self-report interviews with Turkish, Moroccan, Surinamese, and a matched group of white Dutch youth between the ages of 12 and 17, a number of questions were asked about their misbehavior over a certain period. Their responses were compared with the files of the juvenile police. The information provided by the Turkish and Moroccan respondents proved unreliable as a valid source for comparison of ethnic groups. For this reason, the researcher adjusted the data using the official information on crime and delinquency available through the juvenile police. It was found that the ethnic minorities had been in contact with the police for a misdemeanor far more often than their white Dutch peers— Moroccan youth scored especially high in comparison with Turkish or Surinamese youth.

Because this research was based on a relatively small sample, the Ministry of the Interior gave a mandate for more large-scale research of the differential criminal involvement among youth from ethnic minorities. Data was collected on young men between the ages of 12 and 17 who were legal residents of The Netherlands and who during 1990 were held by the juvenile police in the four large cities (Amsterdam, Rotterdam, The Hague, and Utrecht). Police records research showed that the percentage of police contacts among Turkish, Surinamese, Antillian, and especially Moroccan youth in the four largest cities was significantly higher than among their Dutch-born peers. More than two out of three youth arrested by the police were youth of non-Dutch origin and nearly one out of three was Moroccan.[6] It was concluded that non-Dutch youth were responsible for a significant part of the juvenile criminality. In particular, the overrepresentation of young

Moroccan men was seen as noteworthy. When the study was replicated it was found that in 1992 "nearly one out of two youths" involved with the juvenile police were of Moroccan origin (*Integrale Veiligheidsrapportage,* 1994, p. 40).

To what extent this overrepresentation is a matter of selective attention or discrimination by the police, or reflects real differences in juvenile crime, remains subject to debate as does the question of how differences in the crime rate should be explained. These issues will be dealt with shortly.

Organized Crime

Until recently, ethnically organized crime was something that only occurred abroad. Now such developments can be seen in The Netherlands as well, especially in the area of drug trade. It is impossible to determine exactly how many people are involved, but heroin import is presently in the hands of the Turks, whereas Moroccans have an important share in the hashish trade, and the export of cocaine to Europe runs primarily through the Surinamese.

American criminologists have always stressed that ethnically organized crime belonged to the American scene. It met certain requirements in the culture and was not organized from the countries of origin (Block, 1991). This applies in a much smaller degree to the involvement of non-Dutch groups in the drug trade in The Netherlands. Due to intercontinental transportation and banking, the drug trade is organized primarily through the countries or regions of origin. Thus, heroin is brought in from the Near East and Southeast Asia, cocaine from South America, and hashish from North Africa and Pakistan. From The Netherlands as a main port in shipping and transport, these drugs are transported to other places in Europe and the rest of the world. In part, the wares are distributed locally through the channels of the world of ethnic enterprise—a world that has undergone a rapid expansion.

The most important difference from the United States is that the profits from organized crime are not invested in The Netherlands. The profits from the drug trade disappear back into the country of origin, which does not have laws on confiscation of criminal profits or laws against money laundering, or where the governments gain by ignoring illegal activities or granting general pardons, allowing illegal profits to be invested in legitimate firms or enterprises. The Surinamese, Turks, and Moroccans who do the distribution work in The Netherlands for foreign drug networks remain strongly oriented toward their country of origin. This is also true for many who prefer to invest their profits in the economy of their homeland rather than using these profits to improve the position of the ethnic community in The Netherlands. In short, the trade is managed from the outside, the goods are locally distributed by non-Dutch who remain oriented toward their country of origin, and the profits largely disappear back into this country of origin (Van Duyne, 1995).

Undocumented Illegal Foreigners

There is even less known about the involvement of illegal foreigners in criminality than about that of ethnic minorities. On the basis of 1,285 files on foreigners who had been arrested by the police, Aalberts and Dijkhoff (1993) found that 87% turned out to be illegal and 54% had committed at least one criminal offense. Those who had not committed a criminal offense were arrested because they had not been able to identify themselves or produce a permit of residence, and thus were technically illegal. Illegal foreigners were less often arrested and charged with a criminal offense (52%) than legal foreigners (62%). Specific differences between ethnic groups as well as their involvement in different types of offenses, however, were not investigated.

Recently, in the city of Rotterdam, a more elaborate study has been conducted in which such differences were analyzed (Engbersen, Van der Leun, & Willems, 1995). It was, again, found that overall crime rates were lower for illegal foreigners than for legal immigrants.[7] Some categories of illegal foreigners were charged with certain types of offenses more often than others. Differences in recorded crime rates among arrested illegal foreigners reflected known differences between legal immigrant minorities such as Moroccans and Turks.[8] For example, Moroccans were relatively often arrested for felonies (criminal offenses and drug-related crime), whereas Turks were relatively often arrested for misdemeanors (working without a license).

MINORITIES AS VICTIMS OF CRIME

Very little is known about ethnic differences in criminal victimization. There are several reasons for this. The ethnic background of victims of crime is not systematically recorded by the police. And, in the periodically held national crime victimization surveys, the ethnic background of the respondent is not asked. In 1992, however, a small survey was conducted in the cities of Amsterdam (N = 148) and Rotterdam (N = 152) with an equal number of respondents from Surinamese, Moroccan, and Turkish descent (Integrale *Veiligheidsrapportage,* 1993). More than half (55%) of all respondents mentioned being confronted with discrimination from the Dutch one or more times in the last year. One out of seven claims to have been discriminated against often or regularly. There are significant differences among the Turkish (87%), Moroccan (45%), and Surinamese (32%) respondents. Next to being the object of offensive/abusive language by strangers in public, discrimination by officials and police was mentioned most.

Compared to the average for the entire population in Amsterdam and Rotterdam, a study in 1990 showed that ethnic minorities were victims of frequently occurring criminality two to three times as often. For property crimes, the percentage of victims among ethnic minorities is one and one half times higher than that in the total population. In the category of violent offenses, these differences are even greater. For example, the percentage of victims of threat of physical violence is 13%—twice as high among ethnic minorities as the total population (7%), with hardly any differences among the three ethnic minorities. In the case of abuse, however, Moroccan victims are much more common (29%, compared to 7% among Turks, 2% among Surinamese, and 2% in the total population).

In the victim survey mentioned previously, the possible influence of the neighborhood on ethnic differences in victimization was not taken into account. In the 1994 report, this was done by comparing the responses of Turks and Moroccans with those of a "matched" Dutch group who lived in exactly the same neighborhoods. In comparison, Turks and Moroccans appeared to be less often victims of violent and property crimes. The conclusion is drawn that the size of the community and the quality of the neighborhood influences the relatively high percentage of victims of offenses among Turks and Moroccans rather than their ethnic origin (*Integrale Veiligheidsrapportage,* 1994, pp. 38-39). Surinamese and Antillians have been matched in a similar way with Dutch groups and, again, no significant differences were found in general victimization rates of ethnic minorities and Dutch living in the same neighborhood or area (*Integrale Veiligheidsrapportage,* 1994, p. 39).

Thus, no significant differences in general victimization rates appear to exist between ethnic minorities and white Dutch-born who live in the same type of neighborhood. Differences in specific forms of victimization such as racial harassment and discrimination, however, do exist. According to the data that have been compiled from a number of sources, including publications of the official State Security Service and the activist Antifascist Research Collective, the number of reported incidents of racial and right-wing extremist violence increased from a few dozen incidents annually throughout the 1980s, to several hundred in the early 1990s, to more than 1,000 in 1994 (Buis & Van Donselaar, 1994, p. 64). It is not clear whether this trend indicates a real increase in racist attacks, an increasing willingness to report and record these incidents, or both. Research has shown an increase in ethnocentric prejudice and intolerance, especially among the generation that was born between 1968 and 1977. It seems that for these young people the taboo on offensive/abusive language aimed at minorities and discrimination of ethnic minorities has lost much of its strength. This could explain a real increase in hate crimes and racist violence (Scheepers & Coenders, 1996, p. 21).

There are also indications that these incidents are severely underreported. In a 1995 survey among Turks, Moroccans, and Surinamese, it was found that 2% of the respondents reported that they had been a victim of racist violence and 4% had suffered from racist threats. On the basis of this prevalence, the real number of racist violent incidents in 1995 may be estimated roughly at about 10,000 (van Donselaar, 1995, p. 59). This would mean that these incidents are underreported by a factor of 10.

MINORITIES AS EMPLOYEES/PROFESSIONALS IN THE CRIMINAL JUSTICE SYSTEM

Police

At the end of the 1980s, the Ministry of the Interior launched an affirmative action program to increase the representation of ethnic minorities within the police force. Immediately, the percentage of students of foreign descent at the Police Academy increased to more than 25% (1991 to 1994) of the freshmen. In 1995, however, this percentage dropped dramatically to only 5%. Reasons for this drop included a decentralization of the selection, which made it impossible for the Ministry to monitor and control the inflow of students, as well as mistakes made in the early implementation of the plan. Currently, new plans are being developed by the Ministry with what is seen as a more realistic approach.

To increase at least the street visibility of ethnic minorities among the rank-and-file in the police force, a new project, Police and People of Foreign

Descent, was started in 1992. Its aim was to increase the number of people of foreign descent among the rank-and-file of the police and help them in their career development. Data are incomplete, yet it is safe to state that "people of foreign descent" remain seriously underrepresented in the Dutch police force (see Dekkers-Geytenbeek & Snijders, 1995).

The police forces in the four major cities have made an extra effort to hire policemen and -women of foreign descent. An increasing number of so-called city guards, that is, surveillants without formal police power, are hired for foot patrol on the city streets. These low-wage jobs are created as a cheap alternative for more police on the beat. They are part of a large-scale program meant to reduce the two major problems of unemployment and public safety.

Prison Guards

In 1991, the directors of the 52 prisons, employing about 3,000 prison guards, received a letter requesting that they determine how many employees of foreign descent worked in their particular institution. In some cases, directors were opposed to this inventory on principle. Ultimately, data were received from 32 institutions. In 11 institutions, no prison guards of foreign descent were employed. In the rest of the institutions, as of February 1992, 118 prison guards of foreign descent could be found: 94 men and 24 women. Of these persons, the most came from Surinam (59), the Dutch Antilles (23), and the South Mollucans (11). Turks (5) and Moroccans (3) were represented to only a very slight degree (Essed, 1993).

RESEARCH AND THEORY ON CRIME, CRIMINAL JUSTICE, AND MINORITIES

Selectivity

Timmerman, Bosma, and Jongman (1986) found that first offenders who belong to ethnic minorities were more severely sentenced than white Dutch offenders.[9] More specifically, Surinamese and Antillians were sentenced to (partly) unconditional imprisonment for less serious offenses, whereas for similar offenses they received more severe penalties. This result was seen as part of a more general relationship between relative deprivation and severity of punishment through which gender, race, class, and unemployment are reproduced in sentencing.

A more elaborate study (Maas & Stuyling de Lange, 1989) confirmed that ethnic minorities find that their cases are less frequently waived and that they are more severely sentenced than white Dutch offenders for similar offenses. These differences cannot be attributed to differences in previous or repeat offenses. There might, however, be an ethnic difference in the readiness to plead guilty or not guilty. To really explain differential sentencing, more qualitative studies are needed (see Yesilgöz, 1995).

More recently, it has been argued that although differential treatment is apparent in the later phases of the criminal procedure, there are no signs of selectivity in police intervention. Junger (1988, 1989, 1990b), for example, has claimed that there is no evidence of police discrimination against ethnic minorities. A careful reanalysis of all available empirical studies (Bovenkerk, de Haan, & Yesilgöz, 1991) revealed that Junger was selective in the way she interpreted her sources and, in fact, ignored publications by authors who came to different conclusions than her own. Previously, a series of studies had shown that the police were biased in their dealings with ethnic minorities. Esmeijer and Luning (1978) showed that negative stereotypes dominated in the Amsterdam police force. Willemse and Meyboom (1978) found that individuals with a dark skin color were more likely to be regarded as a suspect. And, Junger-Tas and Van der Zee-Nefkens (1977) described how people of color were stopped and searched more often than their white peers. Bovenkerk and Luning (1979), however, found no such differences.

Given the generally negative image of the second generation of Moroccans, it would be almost "unnatural" if this public image did not lead to more attention on the part of the police for this particular group. Police direct their attention selectively to places and circumstances where much criminality occurs, and to the type of individual who fits the bill as a possible perpetrator. In this way, an unavoidable mechanism occurs whereby selective attention sustains the usefulness of applying different standards. Differences in the proportion of suspects from different ethnic groups may be the result of this selectivity. The empirical "fact" that Moroccan youth come into contact with the police for minor offenses relatively often (only to be discharged again) points to this selectivity. Thus, the number of times that members of a specific group are involved with the police is not a reliable measure for "the" criminality in that group. The high crime statistics of ethnic minorities are not facts that speak for themselves; they are constructed and connected with the way the police conduct their tasks. It is important to keep this in mind when considering explanations of ethnic differences in crime.

CULTURAL EXPLANATIONS

A specific explanation for the high rate of criminality among Moroccan youth is the "cultural conflict" between the disciplinary regime of the traditional Moroccan family and the regime of negotiations found outside the family in modern Dutch society. The sociologist, Kapteyn (1987), for example, views the increase in criminality among foreign youth as a consequence of the fact that their parents come from societies in which social control remains the way it used to be in Dutch society before, in the 1960s, the shift took place within the family between parents and children from a disciplinary to a negotiating regime.

In recent sociological research among foreign families living in The Netherlands, it was found that "the so-called disciplinary regime, which so many authors assume, was notably absent" (Cuyver, von Meijenfeldt, von Houten, & van Meijers, 1993, p. 152). No significant differences among ethnic groups in terms of their educational activities were discovered.

> The attitude and opinions of foreign parents in the area of child-rearing . . . did not seem much different than those of Dutch parents. This was particularly true in view of the fact that these parents were nearly without exception from lower social backgrounds. (Cuyver et al., 1993, p. 157)

According to these researchers, the explanation for the problems of children from foreign families does not reside in different family situations or in cultural differences, but rather in the subordinate social position in which they find themselves (Cuyver et al., 1993, p. 159). The problems of Moroccan youth in The Netherlands do not emerge through the "cultural unwillingness" of the parents to give their children a good education, but rather through powerlessness and lack of resources. Based on conversations with the parents of Moroccan youth who have been involved with the police, it appears to be more difficult for Moroccan parents to solve problems that occur within the family due to their poor functioning within Dutch society. Problems occur because Moroccan fathers and mothers often do not have the means to influence their child (Van 'T Hoff, 1991).

The latter is no less true for the situation of the Surinamese[10] and Antillian youth who belong to the "weak" economic classes, and often grown up in Caribbean families with a "matrifocal" character, whereby the mother plays a central role and the role of the husband and father is filled only incidentally or hardly at all by a succession of men. The result is a close tie between mother and child and a family bond that is stronger and broader than usually found in Dutch society, and where family members such as grandparents, brothers and sisters, nieces and nephews play an important role in child rearing (*Integrale Veiligheidsrapportage,* 1993, p. 96). Nevertheless, there seems to be less, rather than more, social control in matrifocal families (*Integrale Veiligheidsrapportage,* 1993, p. 93), which is supposed to explain the relatively high level of criminality.

STRUCTURAL EXPLANATIONS

In the Netherlands, the structural approach has been highly influential, not only in criminology but also in policy on crime control and ethnic minorities. According to van Amersfoort and Biervliet (1975), for example, the relatively high crime rates of immigrants from Surinam in the 1970s must be explained not merely by demographic, urbanizational, and educational differences, but rather, by the relatively high number of young, unskilled, and unemployed (p. 377). In a similar way, the official policy paper on minorities (Minderhedennota, 1983) related the fact that the police and the criminal justice system were being confronted with relatively large numbers of ethnic minorities who had adaptation problems and were handicapped with regard to education, income, and housing. In the more recent report by the Academic Advisory Council for Policy Issues on the policy concerning ethnic minorities (Wetenschappelijke Raad voor het Regeringsbeleid [WRR], 1989), the negative consequences of high unemployment for social relations within the immigrant communities are stressed. Because ethnic minorities tend to live in "problem accumulation areas," they will also be more frequently involved in (violent) crime, either as offenders or as victims. As ethnic minorities become better integrated into Dutch society, current differences in patterns of criminal behavior will diminish (WRR, 1989, p. 21).

Structurally, criminality of ethnic minorities is explained by the same factors that explain the involvement of native Dutch in criminal behavior. Differences merely exist insofar as ethnic minorities suffer from social and economic deprivation. It is hardly coincidental that precisely those ethnic groups with the greatest deprivation in the labor market, housing, and education, also have the biggest problems with juvenile crime.

The theory's advantage is that the issue is not treated as a matter of ethnicity, but rather is situated in the context of the social and economic organization of society. A disadvantage of the differential opportunity theory, however, is that it can only explain differences in scope and not in the type of criminality. Research on the connection between ethnic background and criminality cannot afford to ignore the unique character of some criminality in a particular ethnic group. For example, it has been found that drug trafficking, violence, and aggression are the most usual forms of crime among members of the Turkish community, and interpersonal violence is much more prominent among Turkish males than among the Dutch. The Turkish underworld in The Netherlands is marked by extremely violent action taken within their own circles. As a result, they show the largest number of contract killings of all the ethnic groups. This phenomenon might be seen against the background of a certain tradition of violence in Turkish culture. As Yesilgöz (1995, p. 207) has pointed out, "The Turks and the Dutch differ considerably in their ideas about different offenses, the former being inclined to tolerance of violence and aggression if honor is involved."

REFLEXIVITY

Structural and cultural explanations of ethnic differences in crime have in common that concepts are being used in an unreflected way. Neither the concept of crime nor of ethnicity is submitted to an adequate sociological analysis. The research problem is adopted at face value from the official policy discourses concerning criminal justice, foreigners, and ethnic minorities, whereas the categories are borrowed from criminal justice and crime statistics. These are all categories that have technical, administrative character rather than sociological relevance. In this chapter, I do not expand on the topic of the social construction of crime. As Bovenkerk (1990) has noted, substantial progress has been made in criminology not because racial differences in crime have been established more reliably but because race and crime are considered as social constructs and analyzed as such. Ethnic or cultural differences obtain their specific meaning in a political and historical context in which social (power) relations and inequality are being organized along the lines of these differences. Miles (1982) has pointed out the political and economical consequences of such ideological constructions in which social meaning is attributed to phenotypical difference. As a result, social deprivation and crime may seem to be caused by race. Therefore, the ethnic background of people has to be dealt with not in technical administrative terms but as historical, sociological, and political categories. For theoretically relevant research of ethnic differences in crime, a theory of cultural differences and, more important, of ethnicity is *conditio sine qua non.* Current ethnic categories must be analyzed as normative claims regarding the hegemony of white culture.

Applying a dynamic concept of ethnic identity in cultural explanations of differences in criminal behavior implies that cultural differences are not being seen merely in terms of the dominant culture. Cultural traditions are subject to permanent change. A distinction needs to be made among the dominant culture, the subcultures that immigrants originally came from in their own country, and the new subcultures that emerged in the course of the process of integration in the country of residence (Lea & Young, 1984, p. 131).

ETHNOGRAPHY

Most research on crime of ethnic minorities is a form of naive positivistic, according to some even racist, criminology that ignores the fact that "allochtonic criminality"[11] is a social and political construction in which power differentials and inequality between ethnic groups of allochtones and autochtones are ideologically articulated. The risk of harmful, stigmatizing effects cannot be eliminated merely by methodological rigor or by being cautious when presenting results to the media. These risks are inherent to this type of research and result from the way the research problem is defined. Instead of a methodological defense, an explicit theoretical justification should be required that, as we have seen, cannot be produced in terms of the conventional approaches in current criminology. Thus, when ethnic differences in crime between allochtones and autochtones are methodologically problematic and, moreover, from a theoretical point of view, being applied in an unreflexive way, current positivistic research of ethnic differences in crime should, also given the moral dilemmas involved, be abandoned.

Only qualitative explanations that are grounded in the ethnographic research of criminal behavior by members of ethnic groups can meet the requirements of an adequate explanation and understanding of ethnic involvement in specific types of crime. Good examples of such an approach are to be found in the studies of Jankowski (1991), Katz (1989), Pryce (1979), and Sullivan (1989). In The Netherlands, we have a number of ethnographies concerning the criminal involvement of Surinamese (Biervliet, 1975; Buiks, 1983; van Gelder, 1990; Sansone, 1991, 1992) and

Moroccans (Kaufman & Verbrack, 1986; Wermölder, 1986, 1990). To date, no such study on the Turks has been produced.[12]

DISCUSSION OF LEGAL AND POLICY ISSUES

Whether one employs a general or a specific explanation for ethnic differences in crime has implications for policy. General structural explanations focus on the fundamental similarities among ethnic groups, while attributing any differences among them to social and economic conditions. Specific cultural explanations tend to stress the similarities in the effects of social and cultural conditions on all groups, while attributing specific differences to cultural backgrounds.

In both structural and cultural explanations, however, an ethnocentric perspective prevails. The extent to which ethnic minorities are "different" is measured according to standards of the dominant culture of the majority. In contrast, ethnographically grounded cultural explanations, with their validation of agency and their sensitivity to people's motives and the constraints under which they operate, enable us to discover equality within difference. This paves the way to eventual political acceptance of equality on the basis of a full recognition of difference.

Politics

In The Netherlands, ethnic minorities have been officially subjected to special policy measures since 1983 when a policy plan was launched that targeted a number of specific ethnic groups and aimed at creating a society in which these ethnic minorities both individually and as a group would be accepted and valued as equals. This should be achieved by reducing and eliminating their disadvantage and discrimination and by promoting a tolerant, multicultural society. The formal position of immigrants has been improved by legal reforms concerning the elimination of legislation with discriminating effects. At the same time, discrimination[13] in public, either orally or by writing or image, has been made punishable by law. Less successful, however, are the efforts to implement this legislation. The same holds true for efforts to implement affirmative action and contract compliance in the labor market; these have been controversial from their start in

1994. In response, the point has been made that a special policy for ethnic minorities has become counterproductive and should be suspended.

It is crucial that equality in political rights and difference in culture or ethnicity are reconciled by recognizing differences and integrating them in a notion of equality or, rather, equivalence. Political equality requires a certain amount of "indifference" concerning ethnic and cultural difference. Elimination of all difference, however, cannot be a viable solution. Political equality will have to be granted without having to give up difference or the right to retain one's cultural identity. Particularly with regard to the process of European unification, an increasing awareness will be needed of both the contingent and voluntaristic character of ethnicity. The great danger of rhetorically linking difference in cultural identity to difference in criminality is that a policy of uniformity by enforced elimination of cultural difference may easily be seen as a form of crime control. Enforced assimilation instead of integration would then be seen as a legitimate policy to maintain law and order.

SPECULATION ABOUT FUTURE DEVELOPMENTS

In The Netherlands, just as in many other Western European countries, there is at present considerable concern about the constant stream of refugees, asylum seekers, and the presence of illegal foreigners for economic reasons. Although the most recent figures indicate that their numbers are decreasing rather than increasing, legislation is being developed to restrain the influx from outside the European community. In the context of an open border policy, restrictions of admittance of foreigners are more strictly implemented and policing of undocumented immigrants and asylum seekers has been intensified. Employers of unlicensed workers are now fined, undocumented foreigners are excluded from public services (housing, schooling, health care), and so-called illegals who have been arrested by the police are extradited more effectively. It is to be expected that these policies of discouraging immigrants and containment of illegal populations will be further expanded and intensified.

It is feared that the unrestrained expansion of the number of newcomers will prevent an economic, social, and cultural integration of ethnic minorities into Dutch society. Although the economy is recovering, unemployment, particularly among ethnic minorities, will remain a structural problem. This means that large groups are in danger of becoming socially isolated and chronically dependent on welfare. Anxieties arise concerning processes of concentration and segregation that can lead to the formation of ghetto-like neighborhoods in which social problems and crime become endemic. It is feared that a permanent underclass is in the making, in which unemployment will be chronic and poverty will become intergenerational.

Fortunately, however, a series of studies indicates that these fears are, as yet, unfounded. Although there are unmistakable signs of accumulation in deprivation in certain areas, they cannot be characterized as homogeneous, nor are residents solely from groups with an unfavorable social position. In part, this is the consequence of a high level of social services in the Dutch welfare state, whereby the effects of concentration are hardly noticeable. Moreover, it is notable that concentration occurs primarily among recent immigrants. Thus, it remains to be seen whether the accumulation of deprivation will occur in the long term (Veenman & Roelandt, 1994, p. 165).[14]

The current policy plan, 1995 to 1998, includes an urban revitalization plan for the "big 4" and 15 larger cities. This urban revitalization program aims to improve objectively recorded and subjectively experienced public safety and the quality of life in urban problem areas as well as reduce long-term unemployment and enhance the care for the most vulnerable. As far as public safety is concerned, a safer cities program aims at reconquering the public domain by reducing crime and drug problems. To achieve these goals, the so-called safety chain will be strengthened, that is, additional manpower for the public prosecution and the judiciary, and extra prison cells for the corrections department. Social control in public places is improved by hiring substantial numbers of chronically unemployed for surveillance jobs and by activating social organizations, the business community, and citizens to participate in neighborhood safety plans. Moreover, the plan provides shelter for the homeless and treatment for drug addicts. And finally, it tries to deal with public order aspects of organized crime by preventing corruption and fraud.

Early identification of children with problems at home, in school, or on the street is aimed at through the cooperation in local networks of all relevant services and organizations. Special attention is still given to juveniles of foreign descent. Special policies for ethnic minorities might, however, soon come to an end. In cities like Amsterdam and Rotterdam, about one half of the children are already foreign born or of foreign descent. And in less than 15 years, more than half of the general population of these cities will consist of people of Turkish, Moroccan, Surinamese, or Antillian descent, as well as some other 90 or more nationalities.

CONCLUSION

Research on ethnic differences in criminality is being done mostly for political purposes either to fight current prejudice or to prove the urgency of specific policy measures for the benefit of ethnic minorities. It tends to be "forgotten" that ethnic differences in crime are essentially socially constructed. Ethnicity and criminality are both contingent to a large extent. This creates many problems when studying differences in crime among ethnic minorities, problems that cannot be solved within the confines of the current methodological and theoretical approaches within criminology.[15] Questions of equality and difference in culture and crime require a theoretical reflection on the level of social and political theory, and philosophy, and go beyond the disciplinary boundaries of conventional criminology.

NOTES

1. Parts of this chapter are based on previous Dutch publications written in collaboration with Frank Bovenkerk (Bovenkerk, de Haan, & Yesilgöz, 1991; de Haan & Bovenkerk, 1993, 1995).

2. In several areas such as medical services and higher education, a minimum access to services and care is still guaranteed albeit in combination with a private responsibility of individual citizens for additional insurances.

3. In fact, explaining the relative mildness of Dutch penal policy and sentencing practices during the postwar era is a much more complicated affair. For an explanation that takes a number of additional factors into account, see de Haan (1990b).

4. Only the percentage of unemployed Turkish youth (40%) was lower, but still very high in comparison with their Dutch-born peers.

5. The other half concerns people who have not committed any crime, but are remanded in custody because they have no legal title to stay in The Netherlands.

6. Because Antillians were classified as "other," their involvement could not be estimated.

7. An exception concerned drug-related crimes, for which illegal immigrants showed much higher rates than legal immigrants.

8. Among illegal immigrants, Surinamese are hardly represented because most Surinames have opted for Dutch citizenship.

9. Albeit this difference did not hold for repeat offenders.

10. This refers to the Creole. The family situation of Hindu boys is said to be largely comparable with those of Turkish families (*Integrale Veiligheidsrapportage*, 1993, p. 93).

11. *Allochtonic* is the government term for "foreign born."

12. But see Yesigöz (1995).

13. Discrimination not only on the basis of race but also of religion, ideology, and sexual preference.

14. Recently, Roelandt (1994) rejected the notion of an ethnic underclass in The Netherlands, but argued that the risk is present among Turks and Moroccans, in particular. He immediately added, however, that "very little can be said with any certainty about future developments in the socialeconomic position of persons of foreign descent in The Netherlands" (pp. 218-219).

15. The same holds true for other basic problems of criminology such as problems of morality, justice, and rationality (see de Haan, 1990a).

REFERENCES

Aalberts, M., & Dijkhoff, J. (1993). Illegalen in de criminaliteit, criminelen in de illegaliteit. *Rechtshulp, 11,* 24-28.

Amersfoort, J. van, & Biervliet, W. (1977). Criminaliteit van minderheden. In E. van der Wolk (Ed.), *De bedreigde burger* (pp. 367-384). Utrecht: Spectrum.

Biervliet, W. (1975). The hustler culture of young unemployed Surinamers. In H. E. Lamur & J. D. Speckmann (Eds.), *Adaptation of migrants from the Caribbean in the European and American metropolis* (pp. 191-201). Amsterdam: University of Amsterdam Press.

Block, A. (1991). *Perspectives on organizing crime: Essays in opposition.* Dordrecht, The Netherlands: Kluwer.

Bovenkerk, F. (1990). Misdaad en de multi-etnische samenleving. *Justitiële Verkenningen, 16*(5), 8-28.

Bovenkerk, F., de Haan, W., & Yesilgöz, Y. (1991). Over selectiviteit gesproken! *Tijdschrift voor Criminologie, 33*(3), 309-321.

Bovenkerk, F., & Luning, M. (1979). Surinamers en grote auto's: Een "levensecht experiment" om rassendiscriminatie op te sporen. *Algemeen Politieblad, 128,* 159-162.

Buiks, P. (1983). *Surinaamse jongeren op de Kruiskade; overleven in een etnische randgroep.* Deventer, The Netherlands: Van Loghum Slaterus.

Buis, F., & Van Donselaar, J. (1994). *Extreem-rechts.* Leiden: Leids Instituut voor Sociaal-Wetenschappelijk Onderzoek.

Cuyver, P., von Meijenfeldt, F. von Houten, H., & van Meijers, F. (1993). Allochtone en autochtone jongeren: Hoe groot is het verschil? *Sociologische Gids, 40*(2), 140-160.

Dekkers-Geytenbeek, N., & Snijders, R. (1995). *Registreren, alleen een kwestie van cijfers? Een balans van de stand van zaken omtrent allochtone medewerk(st)ers bij de Nederlandse Politie.* Arnhem, The Netherlands: In opdracht van het Project Politie en Allochtonen.

Donselaar, J. van. (1995). *De staat paraat? De bestrijding van extreem-rechts in West-Europa.* Amsterdam: Babylon-De Geus.

Duyne, P. C. van. (1995). The phantom and threat of organized crime. *Crime, Law, and Social Change, 24*(4) 341-378.

Engbersen, G., Van der Leun, J., & Willems, P. (1995). *Over den verweyenheid van illegaliteit en criminaliteit.* Den Haag: Ministerie van Binnenlandse Zaken.

Esmeijer, L., & Luning, M. (1978). Surinamers in de ogen van de Amsterdamse politie. In F. Bovenkerk (Ed.), *Omdat zij anders zijn* (pp. 136-165). Amsterdam: Boom Meppel.

Essed, P. (1991). *Understanding everyday racism.* Newbury Park, CA: Sage.

Essed, E. (1993). *Tokens binnen vier muren. Een onderzoek naar de werkervaringen van allochtone penitentiair inrichtingswerkers.* Amsterdam: Vrije Universiteit.

de Haan, W. (1990a). Allochtonen en autochtonen: Gelijkheid en verschil in cultuur en criminaliteit. *Justitiële Verkenningen, 16*(5), 29-53.

de Haan, W. (1990b). *The politics of redress. Crime, punishment, and penal abolition.* Boston: Unwin Hyman.

de Haan, W., & Bovenkerk, F. (1993). Moedwil en misverstand. Overschatting en onderschatting van allochtone criminaliteit in Nederland. *Tijdschrift voor Criminologie, 35*(3), 277-300.

de Haan, W., & Bovenkerk, F. (1995). Sociale integratie en Criminaliteit. In G. Engbersen & R. Gabriëls (Eds.), *Sferen van integratie* (pp. 223-248). Amsterdam: Meppel Boom.

Integrale Veiligheidsrapportage. (1993). Den Haag: Ministerie van Binnenlandse Zaken.

Integrale Veiligheidsrapportage. (1994). Den Haag: Ministerie van Binnenlandse Zaken.

Jankowski, M. S. (1991). *Islands in the street. Gang and American urban society.* Berkeley: University of California Press.

Junger, M. (1988). Racial discrimination in criminal justice in The Netherlands. *Sociology and Social Research, 4,* 211-217.

Junger, M. (1989). Discrepancies between police and self-report data for Dutch racial minorities. *British Journal of Criminology, 3,* 273-284.

Junger, M. (1990a). *Delinquency and ethnicity.* Boston: Kluwer.

Junger, M. (1990b). Studying ethnic minorities in relation to crime and police discrimination. *British Journal of Criminology, 4,* 493-503.

Junger-Tas, J., & Van der Zee-Nefkins, A. (1977). Een observatie-onderzoek naar het werk van de politie-surveillance. Den Haag: Wetenschappelijk Onderzoek en Documentatie Centrum, Ministerie van Justitie.

Kapteyn, P. (1987). Publieke moraal en zelfcontrole. *Justitiële Verkenningen, 13*(6), 65-67.

Katz, J. (1989). *Seductions of crime: Moral and sensual attractions in doing evil.* New York: Basic Books.

Kaufman, P., & Verbraeck, H. (1986). *Marokkaan en verslaafd: Een studie naar randgroepvorming, heroïnegebruik en criminalisering.* Utrecht: Gemeente Utrecht afdeling Onderzoek.

Lea, J., & Young, J. (1984). *What to do about law and order.* New York: Penguin.

Lijphart, A. (1975). *The politics of accomodation* (2nd ed.). Berkeley: University of California Press.

Lucassen, J., & Penninx, R. (1994). *Nieuwkomers, nakomelingen, Nederlanders, immigranten in Nederland 1550-1993* (2nd ed.). Amsterdam: Het Spinhuis.

Lutz, H. (in press). Anti-islamism—Rhetorics of exclusion in The Netherlands. A debate on locations of selves vis-à-vis others. In F. Anthias, C. Lloyd, & N. Yuval Davis (Eds.), *Antiracist strategies and movements in Europe.* London: Macmillan.

Maas, C., & Stuyling de Lange, J. (1989). Selectiviteit in de rechtsgang van buitenlandse verdachten en verdachten behorende tot etnische groepen. *Tijdschrift voor Criminologie, 31*(1), 1-13.

Miles, R. (1982). *Racism and migrant labor.* London: Routledge & Kegan Paul.

Minderhedennota. (1983). *Actieprogramma Minderhedenbeleid* (Ministerie van Binnenlandse Zaken). Den Haag: Staatsuitgeverij.

Pryce, K. (1979). *Endless pressure: A study of West Indian life-styles in Bristol.* New York: Penguin.

Roelandt, T. (1994). *Verscheidenheid in ongelijkheid. Een studie naar etnische stratificatie en onderklassevorming in de Nederlandse samenleving.* Amsterdam: Thesis.

Sansone, L. (1991). Marginalisering en overlevingsstategieën onder Surinaams-Creoolse jongeren uit de lagere sociale klasse. *Migrantenstudies, 6*(4), 23-37.

Sansone, L. (1992). *Schitteren in de schaduw.* Amsterdam: Het Spinhuis.

Scheepers, P., & Coenders, M. (1996). Trends in etnische discriminatie in Nederland 1980-1993. *Justitiële Verkenningen, 22*(3), 8-25.

Sociaal en Cultureel Planbureau. (1994). *Sociaal Cultureel Rapport 1994.* Rijswijk, The Netherlands: Author.

Sullivan, M. L. (1989). *"Getting paid": Youth crime and work in the inner city.* Ithaca, NY: Cornell University Press.

Timmerman, H., Bosman, J., & Jongman, R. (1986). Minderheden voor de rechter. *Tijdschrift voor Criminologie, 28*(2), 57-72.

Van Dijk, T. (1994). Brief statement on racism and the press. Some major results of scholarly research on the role of the media in multicultural societies. *ADO Journal, 2*(2/4), 4-6.

van Gelder, P. (1990). *Ik wil een smalle weg volgen Sociale risico's en kansen onder werkloze Marokkaanse jongens in Den Haag.* Den Haag: Rapport in opdracht van het Regionaal Centrum Buitenlanders Zuid-Holland West.

van Swaaningen, R., & De Jonge, G. (1995). The Dutch prison system and penal policy in the 1990s: From humanitarian paternalism to penal business management. In V. Ruggiero, M. Ryan, & J. Sim (Eds.), *Western European penal systems: A critical anatomy* (pp. 24-45). London: Sage.

van 'T Hoff, C. (1991). Gezagsverhoudingen binnen Marokkaanse gezinnen. *Tijdschrift voor Criminologie, 33*(2), 120-131.

Veenman, J., & Roelandt, T. (1994). *Onzeker bestaan. De maatschappelijke positie van Turken, Marokkanen, Surinamers en Antillianen in Nederland.* Amsterdam: Boom/ISEO.

Werdmölder, H. (1986). *Van vriendenkring tot randgroep. Marokkaanse jongeren in een oude stadswijk.* Houten, The Netherlands: Het Wereldvenster.

Werdmölder, H. (1990). *Een generatie op drift. De geschiedenis van een Marrokkaanse randgroep.* Arnhem: Gouda Quint.

Willemse, H. M., & Meyboom, M. L. (1978). Personal characteristics of suspects and treatment by the police: A street experiment, Part I. *Abstracts on Police Science, 6,* 323-331.

Wetenschappelijke Raad voor het Regeringsbeleid—WRR. (1989). *Allochtonenbeleid.* Den Haag: SDU, Staatsdrukkerij.

Yesilgöz, Y. (1995). *Allah, Satan en het recht. Communicatie met Turkse verdachten.* Arnhem, The Netherlands: Gouda Quint.

10

MINORITIES AND CRIME IN EUROPE AND THE UNITED STATES: MORE SIMILAR THAN DIFFERENT!

SOME COMMON CONCERNS

European governments are taking increasingly restrictive measures to deal with minorities and migrants. Reflecting the shift in the nature of immigration and the composition of the migrant population, government policy toward ethnic minorities is more and more subordinated to a security policy toward foreigners and people of foreign origin (cf. Hebberecht, Chapter 7, this volume; Weiner, 1993). There is increased focus on the control of immigration and cross-border crime, organized crime, international criminal networks, and black markets (see Schmid & Savona, 1996). Parallel developments are taking place in the United States.

The authors describing the situation in the United Kingdom, The Netherlands, Belgium, France, Germany, Italy, Spain, and Sweden leave no doubt: Political and public debate on the link between criminality and minorities/migrants in these countries is often highly politicized and volatile, sensitive,

224

and emotionally charged. More often than not, the "minority-crime" connection is enthusiastically embraced by political extremists in Europe. Likewise, in the United States, public and political discourse on native ethnic and racial minorities, "new immigrants," undocumented aliens, and foreigners (and crime) tends to be highly controversial and emotional; Americans also tend to associate criminality and minorities/migrants.

Questions of ethnicity, migration, and crime have polarized intellectuals in Europe and the United States. Some scholars, for instance, refuse to participate in such research because it reifies theoretically and scientifically meaningless concepts (such as "ethnicity" or "race"), because it may have undesirable policy implications, because linking "criminality" and "migrants" (or minorities) has the undesirable consequence of forging an artificial cause-effect association between the two terms, or because it simply is too difficult to do it right.

European countries vary significantly in the amount and sophistication of research on the topic of migrants, minorities, and crime: Britain, The Netherlands, and Germany, for instance, have produced quite a bit more scholarly work on these topics than Spain or Belgium. The amount of writings by U.S. scholars on the topics of race, ethnicity, and crime is huge; U.S. work in the area of migrants and crime (particularly after 1940) is much more modest in scope.

The discussions in this book leave little doubt that a key question in the discourse about ethnicity, migrants, and crime revolves around the criminal involvement of foreigners, recent immigrants, and indigenous (native) or resident nonnative ethnic minorities relative to the larger society. There is plenty of anecdotal evidence, journalistic writing, and "street wisdom" about migrants and minorities, and criminality. Throughout the book, there are some examples of ethnographic research that "allows us to understand better the social dynamics of the foreigners' inclusion and exclusion through participant observation" (Gatti et al., Chapter 5, this volume). But we also need more than ethnographic accounts and anecdotes: We need systematically collected facts to back up theories, to correct them if necessary, and to inform policy. The political Right and Left, in the United Kingdom, Germany, France, the United States, or The Netherlands: All make free use of "facts" and figures to lend credibility to their arguments. Statistics reflect the activities of social control agencies rather than the criminal involvement of individuals—this fact is recognized by almost all of the contributing authors in this volume. Yet, we cannot afford simply to ignore crime statistics; they tell at least part of the story.

Problems With Statistics

Even under the best of circumstances, statistics about migrants, minorities, and crime remain a highly sensitive, politically explosive matter. It is not hard to find instances where such statistics have deliberately been misrepresented and manipulated (FitzGerald, Chapter 2, this volume). The intentional manipulation of crime statistics is a practice not unheard of in the United States, either (see Chambliss, 1995).

More troubling than deliberate misrepresentation for political purposes is the relative lack of reliable and valid statistical information on minorities, migrants, and crime. For example, it is very difficult, if not impossible, to arrive at a reliable estimate of the number of foreigners, immigrants, or even native ethnic or racial minorities. That issue is brought up again and again in most discussions in this book. Most countries have several different conflicting estimates of the actual size of the foreign population; arriving at valid estimates of undocumented immigrants or criminal aliens is even more problematic.

Unlike the situation in the United States, in many European countries there is a principled objection to ethnic monitoring (see Tomasevski, 1994). Thus, the systematic collection of information about nationality, citizenship, race, or ethnic background is either not done at all, or only occasionally and haphazardly, often employing categories so broad that they are virtually of no use. For instance, United Kingdom data do not differentiate between British ethnic minorities and those normally resident abroad (although this has recently changed to include data on nationality). In Germany, there is no separate information on ethnic Germans because they are of German nationality. Comparable problems exist in other European countries. In the United States, the collection of racially and ethnically coded data does not face serious challenges on ideological grounds, but the usefulness of the resulting statistics has been seriously questioned by many.

Frustration with the obstacles created by serious data problems (resistance to being counted and practical problems in doing so) is shared by most scholars struggling to answer questions related to the (differential) criminal involvement of foreigners, minorities, immigrants, or all of these. The question then becomes: Do we simply throw up our hands, lamenting that we know nothing, or do we decide how to make the best use of the available statistics and research, in a responsible and careful manner? The contributing authors in this book obviously find the answer in the latter option.

In the remainder of this chapter, I discuss several general observations about migrants, minorities, and crime; facts that I selected because, to a certain extent, they appear to be consistent (or at least not incompatible) in the eight European nations discussed in this volume and the United States; facts that are primarily drawn from the nine presentations on individual countries in this book. The first part of the chapter divides into two areas: survey findings (self-reports and victimization studies) and official statistics (police data and research, sentencing data and research, and prison data and research). The second half of the chapter outlines the rudimentary beginnings of a theoretical context for interpretation of the observations, including how to make the connection between European and U.S. experiences.

SURVEY FINDINGS

Self-Report Studies of Offending

What simpler way to find out about the world than to go see people and ask questions? With regard to crime, researchers have done just that, starting more than half a century ago. By now, there are hundreds and hundreds of so-called self-report studies of offending, in which samples of (usually young) people are asked about their involvement in a variety of misbehaviors and crimes. Generally, these studies use local samples, often high school students. Occasionally, there are nationwide studies, and there now is also an international self-report survey (Junger-Tas, Terlouw, & Klein, 1994).

This very popular method has several major drawbacks. Surveys are notoriously problematic because they undersample minority groups and highly troubled and deviant youth; the validity of the responses of minorities on these surveys has also been challenged. The offenses included tend to be the less serious ones; because of the sampling problems, the generalizability of the findings is low. The value of these self-report studies may be simply summarized: Self-report surveys provide some useful information about a limited amount and type of illegal behavior among a limited segment of the population (see Marshall, 1996). With this "warning" in mind, what, then, may be concluded from these self-report surveys?

Overall, European self-report surveys of offending (primarily of juveniles) show little or no differences in self-reported criminal involvement between minorities and others. Differences among respondents, if present, tend to be slight; introduction of background variables tend to lower, or eliminate the initial differences. A few exceptions exist (e.g., see Albrecht, Chapter 4, this volume). Also, some studies show differences in kinds of delinquent activities among different minority groups. U.S. self-report surveys tend to find no racial/ethnic differences in nonserious delinquency, but higher involvement of blacks and Hispanic youth in more serious offenses.

Victimization Surveys

Surveys of victims are of more recent origin than self-report studies. Victim surveys have been conducted on a regular basis for almost 30 years in the United States, and they also have become a common data collection method in several European countries. Victim surveys, as a measure of crime, know many critics: There are issues regarding the validity of responses (how do we know that people tell the truth, or that they remember?), and the representativeness of the sample (it is possible that the most highly victimized group is least likely to be included because of frequent moves, that undocumented residents are likely not part of the survey, and that language problems affect responses). From the victim surveys discussed in this book, the following three facts may be drawn.

First, European victim surveys suggest higher criminal victimization of immigrants (minorities), in particular for violent crime. In studies controlling for the effect of social status, neighborhood, age profile, or geographic distribution, the ethnicity effect is significantly reduced, but not eliminated. U.S. victim surveys also consistently show that minorities (blacks and Hispanics) are more likely to be victims of crime (even after controlling for several background variables).

Second, European victim surveys show that criminal victimization to a large degree is intraethnic (i.e., minorities victimize others within their own group). U.S victim surveys also show that victimization is mostly intraethnic and intraracial (one exception is robbery). (Police statistics on violent crime support these survey data, in both the United States and Europe.)

Third, one important exception to the intraethnic nature of victimization is hate crime. The British Crime Survey finds that a small proportion of respondents have been the victim of "racially motivated" crime. Several other European surveys show that minorities feel racially harassed, discriminated against, and feel that xenophobia has increased. Similar findings exist in the United States.[1] (Police data support these survey data. There is disagreement about the evidence concerning the escalation of hate crime: Is there a true increase, a greater willingness of the police to make a formal report about hate crimes, or both?)

OFFICIAL STATISTICS

Surveys provide a useful but rather limited insight into the minorities and crime question; another piece of the puzzle is found in the statistics produced by local, regional, and national government agencies. Official crime statistics (police, courts, prisons) do not represent "real" crime, but rather a filtered "image" of it (cf. Gatti et al., Chapter 5, this volume). There exists a large body of theoretical and empirical work on the "social production of crime statistics" supportive of the view that crime statistics are primarily "organizational products."

Police Data and Research

In many European countries, migrants and migrant-related crime have become a law enforcement priority. In the United States, crime among native-born ethnic minorities, as well as among legal and undocumented immigrants also ranks high as a law enforcement priority. Choices concerning where to allocate police resources, in conjunction with increased budgets, are bound to produce a greater "output" in terms of arrests of target groups. There are cases in which immigrants and minorities are explicit targets; but, sometimes disproportionate police attention to minorities is the consequence of more general policies and priorities (i.e., the disproportionate effect of the "war on drugs" on blacks in the United States, and on *étrangers* in France).

There is ample empirical documentation that in Europe and in the United States the relationship between the police and minorities is strained and marked by verbal and physical abuse, mutual distrust and fear, hostility, prejudice, and occasional violent confrontations. According to the information provided by the authors of this book, in most countries (including the

United States), the police (as well as courts and prisons) employ (very) few
ethnic minorities. With regard to foreigners, the situation is even worse,
partly because of legal limitations.

That police/minority relations are tense is well documented. What does
that mean for the quality of police statistics—statistics that are the formal
reflections of police/citizen interactions? Many of the activities of the police
are "reactive" rather than "proactive." Thus, police statistics mirror, to a
considerable extent, the willingness of the public (victims and witnesses) to
report crime to the police. There is some evidence to suggest that immigrants
and minorities are less likely to report criminal victimization to the police.
There is also some (tentative) evidence that victims and bystanders are more
likely to report minorities to the police. This suggests that the victimization
of ethnic minorities and migrants may be underestimated, and the illegal
behavior of minorities overestimated.

Incidents reflecting unfair or discriminatory treatment of minorities and
migrants by the police can be found all too easily: Some police officers are
racist or prejudiced. Much harder to document is the degree to which the
police are systematically biased against minorities in making arrests. Countries vary in the degree to which they have empirical research on the
antiminority bias of police officers in arrests. What do the studies discussed
in this book say about the arrest practices of police officers?

Although there is some evidence that minorities are more likely to be
the target of police harassment and proactive policing (i.e., being stopped by
police), there is no strong support for systematic antiminority bias in arrest
decisions by the police. This is true for the European countries involved, as
well as the United States. If police discrimination (in making arrests) plays
a role, it probably is most apparent in the less serious offenses, or in cases
related to drugs, prostitution, or gambling (complaintless crimes). When
very serious offenses are involved, legal constraints leave little room for
police discretion.

European police (arrest) statistics do show an overrepresentation of
minorities, migrants, foreigners, or all these in varying degrees. This is also
true for the United States. Because of differences in statistical procedures,
exact cross-national comparisons cannot be made. European and U.S. arrest
data show that not all minority groups of a country are represented in arrest
statistics to the same extent (some are overrepresented, some are underrepresented). European and U.S. arrest statistics show differences with regard
to *types* of offenses for which particular minority groups are arrested. In the
European countries, arrest data show that most minority/migrant arrests are

for drug-related crime, public order violations (immigration offense), and petty offenses (shoplifting, nonviolent offenses). A small proportion involves serious, violent crime. The same is true for the United States. Finally, differences in arrest rates are significantly reduced when controlling for age, gender, and income differences between minority groups and the general population.

Sentencing Data and Research

A second major source of official statistics on minorities, migrants, and crime are those produced by the courts (data on charges, convictions, and types of sentences). The decisions made by prosecutors and judges reflect, in addition to the legal facts about cases (i.e., law-violating behavior), social, political, and organizational forces comparable to those influencing police work. Sometimes, workload pressures or budgetary constraints may play a role; at other times, it may be subtle (e.g., "processing stereotypes") or not so subtle antiminority sentiments. More frequently, the problem is "institutional discrimination," whereby particular ways of "doing things" are organized in such a manner that minorities and migrants are likely to be treated more severely. In both the United States and Europe, there is evidence of indirect discrimination, influenced through factors such as poor legal representation, language problems, (greater likelihood of) preventive detention, type of offense (immigration and drug-related offenses), and employment status.

In both the United States and Europe, there is no strong evidence of systematic, pervasive, and direct discrimination against minorities (migrants) by prosecutors (in charging decisions) and judges (in sentencing decisions). This does not mean that direct discrimination never happens. And, there are some studies in which minorities appear to receive more severe treatment. (Citizenship may be used as an aggravating factor in sentencing. Also, deportation may be used, which is a more serious sanction than some other alternatives used for citizens.) In both the United States and Europe, there is evidence that minorities and foreigners may be more likely to receive a custodial sentence. (This is particularly true for migrant and foreign juveniles.) In both the United States and in Europe, however, there is also some evidence that minorities/migrants are sometimes treated more leniently—intraethnic offenses, or in cases that have weak evidence.

What do European and U.S. court data tell us? Generally, the proportion of minorities in conviction statistics is higher than their presence in the population. In Europe and the United States, however, conviction statistics show that not all minority groups in a country are overrepresented to the same extent; some groups are underrepresented. In Europe and the United States, conviction statistics show that particular minority (national) groups are likely to be convicted for particular types of crime. In both Europe and the United States, conviction statistics show a higher overrepresentation of minorities for serious violent crime (robbery, homicide, rape) and for drug-related crime. The bulk of the convictions of minorities and migrants, however, is for less serious, mundane crime.

Prison Data and Research

There are many reasons to believe that the numbers of foreigners (and minorities) in prisons do not only reflect their patterns of offending, but also changes in migration control, the availability and the length of appeal procedures (cf. Tomaskevski, 1994, p. 10), and a hardening of the general penal climate. Jackson (Chapter 6, p. 144, this volume) for example, refers to Tournier and Robert's (1991, pp. 91-92) summary of the situation for France: "Efforts to reduce illegal immigration . . . have heightened the visibility of minorities as 'potential suspects' attracting police curiosity. That, in addition to efforts to repress illegal drug use and distribution . . . has led to the rapid growth in the presence of *étrangers* in . . . prisons." This observation also rings true for several of the other European countries as well as the United States.

There is a serious overrepresentation of minorities and foreigners in prisons in Europe and the United States. The proportion of minorities and foreigners in prisons in Europe and the United States has increased over the past several years. Drug-related offenses are a major source of the overrepresentation of minorities and foreigners in European and U.S. prisons. Immigration offenses (including having no means of support, or no legal permit to stay) are another major reason for this overrepresentation. A large proportion of incarcerated minorities and foreigners are in preventive custody (pretrial detention), in both the United States and Europe. Minority and foreign women are making up a growing proportion of the female prison population in Europe and the United States; drug-related crime plays an important role. Several authors note that the large population of foreigners and minorities in prison creates serious problems (language problems, overcrowding, lack of education or training, no furloughs, no visitors, interethnic conflicts) for both those detained as well as for the correctional regime.

ANOTHER COMMON OBSERVATION: THE NEED FOR DIFFERENTIATION

Thus far, I have chosen to emphasize the commonalities and parallels among countries. Ironically, most of the authors in this book, implicitly or explicitly, warn against the danger of overgeneralizations about "the" immigrant (or minority) and "crime." A common theme running through most chapters is that of the importance of recognizing the multifaceted and complex character of the phenomena included under the umbrella terms of *minorities* and *immigrants*. The countries discussed parade a large variety of ethnic, racial, and national minorities. There are enormous national differences in these minorities. For instance, England contrasts Asians (Pakistani, Bangladeshi, and Indians) with blacks (of Caribbean or African origin), and Chinese; Sweden has Laplanders, Finns, gypsies, Norwegians, ex-Yugoslavians, and Iranians (with a very small nonwhite population compared to other European nations); Germans are concerned with Italians, Spanish, Portuguese, ex-Yugoslavs, and ethnic Germans; Belgium has Italians, Moroccans, and Turks; the Dutch minority "problem" focuses on Moroccans, Turks, Surinamese, and Antillians; Spain is concerned with gypsies; Italy worries about Moroccans and Tunisians, Germans, French, British, Phillipinos, Albanians, and ex-Yugoslavs. The United States has the traditional "big four" racial/ ethnic groups: blacks, American Indians, Asian Americans, and Hispanics, as well as recent immigrants from virtually all parts of the world.

To further complicate matters, the formal categories used (nationality, citizenship, race, ethnicity) ignore the very real differences between and within each of the minority groups. In the United States, for instance, the "Asian" category lumps together Koreans, Japanese, Filipinos, and Chinese—groups without a clear shared cultural identity, language, and social class status. In the United Kingdom, there are major differences in income, age structure, and employment among Indians and Bangladeshi and Pakistanis. The same holds true for other European countries. A common theme, then, is that minorities are not a homogeneous category, but they typically are a very heterogeneous collection of subgroups. There are not only considerable *cross-national* differences in types of minority groups and migrants, but also major *within-country* variations. It is, therefore, not surprising that we find important differences in the criminal involvement of various immigrant and minority groups, both in terms of the amount of involvement, as well as in terms of the type of offenses: "If the nexus between crime and migration is studied empirically, some of the stronger correlations may apply to some subgroups only" (Schmid & Savona, 1996, p. 22).

MIGRATION AND CRIME: PHENOMENA IN CONSTANT FLUX

Race, ethnicity, migration, citizenship—what is the common denominator here? How do we link these concepts with criminality? Do we see any parallels between the U.S. experience and what we know about the situation in different European countries? I draw from the work of Sun and Reed (1995) to suggest some sort of unifying conceptual framework: The extent and nature of criminality of migrants and ethnic minority groups is shaped by the interaction between characteristics of the migrants (minorities) and those of the host country[2] (including the size, age, and composition of the resident minority group), placed in a global context. Sun and Reed (1995) in their overview of theory and research related to migration and crime in Europe, call for including a temporal framework that "allows us to track the evolution of the research and theorizing on migration and crime." Such a temporal framework, in my view, must include global changes, the history of ethnic communities, as well as generational factors.

Global Changes

The phenomenon of migration is as old as mankind (cf. Mueller, 1996, p. 1); however, the reasons for migration, the push and pull factors, the motivation of the migrants, the reception by the host countries—these factors are in constant flux. There are important differences in historical immigration patterns between the United States and Europe, and among European countries. As is described by several of the authors, in both Europe and the United States, the motives and composition of the recent immigrant population have changed. Asylum seekers and refugees (including undocumented aliens) from Third World countries, the demise of socialism in Eastern Europe and the former Soviet Union, the removal of internal border controls in the European Union, ethnic war in former Yugoslavia—these forces have created a different type of migrant population. Today, immigration reflects the *push factors* of religious and political persecution and poverty rather than the *pull factor* of the need for manpower. It is only reasonable to expect that migrants in the late 1990s encounter a vastly different situation than those who left their home country 100, 50, or even 20 years ago.

Ethnic Communities

The size (and composition) of the migrant/minority group in the host country may affect the type and amount of criminal involvement of members of these groups. "A distinction needs to be made between the dominant culture [i.e., the 'host' country], the subcultures that immigrants originally came from in their own country, and the new subcultures that emerged in the course of the process of integration in the country of residence" (Lea & Young, 1984). These new subcultures differ not only in size but also in recency of arrival in the receiving country and degree of integration in the larger society. Some minority groups have lived in the host country for many generations (i.e., blacks in the United States, gypsies in Spain); some have been there only for two or three generations (i.e., Italians and Moroccans in Belgium). Many of these groups have formed permanent ethnic communities in the host countries. Tomasevski (1994, p. 16) uses the term of *nonnative ethnic groups* to "denote those categories that are no longer foreigners, but not yet citizens." In Western Europe, mostly because of family reunification, immigration (primarily colonial workers and migrant workers) has turned "into an irresistible permanent settlement of ethnic minorities" (Sun & Reed, 1995, p. 232), with a "solidification of ethnic communities" (p. 233). Other migrant groups only recently left their country of origin in sizable numbers, and are thus entering a host country that does not have an already-established ethnic community (i.e., Russians in the United States).

Generational Factors

Finally, at an individual level, it makes a difference whether the individual is a first-, or second- (or later) generation immigrant. It is by now almost a truism: First-generation immigrants have a lower crime rate than their children (or second- or third-generation immigrants; Sun & Reed, 1995). It makes sense, indeed, to speculate that the first-generation immigrant, both in terms of motives and opportunities, differs from second- or third-generation immigrants. Because of changes, however, in the global context of migration, and in the characteristics of the ethnic (migrant) communities in the host countries, the criminal involvement of first-generation immigrants is likely to increase in the near future (see next sections).

THE "NEW" INTERNATIONAL (PROFESSIONAL) CRIMINAL

History knows many examples of people leaving their native society with the explicit motive being to steal, murder, and exploit the land and inhabitants of other societies. Today's sheer volume of these international criminals, however, is unprecedented in the history of mankind. According to Mueller (1996, p. 9), the "recent and massive appearance in the western world (of professional migrant criminals) is attributable to the fall of the iron curtain in 1989 . . . and the easing of U.S. immigration laws covering Asian migration." Several authors in this book referred to these opportunistic migrants. Some of these professional criminals are individual entrepreneurs; others come as part of, or to join, groups with criminal perpetrators (crime that is organized), while yet others are members of organized crime (Mueller, 1996, p. 9). These criminals' primary motive for leaving their country of origin is to pursue crime; in that sense, their behavior is calculating and rational. A disturbing development is that, often, their activities are not confined to a single country. These international criminals frequently are instrumental in getting other migrants and minorities involved in crime (see next section).

CRIMINALITY BY IMMIGRANTS AND MINORITIES

The vast majority of migrants leave their native country to better themselves in legal ways, not to better themselves through a life of crime. Research and theory distinguishes between first-generation and second- (and later) generation immigrants (i.e., the children of immigrants, born in the host country).

First-Generation Immigrants

First-generation immigrants typically have a low level of involvement in crime. This was definitely true in the past, both U.S. (Sellin, 1938) and

European (Ferracuti, 1968) research documented lower crime rates of immigrants than natives. Mueller (1996, p. 7) mentions three factors: (a) the desire to succeed; (b) the availability of support groups of earlier and now settled immigrants from the same areas of emigration; and (c) the fear of deportation. Undocumented immigrants, in particular, are typically believed to be even more law abiding than their legal counterparts: They have much to lose by police detection (Schmid, 1996, p. 22).

This situation may change, however, with regard to the most recent (first-generation) immigrants, in particular the undocumented newcomers. Savona (1996), for example, argues that organized crime (through international criminals) is changing the structure of crime at the local level. Specifically, the widespread trafficking in undocumented aliens is having an impact on the crime involvement of these new arrivals. Immigrants (particularly undocumented aliens) are frequently exploited and extorted by those who imported them in violation of law (Mueller, 1996, p. 8). They are introduced to criminal circuits; they are forced to work as prostitutes, or to get involved in drug dealing (to pay back the debts incurred for their illegal transportation into the country). They are reluctant to go to the police, even though they are victims of criminal exploitation. (Employers who are taking advantage of these undocumented immigrants by hiring them as "slave labor" under unsafe conditions, paying them below-minimum wages, are of course, also guilty of illegal behavior.)

Crime is the product of motivation and opportunity, both legal and illegal. Whereas the economic inequality/deprivation notion emphasizes the marginal social position of minorities and migrants in the legitimate society, illegitimate opportunity structure is important, also (cf. Cloward & Ohlin, 1960). According to Schmid and Savona (1996, p. 21), the main ethnic organized crime groups "are currently trying to use existing migration patterns to nest their own structures and logistics into the stream of interactions and exchanges between legal migrants while exploiting undocumented migrants."

Second- and Third-Generation Immigrants and Minorities

There appears to be a general consensus that, if there are any marked differences between the criminal involvement of immigrants and natives, these are manifested in the criminal involvement of the children of immigrants (second- and third-generation immigrants). It is argued that children of immigrants will have higher expectations; they will have changed life aspirations. Attitudes such as consciousness of deprivation and socioeconomic inequality (Albrecht, 1991 as cited in Sun & Reed, 1995, p. 245), longing for prestigious consumer goods (Brown, 1990 as cited in Sun & Reed, 1995, p. 245; Killias, 1989), and disillusionment with the country of residence (Shelley, 1981 as cited in Sun & Reed, 1995, p. 245), separate the ideological texture of this generation from that of their predecessors (Sun & Reed, p. 245).

The disproportionate criminal involvement of well-established ethnic minorities in the United States, and the greater involvement with the police of second- and third-generation immigrants in Europe reflect comparable dynamics. The situation in the United States is extremely complex; there exist large groups of blacks, Hispanics, American Indians, Chinese, and Japanese who have been American citizens for many generations, but who share with second- and third-generation European (and U.S.) migrant communities two things: (a) a marginal social position, and (b) a distinct ethnic-cultural position (perception and definition—both by self and environment; cf. Penninx, 1994). Whether a person residing in the United States is an eight-generation descendant of an African slave, a fifth-generation descendant of American Indians, a grandchild of a Mexican migrant guest worker, or a recent refugee from Cuba, the odds are that this individual occupies a marginal social position and is subject to negative stereotyping and hostility by the larger U.S. society. In Europe and in the United States, most ethnic minorities and migrants occupy a marginal social position in host society in terms of employment, income, housing, political influence.[3]

Two common explanations (found in virtually all European countries, and in the United States) for the overrepresentation of minorities, migrants, and foreigners in crime statistics are (a) discrimination and (b) deprivation/structural inequality (i.e., social position). Most researchers do realize that the effects of these two (discrimination and social class) need to be taken out (statistically); commonly, there remains some kind of ethnicity effect. This brings us to the second commonality that links the variety of European and U.S. minority and migrant groups: an ethnic-cultural position perceived as inferior by the host society; often, this ethnic-cultural position reflect to a large extent "color" or "race." Ethnic-cultural position includes definition of the minority group by the larger society, as well as self-identification (rather than dramatic differences in cultural values). Stereotyping and prejudice exist in all countries. Of particular relevance for the current discussion are criminal stereotypes. For example, in England, there are popular negative stereotypes of "the black mugger" associating people of West Indian origin in the 1980s with social disorder generally (Solomos, 1988). In the United States, crime (violent crime in particular) is seen as a "black" problem. In virtually all European countries, the media focus on foreigners as criminals, or on organized crime as "threat posed by alien groups" (Albrecht, Chapter 4, this volume).

The ethnic-cultural position of new minorities in Europe is described by Tomasevski (1994, p. 36):

> Mutual accusations between the native and the migrant population abound: The former object that migrants reject integration by transferring their own life style to the host country; the latter object that they are rejected, stigmatized, and discriminated against, often because of their race, color, ethnicity, or religion, or all of these. Nationals equate migrants with increased criminality, while migrants see themselves as targets of racial violence, harassment, or at least prejudice.

This description could be used equally well to refer to the situation of the African Americans (or Hispanics) in the United States. Minorities and migrants are aware of the negative evaluation of their particular ethnic-cultural position by the dominant society; they actively organize specific cultural interpretations of cultural differences (cf. de Haan, Chapter 9, this volume). FitzGerald (Chapter 2, this volume) argues, and rightly so, that the "ethnic-cultural position" (ethnicity or race) needs to be studied in the context of social class and discrimination.

CONCLUSION

Nativists and racists have always viewed the connections among criminality, migrants, and minorities as simple and straightforward: They spell trouble, trouble, and more trouble. That was a popular belief 100 years ago in the United States, and it continues to be the conviction of many Europeans and Americans today. Scholars and social analysts have long taken issue with this simplistic position (e.g., Sellin, 1938). The interconnections among migration, minorities, and criminality have become even more complex in the postmodern world of the late 1990s, with its routine international travel, highly sophisticated technology, global political instability, mass movement of people, and opening of national borders.

The individual chapters have alluded to some changes in the minority/migrant/crime nexus: the fast-growing numbers of professional international criminals, the increasing involvement of organized crime in alien smuggling and other forms of transnational criminality, the formation of ethnic gangs, the victimization of new immigrants (often undocumented) by members of their own ethnic group (including organized criminals) as well as by respectable native-born business people. The "old" question of the criminal involvement of second- and third-generation immigrants is fairly straightforward compared to these newly evolved patterns and styles of criminality. With these new developments comes a need for a shift in thinking. Cultural deviance and structural inequality theories (see Hawkins, 1993) still have a role; however, we have to expand our theoretical horizons. Ethnicity, race, citizenship, or national origin are of only secondary importance; criminality reflects national and transnational macrolevel economic, political, and social processes. We must examine the forces that shape the nature and extent of these newly emerging crime forms, such as transnational drug production and distribution systems, international terrorism and sabotage, transnational organized crime, nuclear material trafficking, electronic international fraud, and trafficking in people. The study of how global developments influence and shape crime locally, be it in U.S. inner cities or German small towns, is also part and parcel of this approach. And most important, we must focus on the social, economic, political, and organizational processes that are at work in the minority/migrant/criminality question, rather than on any inherent characteristics of individual ethnic and migrant groups (cf. FitzGerald, Chapter 2, this volume).

NOTES

1. The U.S. victim survey does not include questions about hate crime.
2. "Host country" reflects the inequality between a traditional host and guests—the guests have no rights, but are dependent on the willingness of the host for food, shelter, and so on. As such, the larger U.S. society is also host to its racial and ethnic minority groups (blacks, Hispanics, Asian Americans).
3. There are, of course, minority and immigrant groups that do not have such a marginal social position. These groups are less likely to be overrepresented in crime statistics; for instance, Japanese in the United States.

REFERENCES

Brown, J. (1990). *Insecure societies*. London: Macmillan.

Chambliss, W. J. (1995). Crime control and ethnic minorities: Legitimizing racial oppression by creating moral panics. In D. F. Hawkins (Ed.), *Ethnicity, race, and crime. Perspectives across time and place* (pp. 235-258). Albany: State University of New York Press.

Cloward, R., & Ohlin, L. (1960). *Delinquency and opportunity.* New York: Free Press.

Ferracuti, F. (1968). European migration and crime. In M. E. Wolfgang (Ed.), *Crime and culture: Essays in honor of Thorsten Sellin* (pp. 189-219). New York: John Wiley.

Hawkins, D. (1993). Crime and ethnicity. In B. Forst (Ed.), *The socioeconomics of crime and justice* (pp. 89-120). Armonk, NY: M. E. Sharpe.

Junger-Tas, J., Terlouw, G., & Klein, M. (Eds.). (1994). *Delinquent behavior among young people in the western world. First results of the International Self-Report Delinquency Study.* Amsterdam: Kugler.

Killias, M. (1989). Criminality among second-generation immigrants in Western Europe: A review of the evidence. *Criminal Justice Review, 14,* 13-42.

Lea, J., & Young, J. (1984). *What to do about law and order.* New York: Penguin.

Marshall, I. H. (1996). De Methode van Zelfrapportage [The self-report method]. *Tijdschrift voor Criminologie, 38*(1), 2-20.

Mueller, G. O. W. (1996, October 5). *The general report.* Paper presented at the International Conference on Migration and Crime, International Scientific and Professional Advisory Council of the United Nations Crime Prevention and Criminal Justice Program [ISPAC], Courmayeur Mont Blanc, Italy.

Penninx, R. (1994). *Raster en Mozaiek* [Framework and mosaic]. Amsterdam: Universiteit van Amsterdam, Instituut voor Migratie-en Ethnische Studies (IMES).

Savona, E. U. (1996, October 5). *The problem.* Paper presented at the International Conference on Migration and Crime, International Scientific and Professional Advisory Council of the United Nations Crime Prevention and Criminal Justice Program [ISPAC], Courmayeur Mont Blanc, Italy.

Schmid, A. (Ed.). (1996). *Migration and crime.* Milan, Italy: International Scientific and Professional Advisory Council of the United Nations Crime Prevention and Criminal Justice Program [ISPAC].

Schmid, A. P., & Savona, E. U. (1996). Migration and crime: A framework for discussion. In A. P. Schmid (Ed.), *Migration and crime* (pp. 5-42). Milan, Italy: International Scientific and Professional Advisory Council of the United Nations Crime Prevention and Criminal Justice Program [ISPAC].

Sellin, T. (1938). *Culture conflict and crime.* New York: Social Science Research Council.

Shelley, L. (1981). *Crime and modernization.* Carbondale: Southern Illinois University Press.

Solomos, J. (1988). *Black youth, racism, and the state.* Cambridge, UK: Cambridge University Press.

Sun, H.-E., & Reed, J. (1995). Migration and crime in Europe. *Social Pathology, 1*(3), 228-252.

Tomasevki, K. (1994). *Foreigners in prison* (Publication Series No. 24). Helsinki, Finland: European Institute for Crime Prevention and Control.

Tournier, P., & Robert, P. (1991). *Étrangers et Delinquences* (travail d'intérêt général). Paris: l'Harmattan.

Weiner, M. (Ed.). (1993). *International migration and security.* Boulder, CO: Westview.

Index

ABOUT THE AUTHORS

HANS-JOERG ALBRECHT received his Ph.D. from the University of Freiburg, Germany. From 1986 to 1991, he was a senior research fellow at the Max-Planck-Institute, Freiburg. In 1992 to 1993, he was Professor of Criminal Law at the University of Konstanz. Since 1993, he has an appointment at the University of Dresden in criminal law, juvenile law, correctional law, and criminology. His work focuses on the system of criminal sanctions, drug criminal law, drug control, environmental criminal law, organized crime, juvenile delinquency, and ethnic minorities. He is coeditor of the French criminology journal *Deviance et Society* and of the *European Journal of Crime, Criminal Law, and Criminal Justice*. He is a member of the Advisory Board of the *European Journal of Criminal Policy and Research*.

ROSEMARY BARBERET received her Ph.D. from the University of Maryland in 1994. She currently is a visiting professor at the Sevilla division of the Andalusian Institute of Criminology at the University of Sevilla, Spain. Her research interests include women and crime and victimization; juvenile delinquency; drug trafficking; and policing.

WILLEM DE HAAN Ph.D., is Professor of Criminology. He teaches at the University of Groningen and the University of Utrecht, The Netherlands. His work is in the field of public safety, street crime, stranger violence, and criminal policy. He has also published on issues concerning ethnic minorities

246

and crime. He is author of *The Politics of Redress. Crime, Punishment, and Penal Abolition* (1990).

MARIAN FITZGERALD is currently Principal Researcher in the Research and Statistics Directorate of the British Home Office, with responsibility for work on race relations/race equality issues in general, including related criminal justice research. She was previously a freelance researcher. Her publications have covered race, politics, and race relations in local government, as well as criminal justice topics.

ELISA GARCÍA-ESPAÑA is a doctoral fellow in the Criminal Law Department of the University of Málaga Law School, Spain. She collaborates in her research with the Málaga Division of the Andalusian Institute of Criminology established at the University of Málaga. The criminality of foreigners in Spain is the topic of her doctoral dissertation.

UBERTO GATTI M.D., is a psychologist and criminologist who currently is Professor of Criminology at the Institute of Criminology and Forensic Psychiatry at the University of Genoa in Italy; he is an expert on juvenile delinquency and juvenile justice. He is a member of the board of directors of the International Society of Criminology, and is the Director of a postgraduate course in Forensic Psychology at the University of Genoa.

INEKE HAEN MARSHALL is Professor of Criminal Justice at the University of Nebraska at Omaha. She studied sociology at the Catholic University of Brabant (The Netherlands), and obtained her Ph.D. in sociology at Bowling Green State University (United States). Her research interests include criminal careers, ethnicity and crime, comparative criminological theory, self-report methodology, and drug policy. She has published in scholarly journals such as *Criminology, Journal of Research in Crime and Delinquency, American Sociological Review, European Journal of Criminal Policy and Research,* and *Justice Quarterly.* She coedited *Between Prohibition and Legalization: The Dutch Experiment in Drug Policy* (1996).

PATRICK HEBBERECHT is Professor of Criminology and sociology of law. He is currently Chair of the Department of Penal Law and Criminology at the Law Faculty at the University of Ghent (Belgium). His research is in the sociology of penal law, fear of crime, minorities and crime, crime prevention, and crime statistics.

PAMELA IRVING JACKSON is the Director of the Justice Studies Program and Professor of Sociology at Rhode Island College. She holds a Brown University Ph.D., and recently served three years as Associate Editor of the *American Sociological Review.* Her book, *Minority Group Threat, Crime, and Policing: Social Context and Social Control,* examines and explains variations in collective support for social control. She has published research articles in several scholarly journals, including *American Sociological Review, Justice Quarterly,* and *Policing and Society.* Her current research involves a comparative investigation of the relationship between minority/majority relations and social control priorities in France and the United States.

DANIELA MALFATTI received her Ph.D. in Criminological and Forensic Psychiatric Sciences at the Institute of Criminology and Forensic Psychiatry at the University of Genoa (Italy). She is a psychologist and a criminologist.

JERZY SARNECKI is Professor of Criminology and Head of the Department of Criminology at Stockholm University. He worked for 17 years as a researcher and later as head of the research division at the National Council for Crime Prevention in Sweden. He has published several studies and textbooks on juvenile delinquency and societal reaction to juvenile delinquency.

HENRIK THAM is Professor of Criminology at Stockholm University. He worked for several years at the Swedish Institute for Social Research where he was involved in the Level of Living Surveys and in research on inequality and social exclusion. This background has influenced his major field of research: The relationship among crime, criminal policy, and the welfare state. His most recent publications concern the development of drug policy and criminal policy in Sweden and a comparison of crime and inequality in Sweden and the United Kingdom.

ALFREDO VERDE is a researcher at the Institute of Criminology and Forensic Psychiatry at the University of Genoa (Italy). He is a psychologist and psychotherapist with a Ph.D. in Criminology. He is a member of the Scientific Council of the Italian Society for Criminology.

HANNS VON HOFER is Associate Professor of Criminology at Stockholm University. He studied law in Germany and criminology in Sweden. He has worked as a senior statistician at Statistics Sweden. He has published several studies on crime and criminal justice statistics. His research interests are in time series analysis, international comparisons, and historical perspectives on crime and reaction to crime. He is currently a member of a group of specialists on trends in crime and criminal justice statistics appointed by the Council of Europe.